THE SUVLA BAY LANDING

Other Books by John Hargrave

GENERAL

Words Win Wars
The Life and Soul of Paracelsus

NOVELS

Harbottle
Young Winkle
And Then Came Spring
The Imitation Man
Summer Time Ends
Etc.

1. THE MOMENT OF DECISION

A little-known snapshot of Mustafa Kemal, the Turkish Commander, looking down on our troops at Suvla Bay on August 9, 1915, at the moment of his decision to order a mass attack from the hills in an attempt to drive the British into the sea.

[See page 161]

The
SUVLA BAY
LANDING

JOHN HARGRAVE

MACDONALD:LONDON

"The story of the IXth British Corps and of the whole Suvla landing would be incredible if it were not true."

Churchill, *The World Crisis*

First published in 1964 by
Macdonald & Co. (Publishers) Ltd.,
Gulf House, 2 Portman Street,
London W.1
Made and printed in Great Britain by
Waterlow & Sons Limited,
Dunstable and London

ACKNOWLEDGEMENTS

I wish to thank Sir Winston Churchill for giving me permission to quote from his work *The World Crisis* (published 1923–29), and also Odhams Press Ltd., the publishers and proprietors of the copyright, for according me the same privilege.

My thanks are also due to the publishers, Edward Arnold Ltd., for allowing me to quote extensively from Sir Ian Hamilton's *Gallipoli Diary* (published 1920).

Indebtedness is hereby acknowledged to the official history of the campaign, *Military Operations: Gallipoli* (Heinemann, 1929–32), by Brigadier-General C. F. Aspinall-Oglander; to *The Final Report of the Dardanelles Commission (Part II—Conduct of Operations, &c.)*, published by H.M. Stationery Office, 1918 [Cmd.371], from which I have made a number of extracts; to John North's *Gallipoli: The Fading Vision* (Faber, 1936), one of the most accurate and exhaustive accounts of the campaign as a whole; and to Alan Moorehead's panoramic masterpiece *Gallipoli* (Hamish Hamilton, 1956), from each of which I have drawn factual information.

In checking my own data relating to the Suvla operation, I have found Major Bryan Cooper's *The Tenth (Irish) Division in Gallipoli* (Herbert Jenkins, 1918) of great value, and the same must be said of a slim paperbacked volume by a Sergeant of my own unit, C. Midwinter, entitled *Memoirs of the 32nd Field Ambulance, Xth (Irish) Division* (privately printed, 1933, now out of print).

Finally, I wish to thank my old barrack-room comrade, R. C. Holmes, one-time Water-cart Orderly (and later Provost Corporal) at Suvla, for supplying written replies to innumerable questions, and for his meticulous care in checking my facts against his own recollections of the Suvla Bay Landing.

JOHN HARGRAVE

Royal Societies Club, 1964

PREFATORY NOTE

Those who feel inclined to look upon the Gallipoli Campaign as little more than a "side-show" to the Western Front in the 1914–18 war—as many certainly did in 1915—and who feel that even had it been successful, it could not have "won the war," may find it worth while to ponder the words written by Admiral von Tirpitz on August 7th, 1915, the morning after the Suvla Landing:

"Heavy fighting has been going on since yesterday at the Dardanelles ... The situation is obviously very critical. Should the Dardanelles fall, the World War has been decided against us."

CONTENTS

MAPS AND DIAGRAMS

LIST OF PLATES

The author and publishers wish to thank the following for supplying photographs: Central Press Ltd. for 17; The Imperial War Museum for 5, 6, 7, 8, 9, 10, 11, 16, 18, 19, 23, 24, 25, 26, 29, 30, 34, 35, 36; Paul Popper Ltd. for 21; The Radio Times Hulton Picture Library for 2, 3, 4, 27, 28; and the Turkish Embassy, London for 1 and 22.

1

PLAN OF CAMPAIGN

Napoleon, at the height of his powers, marched his *Grande Armée* against the Russians, and arrived in Warsaw on January 1, 1807. At Eylau in East Prussia, during a blinding snow-storm at 7 a.m. on February 8, he received the full force of an unexpected blow from the Cossacks. It was a blow that winded the *Grande Armée* and left it sagging at the knees for several days.

Fortunately for Napoleon, Turkey declared war on Russia, compelling her to draw off troops from her western front in order to defend the south.

Russia asked for help, and the British sent a naval squadron under Admiral Duckworth to the Dardanelles.

Sir John Moore, then second-in-command of the British garrison in Sicily, urged that troops be sent with the expedition. "There are none to spare," came the reply, although this was not a fact. After the squadron had sailed, Sir John wrote: "It would have been well to have sent 7,000 or 8,000 men with the fleet to Constantinople, which would have secured their passage through the Dardanelles and enabled the admiral to have destroyed the Turkish fleet and arsenal, which from the want of such a force, he may not be able to effect."

Nevertheless, the admiral with seven ships of the line and some smaller vessels forced his way through The Narrows in February, 1807, silenced the forts, and destroyed a Turkish squadron. Then, within eight miles of Constantinople, his sails hung limp. He waited a week becalmed in the Sea of Marmara, whistling for a wind. Fearing he might never be able to get back if the Turks, helped by French engineers, had time to repair and improve the fortifications, and being unable to train his guns on Constantinople, he decided to turn about and allow the swift current of three knots to bear him away through The Narrows. But the return journey was more hazardous. Although no ship was lost, the frigate *Endymion*, forty guns, was hit in her hull by two stone shots of twenty-six inches each in diameter, and among the sailors there were 150 casualties.

This seems to be the first and only time that the Dardanelles have been forced since they were fortified by the Turks in 1460.

Even so, it had been a fruitless errand—a failure.

A century later, in 1915—astonishingly, if we did not know that history repeats itself with variations—almost the same set of circumstances arose.

On August 4, the date on which Britain declared war on Germany in 1914, the British fleet in the Mediterranean sighted the fast German battle-cruiser *Goeben* with her attendant light cruiser *Breslau*, and shadowed them throughout that afternoon, unable to sink them because the British ultimatum to Germany did not expire until midnight. The two vessels escaped in the darkness, and finally entered the Dardanelles on August 10. On September 21 a British squadron was sent to the mouth of the Dardanelles with orders to sink the *Goeben* and the *Breslau* should they show their noses outside the Straits.

As they were now bottled up they turned in the opposite direction and with some Turkish warships sailed into the Black Sea where they bombarded the Russian fortress of Sevastopol on October 29–30, raided Odessa, and practically destroyed Novorossisk.

The British Foreign Office sent an ultimatum to Turkey on October 30. Russia declared war on Turkey on October 31.

In agreement with the Foreign Office—but without consultation with the Cabinet—Churchill ordered naval hostilities to begin against Turkey, and on November 1 Admiral Carden was instructed to bombard the outer forts of the Dardanelles at long range.

On November 3 he shelled the batteries at Sedd-el-Bahr and Cape Helles, while French battleships fired at the Asiatic batteries at Kum Kale and Orkanieh. The bombardment lasted twenty minutes, and about eighty rounds were fired, damaging the forts and inflicting several hundred casualties on the Turks and Germans who manned them.

Churchill says:

> "The reasons for this demonstration have been greatly canvassed. They were simple though not important. A British squadron had for months been waiting outside the Dardanelles. War had been declared with Turkey. It was natural that fire should be opened upon the enemy as it would be on the fronts of hostile armies. It was necessary to know accurately the effective ranges of the Turkish guns and the conditions under which the entrance to the blockaded port could be approached. It has been stated that this bombardment was an imprudent act, as it was bound to put the Turks on their guard and lead them to strengthen their defences. That the organisation of the defences of the Straits should be improved steadily from the declaration of war was inevitable. To what extent this process was stimulated by the bombardment is a matter of conjecture."
>
> (*World Crisis*, 1911-18, p. 285.)

The reasons may have been "simple", but if they were also "not important" how can they be held to justify this initial bombardment? True, a British squadron had been waiting outside the Dardanelles for two or three months, and that war had been declared on Turkey. But there is no rule of war requiring that guns must be fired the moment war is declared.

As for the third and final reason: a British Naval Mission had been in Turkey for years, and must have known all there was to know about these fortifications, gun by gun. One would imagine it was only necessary to ask Admiral Limpus, Chief of the British Mission (withdrawn from Constantinople on or soon after September 9), for the required information. That this does not appear to have been done is the more surprising when we read in Churchill's own words:

> "It was my intention to appoint the head of our naval mission to Turkey, Rear-Admiral Limpus, to command the squadron watching the Dardanelles, and orders were sent definitely to that effect. This project was not, however, pursued, it being thought that it would be indelicate to employ on this station the very officer who had just ceased to be the teacher of the Turkish Fleet. No doubt this was a weighty argument,

but in bowing to it we lost the advantage of having at this fateful spot the Admiral who of all others knew the Turks, and knew the Dardanelles with all its possibilities."

(*World Crisis*, 1911-18, p. 283.)

Finally, as to whether the bombardment of November 3 was "bound to put the Turks on their guard and lead them to strengthen their positions"—after the war the Turkish fortress commander wrote: "The bombardment of November 3 warned me, and I realised that I must spend the rest of my time in developing the defences of the Straits."

The bombardment was in fact tantamount to sending the Turks a postcard to say "*Look out! We're coming!*" It had revealed to the Turks how old and ramshackle their outer defences were. At Sedd-el-Bahr, for example. the forts were destroyed, and when the magazine blew up all the guns were dismounted. It was clear to the enemy that the British Navy, while keeping out of range itself, could at any time wipe out these fortifications. Repairs were made, but the Turks (or their German advisers) had learned that they must rely upon strengthening the inner defences, and, in particular, upon minelaying. This they did.

This impetuous naval action could be more easily understood if an attack on the Gallipoli Peninsula had not yet occurred to Churchill's bold imagination. But it had, as the following note dated December 31, 1914, to Asquith (Prime Minister) shows:

"I wanted Gallipoli attacked on the declaration of war ... Meanwhile the difficulties have increased ..."

(*World Crisis*, 1911-18, p. 321.)

There can be little doubt that the bombardment of November 3 had helped to increase these difficulties, and perhaps we may conclude that Churchill, from the moment we declared war on Turkey, was all for action, and just a little too "quick on the trigger".

In war, however, it is better to have a man of action—even one liable to act a moment too soon—than someone who, from lack of enterprise, lets the moment of opportunity slip away.

Whatever mistakes may have been made at this early date, Churchill, then forty years of age, was the man who had The Idea—the only idea that could have won the war in 1915.

Stalemate on the Western Front set in after the Battle of the Marne, September, 1914. It was this deadlock in trench-warfare, grinding away month after month as a war of attrition, that became the compelling factor in bringing forward the idea of an attack on some other front: an attack that might put an end to what seemed to be an interminable slaughter waged by enormous troglodyte armies elaborately dug-in and sitting opposite each other. Unless this sit-down war could be turned somehow into a war of movement, Britain might be bled to death. Neither side could budge, and the armies had been stuck in the mud of France and Flanders for four months.

Already the Russian armies—then called the "Russian Steamroller"—never well-equipped, had slowed and come to a halt before the German lines for lack of shells, rifles, and ammunition. By January 2, 1915, the Grand Duke Nicholas was asking if Lord Kitchener could arrange "a demonstration against the Turks" to draw them off from his hard-pressed Army of the Caucasus. It had therefore now become essential to find some way of helping our Russian allies.

Three plans had been put forward during the winter of 1914 with a view to ending the stalemate on the Western Front:

1. Churchill (First Lord of the Admiralty) wanted a land and sea attack in the Dardanelles.
2. Fisher (First Sea Lord) wanted to open up the Baltic.
3. Lloyd George (Chancellor of the Exchequer) wanted a Salonika landing.

Kitchener was opposed to any plan that would take troops from the West. His reply was always the same: "We have at present no troops to spare."

At first Fisher seemed to be opposed to any plan but his own. But before long he had abandoned the Baltic and was fired by the idea of an attempt to land troops on Gallipoli and at the same time force the Dardanelles, using old battleships only. In fact the First Sea Lord was fantastically enthusiastic—like a schoolboy who has found a catapult and is all agog to try it. And like an excited schoolboy he wrote to Churchill on January 3:

"... I CONSIDER THE ATTACK ON TURKEY HOLDS THE FIELD!—but ONLY if it's IMMEDIATE!" ... (and

went on to outline his plan under four main points, ending
with the words):

"... But as the great Napoleon said, 'CELERITY'—without
it—'FAILURE'! In the history of the world—a Junta has
never won! You want *one* man!"

As there were no troops to spare from the Western Front,
and Greece was blowing hot-and-cold the whole time, the
military part of Fisher's plan was out of the question. But
Churchill seized upon Fisher's fourth point, which read:

"IV. Sturdee forces the Dardanelles at the same time [as
the proposed military landings] with 'Majestic' class and
'Canopus' class! God bless him!"

"Here for the first time," Churchill wrote after the war,
"was the suggestion of forcing the Dardanelles with old battleships." On the principle that half a loaf is better than no bread,
he put this idea before the War Council on January 5.
Kitchener approved of it because no troops would be called for.
But by January 20 Fisher had turned against the Dardanelles
plan because it did not combine large land forces with the
naval attack.

On January 28 all members of the War Council (except
Fisher, who left the table in a huff) decided in favour of the
proposed naval action. In a private talk after this meeting,
Churchill, with tremendous patience and tact, brought the
First Sea Lord round again. "When I finally decided to go
in," Fisher said later, "I went the whole hog, *totus porcus*."

That may be, but it is clear enough from all accounts
(including Churchill's) that Fisher was an "awkward cuss" to
deal with, liable to go "*totus porcus*" first in one direction, then
in another.

What with Fisher whole-hogging on one side, and K. of K.
sphinxing on the other, Churchill had his work cut out to get
any sort of agreement at all.

Within the next few weeks it was found that the purely naval
plan called for some modification. Landing parties would be
needed to destroy guns and forts disabled by the Navy, and
Fisher at once began to press for troops to be used not only in
this way but in support of the attack.

This was what Churchill had originally wanted, but as there
were "no troops to spare" he felt it wise to stick to the naval

plan. So Totus Porcus had to be headed off his latest acorn-hunt—unless of course the Sphinx would unriddle the whole situation by agreeing to send a sufficiently large British army for the purpose. And that was exactly what happened when the War Council met on February 16, 1915. Kitchener was present.

On that day it was decided to send a military force "to be available in case of necessity to support the naval attack on the Dardanelles". This force was to include the 29th Division of the Regular Army, without which it would be too small.

Thus February 16 marked the turning-point when what was to have been a purely naval project became a combined operation. Before long we shall see how the whole thing turned turtle once again, by sheer force of circumstances, and became *a military operation with the Fleet in support*—a totally different proposition from that agreed upon by the War Cabinet on January 28.

On February 17, the very day after the decision to send troops in support, Kitchener changed his mind about diverting the 29th Division from France. He was torn between the claims of the two opposing camps: those who supported the "Western policy" ("every man is needed to kill Germans in France"), and the advocates of the "Eastern policy" ("the stalemate can and must be broken by a break-through in the Near East").

He wobbled badly, almost pathetically, and at the meeting of the War Council on February 19 announced that he could not now agree to send the 29th Division.

On this very day, February 19, at 9.51 a.m., the British and French fleets bombarded the outer forts of the Dardanelles. *The Gallipoli Campaign had begun.*

And by some quirk of fate, some strange coincidence, this very date was the 108th anniversary of Admiral Duckworth's successful but unlucky thrust into the sea of Marmara!

So the present stepped unknowingly upon the ghost of the past.

Meantime, on February 20, Kitchener sent word to Fisher and the Admiralty Transport Department—without consulting Churchill—that the 29th Division was not to go. In consequence the transports held in readiness for these troops were dispersed *without the First Lord knowing a thing about it.*

In fact, Churchill thought these twenty-two ships were ready to sail in case of need, and did not discover until six days later that they had all been released for other duties. Churchill writes: "I was staggered at this, and wrote at once to Lord Kitchener in protest."

Alas, the transports could not be reassembled and fitted before March 16—two days before the naval attack on The Narrows was resumed.

We see, then, how the plan of campaign was conceived and how the arrangements for carrying it out were being handled. The battleships were already engaged in an attempt to force the Straits nearly three weeks before adequate military support was decided upon in Whitehall. It was not until March 10 that Kitchener again changed his mind and agreed to the despatch of the 29th Division.

All this, viewed at the time from 10 Downing Street, the War Office, and the Admiralty, under the day-to-day stresses and strains of war, no doubt seemed inevitable. There are always hitches and delays in the initial stages of any new undertaking, but after making full allowance for the fact that this was the *first* World War, and that no one quite knew how to cope with such a thing, anyone who takes the trouble to set down a time-table of events from official sources relating to the Gallipoli Campaign will find that from first to last it reveals hesitation and muddle at the highest level. We shall see, as we go on to tell exactly what happened, how crazy it becomes. Laughable? It would be, but for the torn-out guts—and the cry of *"stretcher-bearers! stretcher-bearers!"* ... and the young dead, the boy corpses, lying on the beaches in the hot sunshine. ...

Since the plan of campaign was in reality a brilliant idea flung into action and left to be battered into this shape or that by the pitch-and-toss of war itself, there is nothing for it but to follow the desperate course of events as they were played out on the Aegean front and in Whitehall.

The long-range naval bombardment of the outer forts of the Dardanelles on February 19 went unanswered. The Turks and their German advisers held their hands from 9.51 a.m. until

4.45 p.m., when the battleships closed to within 5,000 yards. Then two of the forts opened fire, proving that their guns had not been damaged. Five battleships replied, and one of the forts was put out of action for the time being. By now the light was fading and the action was called off for that day.

During the next five days no action was possible owing to stormy weather.

At the War Council in London on February 24, Kitchener said that he "felt that if the Fleet could not get through the Straits unaided the Army ought to see the business through. The effect of a defeat in the Orient would be very serious. There could be no going back." He then relapsed into his usual silence, and no plans of any kind were worked out at the War Office or elsewhere in readiness for such a contingency.

On February 25 the naval bombardment was resumed, and minesweeping to clear the entrance to the Straits had begun.

Landing parties of bluejackets and marines were put ashore on the 26th and following days, to blow up the guns in the abandoned forts on both sides of the sound. Apart from a few snipers, they met with hardly any opposition. At this date Achi Baba could have been taken and held by one brigade with hardly a shot fired—but it was still hoped that the Navy could do the job on its own, and it now looked as though this might be possible.

Things seemed to be going well. Drooping spirits rose. The attention of the world was fixed upon the Dardanelles, and for a little while what had been looked upon as a "side-show" suddenly became all-important.

But from March 3 onwards the naval operations slowed and wavered. The Turks brought up mobile howitzers in large numbers along both shores. Our minesweeping trawlers were picked out by glaring searchlights and raked by field gun fire. The crews (civilians in peace-time) could not face it, and on one occasion at least were driven back by these heavy onslaughts, which, Admiral Carden reported, had "caused no casualties"! It was clear to Churchill that the direction of the whole operation lacked determination and drive.

In the meantime Kitchener had sent General Birdwood (commanding the Australian troops in Egypt) to the Dardanelles to make a first-hand report on possible military action.

Birdwood telegraphed to Kitchener on March 5: "I am very doubtful if the Navy can force the passage unassisted. . . ."

The method of bombardment in the Dardanelles was now changed. The *Queen Elizabeth* took up a position on the Aegean side and fired her 15-inch guns across the peninsula.

Then, in the squall-flustered darkness of early dawn on March 8, one of those small sea-urchin events took place that— by chance, destiny, *karma*, or whatever it is—change the course of history. A Lieutenant-Colonel Geehl, a mine expert, thought it would be a good idea to lay a few mines where he had seen British ships manœuvring the day before. So he took the little Turkish steamer *Nousret* into Eren Keui Bay and put down a line of twenty new mines just inside slack water, and running parallel to the Asiatic shore. It was just an idea. No harm in having a few mines below The Narrows, in waters already cleared by the minesweepers.

Three of them were swept up on March 16, but as no more were found the remaining seventeen lay there for the next ten days unsuspected.

On March 10 Kitchener swerved back to his decision of February 16, and announced to the War Council that "he felt that the situation was now sufficiently secure to justify the despatch of the 29th Division". *But three precious weeks had been lost*, and the transports that could have sailed on February 22 were still being brought together and fitted out. And even now—now that he had once again agreed to send an adequate military force—nothing was done, no plans put in hand, no systematic study of the problem undertaken, no commander appointed.

And all the time the Fleet was pounding away at the forts in The Narrows, fumbling about trying to fish up mines with trawlers that were not suitable for sweeping under artillery-fire, and not really making much headway. The naval bombardment went on by fits and starts, but the forcing of the Dardanelles had not been attempted. After all, Admiral Carden's original instructions "laid stress on caution and deliberate methods", and he was not the man to take chances.

Now at long last, on March 12, Kitchener sent for Sir Ian Hamilton to come to see him at the War Office. The Secretary for War was writing at his desk when Hamilton walked in. After a moment the great man looked up and, as casually as you might say "I want you to get me a packet of cigarettes", said: "We are sending a military force to support the Fleet now at the Dardanelles, and you are to have command."

Kitchener went on writing at his desk. Hamilton stood, waiting, cap-in-hand (so to speak). At last the Strong Silent Soldier, the Man of Few Words, looked up and said, "Well?"

This was the first Hamilton had heard of the project.

A little taken aback by this off-hand appointment to the command of a vast new military enterprise thousands of miles away (although he knew the terse and sometimes taciturn injunctions of his old chief only too well), Hamilton replied:

"We have done this sort of thing before, Lord K. We have run this sort of show before, and you know . . . that I will do my best and that you can trust my loyalty—but I must say something—I must ask you some questions."

At that Kitchener frowned, and shrugged his massive shoulders. Hamilton thought he was "going to be impatient", and to begin with his answers were curt. Gradually he opened out and became quite talkative, "until at the end" (Hamilton wrote in his *Gallipoli Diary*) "no one else could get a word in edgeways."

In spite of that the information obtained amounted to very little. The Director of Military Operations was called in. He produced a map of Gallipoli (later found to be hopelessly inaccurate). Beyond this, the only information he could give was that the Greek General Staff had estimated that a landing at the tip of the peninsula would call for 150,000 men.

Kitchener instantly brushed that aside. Half that number would be more than enough, he declared. Then the Chief of the Imperial General Staff and the Inspector of the Home Forces were called in, together with General Braithwaite, who had just been appointed Hamilton's chief-of-staff. Up to this moment *none* of these gentlemen had heard anything of the proposed Gallipoli campaign! The C.I.G.S. and the I.H.F. were so thunderstruck that they never uttered a single word during this extraordinary conference. They could only suppose that the great K. of K. knew what he was doing.

Braithwaite had the nerve to beg that a number of up-to-date aircraft, pilots, and observers be sent out with the expedition. That removed the pin from the hand-grenade. Kitchener exploded. "*Not one!*" he bellowed. And that was that.

Hamilton has left a detailed account of this capricious and crotchety interview that sealed the doom of the Gallipoli Campaign before a man set foot on the beaches. It was in fact doomed the moment Kitchener looked up and said "Well?" to the newly appointed Commander-in-Chief.

In effect Kitchener said: "If the Fleet can't get through, you are to take the Gallipoli Peninsula. Off you go!" But this bold gesture, that seemed to capture the Golden Horn at one perfunctory blow, was hedged about by a beggarly policy of cheese-paring and candle-ends. Thus, Kitchener had "given definite orders" to the C.I.G.S. that Hamilton's headquarters was "not to include more than about three staff officers". Yet within a few hours he had put his "K" monniker to the document sanctioning an establishment of twenty-three staff officers (the smallest possible number) without a word. So much for "definite orders". The psychological weakness in all this is painfully clear: the rapped-out word of command, followed by drift, hesitation, and (sometimes) countermanding action.

Hamilton was due to leave for the Dardanelles the very next day. He had only a rough idea of the strength of the forces under his command. He knew nothing of Turkey or the Turks. His chief-of-staff ransacked the War Office Intelligence Branch. All they could produce was a textbook on the Turkish Army (three years out of date), and a pre-war report on the Dardanelles defences.

"The Dardanelles and the Bosphorus might be in the moon for all the military information I have got to go upon. . . ." Hamilton wrote at that time in his diary. "There is no use trying to make plans unless there is some sort of material, political, naval, military or geographical to go upon."

It is a question what a Commander-in-Chief ought to do in these circumstances. Instead of writing doleful complaints in a private diary, ought he not to report his findings and his dissatisfaction at once to the Secretary of State for War, and if nothing is done about such serious deficiencies, ought he not to decline or resign the command?

Although he knew the whole thing was as ramshackle-crazy as a child's soapbox scooter held together with a few rusty nails, Hamilton could not bring himself to do that. His heart ruled his head, his innate gentleness of nature was fatal.

"So I said goodbye to old K.," he wrote in his diary, "as casually as if we were to meet together at dinner. Actually my heart went out to my old chief. He was giving me the best thing in his gift and I hated to leave him among people who were frightened of him."

Hamilton was not frightened of him, but the effect was the same as though he had been. A deep and abiding loyalty to his old chief forbade him to ask even for bare essentials, let alone demand them. At a moment's notice he had been given an impossible task to perform, and somehow or other he must perform it. It wasn't bricks without straw—it was bricks without clay, straw, kiln, hod, or anything else. But he could not bother "old K." with such matters at a time when the entire war organisation and direction rested upon him. He must do the best he could, with next to nothing.

He was, moreover, under the spell of a heavily dominating, domineering, and erratic personality. Almost to the last he half expected the magic of "old K's" luck and will-power to "pull it off" by some unforeseeable fluke. "Sir Ian Hamilton appears to have regarded [Lord Kitchener] as a Commander-in-Chief rather than as a Secretary of State," says the Final Report of the Dardanelles Commission (Part II).

And so, on Friday, March 13, 1915, Hamilton and his hastily scraped-together headquarters staff left Charing Cross on their way to the Dardanelles, armed with one useless map, one out-of-date textbook on the Turkish Army, one pre-war report on the coast defences, and Kitchener's written instructions, which last contained no facts relating to the enemy, the political situation in the Near East, the topography of the peninsula, nor the possibility of co-operation by our Russian allies. In fact these "instructions" merely told Hamilton that he was not to use his troops unless the Fleet failed to force The Narrows, and thereafter left him almost entirely to his own devices.

No administrative staff went with them, and none had so far been appointed.

As the train pulled out, Hamilton turned to Aspinall, and

said: "This is going to be an unlucky show. I kissed my wife through her veil."

It was an unlucky thing to say. It set the wrong note from the start. It revealed a strange flaw in the Commander-in-Chief's psychological make-up. The subsequent day-to-day entries in his diary show an extraordinary succession of forebodings, portents, premonitory dreams, and ominous presentiments, which may account for far more than military and other historians would be likely to acknowledge.

Indeed it is a wonder he did not remark upon the fact that he was setting forth upon what he felt was going to be "an unlucky show" on Friday the 13th!

With this momentary snatch of fortune-telling by lucky or unlucky omens, the military phase of the campaign plunged into action. Perhaps for the first time in history a Commander-in-Chief set out with no army, no plan of campaign, no details of transport or supplies, and no administrative staff, to fight an enemy whose strength and dispositions were unknown, on a battlefront that could be anywhere on the 53-mile coastline of a rough and tumbled peninsula that had never been accurately mapped.

It cannot be said that Sir Ian was not given a free hand. In fact at the outset he was given nothing else.

What, in all the last-minute search for essential information, had become of Admiral Limpus, late of the British Naval Mission to Turkey? Churchill has told us that he "of all others knew the Turks, and knew the Dardanelles with all its possibilities". We know that it was thought "indelicate" to appoint him to command the naval forces at the Dardanelles. The strange thing is that his information (that must have included the ranges of the guns in the forts) seems to have been of so little use to Admiral Carden. He had to find out by hazardous trial-and-error what these guns could do.

Is it possible that this source of information was never tapped by anyone? Can it be that Admiral Limpus was recalled and somehow dropped out of things, never consulted, perhaps forgotten? It could be so. The whole set-up was certainly as drifty and screwloose as that.

Hamilton—62 years of age, good-natured, shy, dreamy,

optimistic, and, alas! omen-haunted—was now speeding on his way aboard the 30-knot light cruiser *Phaeton* to the scene of action.

Meantime the Carden plan of a fort-by-fort and mine-by-mine clearance of the Straits had slowed almost to a standstill. The outer forts had been silenced, but The Narrows were protected by ten minefields (totalling 373 mines) and dominated by the forts at Chanak and Kilid Bahr. The mine-sweepers were old, bad, and slow, with worn-out engines, and they were under fire from twelve hidden mobile howitzers. The naval seaplanes were too heavy to rise out of rifle range, and so could not be used to spot enemy positions.

Add to all this Carden's caution—his fear of risking the loss of even a few of his old scheduled-for-scrap battleships in any attempt to "make a dash for it"—and the cause of the slow-down since the attack opened on February 19 becomes clear.

There was one man who had the dash and go to take a chance and risk everything in an attempt to get through, and that was Carden's 43-year-old chief-of-staff, Roger Keyes. He was straining at the leash, but he never got the chance. "Have a go!" was his watchword, and day and night he did his best to put a bit of Trafalgar into the enterprise.

Churchill was trying to do the same from Whitehall. On March 11 he had sent a telegram to the Admiral urging him in so many words to "press on regardless". It ended by saying: "We shall support you in well-conceived action for forcing a decision, even if regrettable losses are entailed."

Three days elapsed with no reply. The Admiral could not make up his mind. The truth is, he was already a sick man on the verge of a nervous breakdown. He dreaded the whole thing. The strain was too much. He could neither eat nor sleep. On March 14 he replied that he agreed that now was the moment to push on but felt that "military operations on a large scale should be commenced immediately" in order to ensure communications when the Fleet entered the Sea of Marmara.

On March 15 he was told to confer with Hamilton who would be arriving on the 17th, and was again urged to "press forward without hurry, but without loss of time". On the same day Carden replied that he intended to make a vigorous attack

on the forts at The Narrows at the "first favourable opportunity".

No sooner was the decision made, and the message sent, than
the Admiral told Keyes he was too ill to carry on, and that his
second-in-command, Vice-Admiral de Robeck, must take
over.

At such a critical moment—two days before the main attack
on The Narrows was due to begin—this might have been as
dangerous as swapping horses in mid-stream. As it turned out
it made very little difference. All arrangements went forward
as planned, and, as we shall see, de Robeck not only took over
a hazardous undertaking, but also a full measure of Carden's
fatal caution.

On March 16 the first of the delayed transports sailed from
England, carrying men of the 29th Division on their long slow
journey to Lemnos.

At 3 p.m. on March 17, Admiral Carden sailed from
Tenedos harbour. And at that very moment the light cruiser
Phaeton sailed in, with Hamilton and his H.Q. staff on board.
Within an hour the Commander-in-Chief had a consultation
with Admiral de Robeck, who announced that his attack on
The Narrows would begin the next day. He was confident of
pushing through to the Marmara without the help of troops on
any large scale—which was just as well, because there were no
troops ready for any such operation.

The next day Hamilton landed on Lemnos and found that
the Naval Division transports from Alexandria had been
"loaded up as in peace time"—"water-carts in one ship:
water-cart horses in another: guns in one ship: limbers in
another: entrenching tools anyhow", and in fact everything
topsy-turvy and wrong-way-about. They would have to be
"completely discharged and every ship reloaded" before troops
could land under fire.

None of this could be done at Lemnos, where there were
"neither wharfs, piers, labour, nor water". So the wrongly-
packed transports would have to sail all the way back to
Alexandria—over 600 miles—to be emptied and reloaded.
The naval men reckoned six days per ship as the best they could
do.

Thus the days and weeks slipped by while the Turks were

busy fortifying every possible landing-place in the south of the peninsula day and night with ant-like energy.

March 18, 1915: *Vice-Admiral de Robeck to Admiralty:* "Weather fine. Operations about to begin."

Already a month had drifted into eternity since operations had begun, but to read de Robeck's message you would think they were just beginning.

Soon after dawn on March 18 the British and French Fleet, with a total strength of seventeen battleships and one battle-cruiser, was cleared for action. Of these, fourteen battleships (ten British and four French) were old. This armada sailed from its anchorage at Tenedos in the morning haze. The weather was perfect, the sea smooth.

At 10.30 a.m. the first ten battleships entered the Straits, and at 11.25 the bombardment of the five main forts at Chanak, Kilid Bahr, and Kephez Bay began from 14,000 yards.

Just after midday the French squadron went forward to engage the forts at closer range. Hell broke loose from sea and land in a deafening uproar, volcanic in its eruptive violence. Gun-thunder cracked and rolled. Vast dust-clouds billowed from muffled explosions in the forts. Livid gunflashes made the sunlight blink. Coils of thick black and yellow smoke belched and hung in a choking sulphurous pall. Plunging shells whipped the mouth of The Narrows into foaming stalagmites of shooting spray. For nearly two and a half hours the battle-fury echoed and re-echoed in the barren hills on either side.

By 1.45 the forts were almost silent. Up to now the plan was going well. Some of the French ships had been severely battered, but the British had suffered hardly any damage. Not one had been put out of action. Killed and wounded numbered less than forty. For the time being the enemy gunners, smothered in dust and debris, were demoralised. The forts were dominated. But for the minefields the Fleet could have sailed through. The minesweepers were therefore ordered forward to deal at once with the Kephez minefield.

Ah, if de Robeck had only known that the nine remaining fields had been in position six months: that a large number of the mines, half-waterlogged, had sunk below keel-level: that some had broken loose and been carried away by the current,

c

that others were out of date in design and unreliable, and that
all were spaced ninety yards apart—three times the beam of a
ship—because there was such a shortage.

Where was Admiral Limpus? He had been in charge of the
Turkish Navy up to the end of August 1914, and must have
known something of these antiquated mines. Apart from that,
had we *no* agents in Turkey capable of getting up-to-date
information?

The nerves and discipline of the minesweeping crews were
still unsteady. As they approached Kephez Point and came
under fire from 6-inch guns, they again funked it, put about,
and made off south for Cape Helles. And at that moment—
1.54 p.m.—disaster struck.

The French battleship *Bouvet* exploded, heeled over, and
sank as she was coming out of action through Eren Keui Bay
in waters that were thought to be entirely free of mines. At
4.11 the *Inflexible* struck a mine in the same waters, and took a
dangerous list. Three minutes later the *Irresistible* struck a
mine about a thousand yards away, listed, and had to be
abandoned.

This triple calamity—swift, unaccountable, sinister—was a
stunning blow. With mines—if they were mines?—drifting
about in the mineswept waters of the bombardment area, and
with panic-stricken trawler-crews who would not face the task,
there was nothing for it but to break off the action. At 5 p.m.
de Robeck ordered a general retirement, leaving the *Ocean*
to try to salve the *Irresistible* which was drifting helplessly under
heavy Turkish fire towards the Asiatic shore.

Then came the final disaster. The *Ocean* struck a mine, listed
heavily, and with her steering-gear out of order began to turn
in circles. The Turkish gunners now had two crippled battleships to pot at. Despite the splendidly daring efforts of Keyes
to take the *Irresistible* in tow, both she and the *Ocean* foundered
during the night in deep water.

When the Turks saw the Fleet turn and steam away down
the Straits towards the open sea, leaving them to the empty
darkness and the uncanny silence of oncoming night, they
could not believe their eyes. For at this moment they were
running short of armour-piercing shells and other ammunition,
and there was no hope of further supplies. The Turkish govern-

ment, certain that the Allied Fleet would be successful, was already preparing to quit Constantinople. The Turks were at the end of their tether, and, notwithstanding the enheartening finale to the day's battle, the expectation of defeat was gnawing at the heart of the Turkish command.

But de Robeck did not know this, and no inkling of it had reached the War Council in London. Nor was it known until after the war what invisible force had struck *Bouvet*, *Inflexible*, *Irresistible*, and *Ocean*.

It was the little French steamer *Nousret* that had, all unknowingly, saved Turkey (and perhaps the Central Powers) from defeat when she laid that line of twenty mines in Eren Keui Bay on the morning of March 8, thereby changing the entire course of the First World War. But for that little steamer and her twenty mines Russia might not have collapsed, and Lenin and his Bolshevik Party would have found little opportunity for effective agitational propaganda—thus changing the development of what is today called "World Communism".

There ought to be an enormous monument to the little steamer *Nousret* in Red Square.

In the pitch blackness of the night Commodore Keyes was searching every creek and inlet along the Kephez Bay coast for any sign of the *Irresistible* or the *Ocean*. While that was going on de Robeck, in a state of dejection, telegraphed to Rear-Admiral Wemyss, commanding the naval base at Mudros, saying "We have had a disastrous day" and asking him to come to Tenedos to discuss the position.

Having made sure that the two battleships were lying at sea-bottom, Keyes returned to the *Queen Elizbaeth* and found de Robeck dispirited and distressed.

"After losing so many ships," said the Admiral, "I shall obviously find myself superseded tomorrow." This in spite of Churchill's telegram to Carden of March 11 that stated clearly: "We shall support you . . . even if regrettable losses are inevitable."

The Carden-bacillus—fear of the loss of a few old surplus ships—was already at work.

That night de Robeck made his report on the day's action to the Admiralty (received 8.35 a.m. March 19), and in a further message said: "With the exception of ships lost and damaged, squadron is ready for immediate action, but plan of attack must be reconsidered and means found to deal with floating mines."

The sea-change is already discernible.

Next morning Wemyss arrived, and the two admirals had a long private talk, *during which they agreed that the Navy could do no more until the Army had taken the peninsula.* (See Wemyss's Memoirs published long after the war.)

For sheer heave-to and stand-by-to-go-about old sea-doggery you can't beat it. And of course the line of argument was screwtight-logical, as it always is at such moments of touch-and-go (or touch-and-don't-go):

(a) The Navy can't get through until the minefields are cleared.
(b) The minefields can't be cleared until the mobile guns defending them are destroyed.
(c) The mobile guns can't be destroyed until the Army has taken the peninsula.

So we can't do anything? Pity, but there it is. Have another pink gin? . . .

Usually de Robeck took Keyes into his fullest confidence, but he made no mention of this meeting to him nor to any other member of his staff.

While the Admirals were having their long private palaver, during which they agreed, among other things, that Keyes was too optimistic about getting through and had perhaps a little too much of the "Nelson touch" in his make-up, Churchill was reading de Robeck's report.

With an unerring nose for nuances he seems to have sensed that the words *"but the plan of attack must be reconsidered"* might indicate an inclination to slacken-off, for his reply of March 20 said: "It appears important not to let the forts be repaired, or to encourage enemy by an apparent suspension of operations."

If that meant anything, it meant: *"Don't wait—push on!"*

In his reply of the same date de Robeck gave details of essential minesweeping reorganisation, and ended by saying that delay was inevitable, but that he "hoped to be in a position to commence operations in three or four days".

It is difficult to know what to make of this, bearing in mind the attitude taken by the two Admirals when they were closeted together the day before.

Imperceptibly the plan of campaign was beginning to drift clean away from a naval operation with the Army in support (as soon as there were troops ready for that purpose), and was becoming exactly the opposite—*a military operation with the Fleet in support.* That perhaps was not de Robeck's intention, but that was the direction in which fear of minefields and floating mines was, willy-nilly, drifting him.

There was never any more talk of hoping to be or of being "in a position to commence operations in three or four days". De Robeck's No. 1 personality had shelved the naval operations until the Army had been able to take the peninsula, while his No. 2 personality went forward with all preparations for reorganised minesweeping and the immediate resumption of the attack—without mentioning to anyone what his No. 1 personality had decided!

If some form of schizophrenia is not the explanation, we are left without any.

"We are all getting ready for another go," de Robeck (No. 2) wrote to Hamilton at this time, "and not in the least beaten or downhearted." No doubt that was perfectly true. But personality No. 1 was still keeping "mum"—clamtight, in fact.

It is important to bear in mind that even after the "disastrous day" of March 18 de Robeck (No. 2?) had told Hamilton that he felt he had a fair fighting chance of getting through without large-scale military support.

On the morning of March 22 the Admiral had a conference with Hamilton and his Generals at Mudros. Wemyss was also present.

In reality it was not so much a conference as a statement. "There was no discussion," Hamilton recorded in his diary. "The moment he sat down de Robeck told us he was now quite clear *he could not get through without the help of all my troops.*"

Keyes was too busy with the minesweeping reorganisation to attend this meeting. When he rejoined the flagship later in the day he was told by Captain Godfrey that the naval plan had been scrapped, and that de Robeck had decided not to resume the attack on The Narrows until the Army was "sufficiently in occupation of the peninsula to ensure passage of the Fleet into the Marmara". The Commodore was astounded—and hopping mad. This was not at all what the Admiral had led him to understand up to now, and he was all for going ahead according to plan.

No one was more astounded by the turn of events than the Turks themselves. According to an officer of the Turkish ship *Hamidieh*, when the attack was called off and the Fleet left the Straits, the reaction among Turkish naval men was: "The English have only gone home for tea—they'll come back again as soon as they've had breakfast tomorrow morning."

Churchill has recorded that he read de Robeck's telegram of March 23 "with consternation". It began:

> "At a meeting with Generals Hamilton and Birdwood the former told me Army will not be in a position to undertake any military operations before April 14."

And went on to say:

> ". . . It is necessary to destroy all guns in position guarding the Straits . . . Destruction of guns will have to be carried out [by the Army] in face of strenuous and well-prepared opposition."

And then:

> ". . . The mine menace [is] much greater than was anticipated. It must be carefully and thoroughly dealt with. This will take time to accomplish, but our arrangements will be ready by the time Army can act."

Churchill says: "I had no doubt whatever what orders should be sent to Admiral de Robeck", and he drafted a telegram that ended by saying:

> "We do not think the time has yet come to give up the plan of forcing the Dardanelles by a purely naval operation . . . all your preparations for renewing attack should go forward."

But this telegram was never sent. Fisher would not agree to it. He held that the men on the spot knew best. Besides, he had all along wanted a combined operation, and he was in fact "immensely relieved" that the plan was now taking that form. There were "high words" between the First Lord and the First Sea Lord, but Fisher won. Next day he sent a characteristic note to Churchill:

" . . . *You are very wrong to worry and excite yourself.* Do try and remember that we are the lost ten tribes of Israel. We are sure to win! ! ! I know I am an optimist! *Always have been*! ! Thank God . . . *Send no more telegrams! Let it alone!*"

Totus Porcus was now whole-hogging for delay at the very moment when the forts at Chanak, Kilid Bahr, and Kephez Bay had been knocked half-silly.

Churchill was right in pressing for immediate follow-up action by the Navy after March 18, because up to this time—thanks to Kitchener's masterly inactivity—*no preparations had been made for any full-scale military assault.*

But the Old Admirals (Fisher was 74) had defeated the Young Hotheads (Churchill and Keyes). "We are sure to win! ! !" Alas, the plan of campaign had once again turned turtle. The Navy was to wait for the Army to act—and the Army was not ready. Meantime, the Turks were repairing the forts and reinforcing the garrisons with all possible speed.

So now the campaign switched to Hamilton and the Army, in spite of the fact that no ship of real value had been sunk, and the killed and wounded were, so far, less than those frequently listed after a trench-raid across no-man's-land on the Western Front.

It was still possible to pull out of the Dardanelles altogether and have done with it. But events have their own momentum, their own grip upon human beings. Kitchener telegraphed to Hamilton after March 18:

> "The passage of the Dardanelles must be forced, and if large-scale military operations on the Gallipoli Peninsula are necessary to clear the way, they must be undertaken and must be carried through."

"*Must—must—must!*" From Kitchener, who—by delaying the despatch of the 29th Division, and by making no proper plans from the outset—had already knocked the bottom out of any successful military operation!

Neither the Cabinet nor the War Council took any formal decision on this new and stupendous military exploit. Events—like floating mines—broke loose, bumped into each other, and sailed off in contrary directions. In any case the Navy could do no more at the moment: the weather was too rough for minesweeping. Far better to wait for Hamilton and the Army. . . .

And what did Hamilton find on March 21 (the day before de Robeck told him he would need the help of all his troops) when he glanced around at the military preparations?

Hardly any small craft for landing. No accurate maps. No information about springs or wells ashore. No provision for the carriage and storage of water. No arrangements for getting off the wounded. No administrative staff, and therefore no medical staff to study the problems on the spot. No prepared base at Lemnos (which meant the transfer of troops already on the island back to Egypt, and the use of Alexandria and Port Said as base). And the 29th Division still on their way from England. "The Navy, *i.e.*, de Robeck, Wemyss and Keyes", he wrote in his diary, March 21, "entirely agree. They see as well as we do that the military force ought to have been ready before the Navy began to attack."

It never seems to have struck Hamilton that—even at this late hour—he ought to have told Kitchener flatly that the whole military project had been hopelessly botched-up from the start and was bound to fail.

Instead, this strange, poetic figure, knowing that everything was at sixes and sevens, remained quixotically loyal to "old K.", and by doing so was, alas, disloyal to the cause of victory.

Although not a shot was being fired in the Straits, the Battle of the Dardanelles was taking another strange turn in White-hall.

Totus Porcus wrote to Churchill, April 5:

"... You are just simply eaten up with the Dardanelles and cannot think of anything else! Damn the Dardanelles! They will be our grave! ..."

From March 17 to April 24 Hamilton did a Herculean job in equipping, assembling, and preparing his army. A whole month was taken up in unpacking and repacking the transports in Egypt. And during the whole of that time, of course, the Turks were hard at work on their defences. Enver Pasha said later: "If the English had only had the courage to rush more ships through the Dardanelles, they could have got to Constantinople: but their delay enabled us thoroughly to fortify the peninsula and in six weeks' time we had taken down over two hundred Austrian Skoda guns."

The element of surprise had vanished long ago. April 14 came and went. It was not until April 25 that Hamilton began his assault upon the peninsula.

There is no need to retell the story of the first six landings by British and Anzac troops: five at the tip of the peninsula, and one at Anzac Cove*. They were terrible and bloody. All were successful in getting a foothold, none in pushing forward more than three-quarters of a mile. At Anzac they clung to the precipitous cliffs like clawing cormorants on a storm-battered rock ledge. On the sandy spits and steep crests of Cape Helles—the spearhead of the offensive—the fighting was even fiercer. Here the 29th Division was thrown into action. At Sedd-el-Bahr the landing became a slaughter. Hundreds were killed in the landing-barges before they could reach the shore or fire a shot—and the barges, packed with dead, drifted away. . . . Nevertheless, having suffered nearly 20,000 casualties, the British managed to get 30,000 ashore. And at all points they held on.

But the men were worn out. Food, water, and ammunition were running short. By April 28 the initial impetus had spent itself. As the days dragged by and the heat of the sun increased, the position became as stalemated as it was in the trenches of France and Flanders. The Army was checked. No advance was possible without adequate reinforcements.

At last, on May 10, Hamilton sent a message to "old K.", saying: "If two fresh divisions organised as a corps could be spared me I could push on with good prospects of success."

Watching soldiers getting killed on the beaches while the Navy stood by doing nothing drove Keyes nearly frantic. He felt they ought to help the exhausted army by making a hell-for-leather dash through The Narrows with his reorganised minesweepers and the most powerful of the battleships. On

---

* The French made a wholly successful diversionary landing with a regiment of native African troops near Kum Kale on the Asiatic shore opposite Cape Helles on April 25th. They went ashore at Orkanie Mound (traditionally the tomb of Achilles), and forced the Turkish garrison holding the ruined fortress of Kum Kale to surrender at the bayonet-point.

May 9 a special conference had taken place on board the flagship. De Robeck was against the idea, but finally agreed to refer it to the Admiralty. The message sent on May 10 was halfhearted to a degree, as who should say: "We will try again if you say we must, but if we fail the whole campaign may be jeopardised."

On May 11 Churchill and Fisher met to consider the Admiral's telegram. Churchill was, as always, in favour of renewing the attack. But Fisher, old, and "worried almost out of his wits" (as Churchill relates) by the ever-increasing strains of the war, was in a dither of distress and anxiety. He would have nothing to do with any further attempt to force The Narrows. That was that, and that was flat.

Things were going very badly in France and on the Russian front. The facts about the shell shortage were about to break in the British Press. When the War Council met on May 14 the whole atmosphere was one of gloom, anxiety, and frayed tempers. Kitchener's report to this meeting was depressing in the extreme. He was particularly bitter about Fisher's order of May 12 withdrawing the *Queen Elizabeth* from the Dardanelles (because of the U-boat danger that had suddenly developed in the Aegean) at the very moment when the army on the peninsula was fighting for its life with its back to the sea. At this Fisher could contain himself no longer—"I was against the Dardanelles from the beginning, as the Prime Minister and Lord Kitchener know very well!" he roared.

Kitchener was just as "humphy" and difficult. By the end of the meeting he had given no indication as to what he would or would not do in the question of reinforcements for Hamilton. It was decided that Kitchener should ask Hamilton what force he would need to ensure success—in spite of the fact that Hamilton had already begged for "two fresh divisions organised as a corps" in his message of May 10.

As for Fisher, he now hated everything to do with the Dardanelles. It had become a bugbear. If there had been half a chance, he would have cut loose from the whole thing. But that was impossible. The Army was there, and the Navy must give it protection—if nothing more.

The close friendship between the young First Lord and the old First Sea Lord was at breaking-point.

So was Asquith's Liberal Government. A first-class political crisis was brewing.

Next day, May 15, Churchill received Fisher's note of resignation:

"First Lord,

After further anxious reflection I have come to the regretted conclusion I am unable to remain any longer as your colleague ... I find it increasingly difficult to adjust myself to the increasing daily requirements of the Dardanelles to meet your views—as you truly said yesterday I am in the position of continually veto-ing your proposals.

This is not fair to you besides being extremely distasteful to me.

I am off to Scotland at once so as to avoid all questionings.

Yours truly, Fisher.

As he had threatened to resign on a number of occasions, Churchill was not at first unduly bothered about it. This time, however, he was nowhere to be found. Asquith had to send a written order commanding the First Sea Lord, in the name of His Majesty the King, to return to his duties. When he was finally run to earth (in a room in the Charing Cross hotel) he was in a smouldering rage. He refused pointblank to go back to the Admiralty. "I have resigned," he growled. "I can stand it no longer! I will have no further part in the Dardanelles foolishness!"

In his last outburst to Churchill on May 16 the old swash-buckler wrote:

"YOU ARE BENT ON FORCING THE DARDANELLES AND NOTHING WILL TURN YOU FROM IT— NOTHING. I know you so well! ...

You will remain and I SHALL GO—It is better so . . ."

Hamilton replied the next day, May 17, to Kitchener's enquiry of the 14th, saying: "If the present situation continues I shall want the Army Corps asked for on May 10, and an additional Army Corps, *i.e.*, two Army Corps in all." (That was four divisions, about 100,000 men.)

Kitchener replied on May 18 that he was "disappointed" about the hold-up on the peninsula, and that Hamilton's request for four new divisions would require "grave considera-tion".

The rumpus about Fisher's walk-out and the resulting political upheaval completely blotted out Cape Helles and Anzac Cove. The government itself was now "under fire", and the beaches of Gallipoli were far away.

Next day, May 19, Fisher sent a crazy six-point ultimatum to Asquith, saying that he would return to the Admiralty only on condition that he was given absolute control of the entire Navy—lock, stock, and barrel: bilge-keel, crown and anchor— and that Churchill was sacked forthwith! If these things were agreed to, he wrote: "I can guarantee the successful termination of the war."—"P.S. These six conditions must be published verbatim, so that the Fleet may know my position."

This final broadside sank the good ship *Porcus* with all hands.

Asquith accepted his resignation. What else could he do? But now the Conservative Opposition and all the other critics of the Dardanelles venture were up in arms. They turned upon Churchill, the young amateur who had made a mess of the whole show by refusing to take the advice of the naval experts and the Admirals, including Fisher, the Grand Old Fighting Téméraire who had served seventeen years at the Admiralty under nine First Lords.

There was no escape for the scapegoat. The full fury of the storm burst upon him. The *Morning Post* was out gunning for him almost every day with such headlines as: "Too much Churchill"—"The Amazing Amateur"—"The Amateur Admiral"—"Politician versus Expert". Churchill brushed all this aside as nothing more than Tory propaganda. He did not fully realise what was happening.

As soon as Bonar Law, leader of the Conservative Opposition —a dry-as-dust politician who hated Churchill's flamboyant ability with a bitter hatred born of deep distrust—heard of Fisher's departure from the Admiralty, he forced Asquith to form a Coalition Government. There was no other way of calming the political hullabaloo. Churchill still hoped to retain his position, and Asquith was agreeable to this. But the Conservatives were determined to have him out of it.

On May 26 the Coalition Cabinet was formed, and on that day Churchill left the Admiralty, and Balfour became First Lord in his stead.

The Amazing Amateur was out. Totus Porcus was out, never to return.

All this might be written off as little more than a gang of kids kicking up a shindy in a backyard, pushing, catcalling, and chi-ikeing at the top of their voices—but for the ominous lull on the far-away beaches: the soft molelike thuds of men digging-in, gasping for water: the words *"If we don't get reinforcements soon—"* suddenly silenced by larynx-slitting shrapnel, and the despairing call for—

"stretcher-bearers! stretcher-bearers! . . ."

The first meeting of the newly formed Dardanelles Committee did not assemble until June 7. Thus, for three weeks—during the government crisis and change-over brought about by Fisher's petulant bloodymindedness—Hamilton's telegram of May 17, asking for reinforcements, lay unheeded.

At the most critical period of the Gallipoli Campaign there was no one to make a decision. In effect there was no government.

On June 7 the Dardanelles Committee (of which Churchill was a member) unanimously decided to send Hamilton three divisions of the First New Army, K.1., or "Kitchener's Army" as it was popularly called. One of these was the Xth (Irish) Division, in which I had the honour, the fortune, and the misfortune to serve.

It was not, however, until June 9 that the decision to send these reinforcements for a new attack on the peninsula was ratified by the Coalition Cabinet. In the meantime *ten new Turkish divisions* were being organised under German supervision.

2

KITCHENER'S NEW ARMY

Enlisting in the Royal Army Medical Corps on September 7, 1914, it was natural to expect to be fitted out with a uniform within a few weeks. But after seven months we were still clad in our own civilian clothing. Five of the seven months were devoted to hard training in Ireland, most of the time drilling on the barrack square. This reduced us at last to such raggedness that many men were through at the knees, out at elbows, threadbare in the seats of their trousers. Before long a shirt-tail showed here and there, like the white scut of a rabbit. Our civilian boots wore paper-thin. Sometimes the soles came adrift as we marched. Heels twisted off as we "right turned".

We became such a ragamuffin crew that, as we marched through the streets of Limerick, the girls jeered at us—"What would they be callin' you—Kitchener's Ragtime Army, is it?"

And a gang of street-corner yahoos came yelping after us, chanting—"Here comes my boy with his arse hanging out! *Ta-ra, ra-ra! Ta-ra, ra-ra!*" The time came when we could not be allowed out of barracks without overcoats. Immediately opposite those barracks a cloth factory was turning out khaki uniforms for the British government every hour of the day.

"D'ye think we'll ever be getting any uniforms at all?"

"Ach, listen now! The English wouldn't be spending a penny piece on uniforms for the Irish Division."

And then uniforms began to arrive at the quartermaster's stores in dribs and drabs, and now and then a batch of men were put into khaki. The sprinkling of khaki increased each time we came on parade, until one day the whole of the 30th, 31st, and 32nd Field Ambulances were fitted out.

Already the 32nd had been placed under the command of a Lieutenant-Colonel who turned out to be one of the most

46

eccentric, crotchety, and capricious characters that ever
walked the earth. Erratic, tetchy, unjust, moody, his punish-
ments were often savage and stupid. Smirking like a prima
donna one moment, he was a bear with a sore head the next.
He was in fact cruel and absurd. Before long all ranks came to
fear and despise him. We lived in a state of nervous tension
from morning to night, like a group of little children huddled
together in a corner, afraid of some story-book ogre.

His appointment to the command was a misfortune, if not a
calamity, for us all. Like so many of the officers in Kitchener's
New Army, he was a Regular who had seen service in South
Africa. "Mad Jack" they called him in the Boer War, with
good reason. To us he was known as "Okie Mutt", a nickname
that stuck to him like a burr.

He particularly detested the civilian volunteers of this New
Army. He regarded all temporary officers with venomous
contempt, and made no effort to conceal it. He treated his two
adjutants abominably, taking a special delight in humiliating
them in front of us all, sneering at one, snubbing the other.
He bullied and browbeat the sergeant-major, intimidated the
lesser N.O.C.s, glared threateningly at the rank and file—or
suddenly beamed upon them as though he had just come down
from heaven to present each one with a shining halo and a
packet of manna as a free-gift iron ration. Then, catching sight
of a tunic button undone, he would point with his Malacca
cane, and bellow—his face flushing beetroot-crimson—"What's
the meaning of this? Improperly dressed! Sergeant! put that
man under close arrest!"

Close arrest for an undone button! *King's Regulations and
Orders for the Army*, 1912 (Reprinted, with Amendments up to
August, 1914), allowed no such procedure. We soon found,
however, that the Colonel concocted his own version of *King's
Regulations* on the spur of the moment to suit these sudden
whims and crotchets—and who could say him nay?

To make matters worse, his physical structure exactly fitted
his high-handed antics. Big head, red face, stick-out ears,
bulging eyes, skinny neck, hairpin arms, and bandy legs: a
ludicrous jack-a-dandy, who seemed to prance rather than
walk: a curiously mincing gait that was both pedantic and
cock-a-hoop.

The last thing I wanted was to fall foul of this preposterous Springheeled Jack, and I took pains to avoid getting on the wrong side of him. With three stripes on my arm this was difficult enough. It was sheer bad luck that his physical peculiarities led me, inadvertently, into exactly that unfortunate position.

It was all so swift, so simple. I had made a pen-and-ink caricature of the Colonel. Lieutenant ———, who was in charge of my section, heard of it, asked to see it, saw it, begged me to let him have it, and took it. I supposed he wanted to show it to one or two of his brother officers. They would have a laugh or a chuckle, no doubt. What harm was there in that?

But at the next morning parade of the ambulance the Colonel's normally baleful glance in my direction had changed. His bulging, bloodshot eyes were vengefully splenetic. I knew I was on his black-list.

A few days later, Lieutenant ——— drew me aside, and said laughingly: "You know that caricature you did of the Colonel? I stuck it up in the officers' mess, just for the joke of it. He was furious!"

So was I. But there was nothing to be done about it.

We moved from Limerick to Dublin on April 13, 1915. It was still, no doubt, Joyce's Dublin. Alas, we saw little of it. We got the whiff of niffy-Liffy, the smell of Plurabelle, the reek of the tanyard mixed with the rich malting-house stinkomalee of the brewery. All the trees out-bursting. And not a Fenian in Phoenix Park. The lolling air damply indulgent. The sun's gleam dropping down on Trinity College and the Four Courts as pale as honey.

No wonder they have the soft buttermilk-lilt to their words. And never a whisper of Sinn Fein to be heard, though there was only a year to go before the Easter Week Rising went off at half-cock. All so peaceful you wouldn't think there was a war on anywhere.

All the same, you might think, khaki doesn't march with the ghost of Brian Boru, and the ghost of Daniel O'Connell—not khaki worn by Irishmen going off to fight "over there" for an English king. But this was the Irish Division, don't forget—the first Irish Division ever to take the field in war. Sons of Ireland,

2. ADMIRAL
   LORD FISHER
   FIRST SEA LORD
   1903–1909 : 1914–1915

3. THE RIGHT HON.
   WINSTON S. CHURCHILL
   FIRST LORD OF THE
   ADMIRALTY
   1911–1915
   leaving 10 Downing Street, March
   1914

4. GENERAL SIR IAN HAMILTON
COMMANDER-IN-CHIEF, GALLIPOLI CAMPAIGN

every one of them—Dillons, Boyles, Kellys—(except about thirty per cent.).

And so, in the splendid confusion of its back-history and stubborn patriotic loyalties—and never imagining for one moment that Easter Monday a year hence would see the streets ablaze—dear dirty Dublin took us to its great big Firbolg heart of pure Danaan gold.

What a send-off they gave us when we marched from the Portobello Barracks down to the North Wall on April 29th! The whole of Dublin seemed to have turned out. They crowded the streets from the barracks to the dockside. They cheered, they swarmed after us, they broke our ranks—they jostled us, linked arms with us, thrust apples, cigarettes, lucky trinkets, rosaries, scapulas, packets of sweets into our hands.

You'd think we were Cuchullin-heroes one and all, with all the old drabs and trulls, and all the young bubsy Biddies from "the Liberties" (as the backstreet slums were called) slummocking along with us, trying to keep in step with the drums and fifes wheezling and whingeing the regimental march of the Royal Army Medical Corps—*Her sweet smile haunts me still*. The high-screaming Irish pipes wailing *The Wearin' o' the Green*: the Connaught Rangers crashing our *Saint Patrick's Day*, and the Leinsters' fife-band sweeling-in so sobbing sad with *Come Back to Erin*—and the Faugh-a-Ballaghs* swinging to *The Battle of Barrosa* with its defiant yell leaping in the last bar.

All the ships in Dublin Bay sounded their sirens. Even the

---

* Miss Veronica Kennedy, writing from the Department of Folk Music and Song, University College, Dublin, Eire, (March 20, 1959) was good enough to inform me that the words "Faugh a Ballag" are a rough phonetic rendering of the Irish "*Fag a' bealach*", meaning "get out of the way", or "clear the way"—literally, "leave the way".

The Royal Irish Fusiliers were known as "Faugh-a-Ballaghs", or "The Faugh-a-Ballagh Boys", from the order given to them at the battle of Barrosa (1811) in the Peninsula War. As the Irish spoke their own language in those days, their commanding officer, Colonel Hugh (later Field Marshal Viscount) Gough, gave the order "Fag a' bealach!"—"Clear the way!" This they did in a spirited attack on the French line. From that time "Faugh-a-Ballagh" has been the regimental motto, and it is also the motto of the Gough family.

A "Faugh-a-Ballagh" march has long been associated with the regiment. Miss Kennedy says: "The air is related to the Scottish one of 'Highland Laddie, Highland Laddie', but whether it is also known as the 'Battle of Barrosa' or whether this latter is another march commemorating the same battle I cannot say."

D

North Wall seagulls wheeled and squealed over the quayside.
Soon the cheering crowds, the docks, quays, breakwaters, the
whole sky-pointing array of steeples and spires, the blue
Wicklow hills, and at last the Howth lighthouse drifted astern,
dwindled, hazed, shrank to a pencil-line, and vanished.

Long after the coast became invisible, a huddle of young
Irish soldiers stood on deck staring into the grey nothingness,
silent and disconsolate. . . .

Later that evening they had us battened down under hatches
in the hold of the ship, sitting on the bare boards in the pitch
darkness, with only the flare of a match or the red glow of a
cigarette to see by, as we steamed dead slow through the minefields. The fug was indescribable. No one knew why we were
locked in below docks. Someone said we were zig-zagging
because of enemy submarines. Lack of oxygen did not induce
sleep. We dozed and woke again at the slightest sound.
Darkness and dread killed the spoken word. The hours stretched
into eternity.

We disembarked at Holyhead blear-eyed, yawning, half-
asphyxiated, hungry, and dejected. In the semi-darkness we
marched across windy space, stumbling over quayside rail-
tracks to the dark empty train standing in a siding. A corporal
tried to bring some sort of military rhythm into the lurching
straggle by shouting—"*Left!—left!—left!*——" and a weary
voice from the ranks came in with the antiphonal response—
"I had a good home and I—*left!*" and a rich Kilconnel voice
from County Galway rolled out the climax——"*Right!—right!—*
serves me bloody-well *right!*"

When daylight broke we found ourselves in Liverpool.

They slid us straight down through the five shires from
Cheshire to Hampshire, and dumped us in the green fields
near Basingstoke for nine weeks divisional training along the
white dusty roads. *Sumer icumen in* (*sing cuccu!*) and all along the
leafy hedgerows tricked and flaunty, blowing pink-and-white
with wild roses—soon to be smothered in the choking dustcloud
billowing up from the 50,000 army boots of our longdrawnout
divisional column.

Hideously incongruous, cluttered in kit, sweating in our
heavy khaki serge. A giant khaki centipede marching—"*left-*

—right! left–right!–left!–left!—pick 'em up there!"—across the bee-drowsed, beer-fuddled, clover-scented countryside. With gun-carriages and limbers jolting and clattering.

Our marching discipline is clockwork-true—*click-clack! click-clack!*—all the way from our campsite on the huge, gently-sloping field at Viable's Farm, swinging north-west on the Newbury road, wheeling north-east through Wolverton, along the twenty-mile trek to Silchester Common on the Icknield Way. All on a May morning, and all so English the Irish must have felt they had been transported to some other planet. The Old Bull Inn, The Green Man, The Rose and Crown. . . .

Our cap-badges and buttons flash like stars in the blazing sunshine—all button-stick bright, anointed with Brasso, scoured with an old toothbrush, and vigorously rubbed. The magical result? A thousand scintillating serpents of Aesculapius entwining a thousand scintillating staffs of that same Greek god of medicine!—the badge of the Royal Army Medical Corps shining resplendent in a thousand khaki caps. Proudly worn by one and all: the symbolic meaning totally unknown to almost all of us. "The old snake-and-walking-stick," as it was sometimes called. Once, in a barrack-room at Limerick, someone asked: "Why do we wear a snake, anyway?" and was answered instantly—"Because it's bloody poisonous!" Not satisfied, the enquirer probed further: "What's the walking-stick for?" The reply darted like a forked tongue—"To bash it's bloody 'ead in, o' course!" So we had our myth concocted on the spur of the moment. What's wrong with it?

Nothing. "*March at–ease!*" Now we can sing. We can undo the hook-and-eye fastening of our buckram-stiffened tunic collars. We can wipe the trickling perspiration from the sodden-dark leather sweatbands of our thick khaki caps. We can push them back, and mop our beaded foreheads. And sing.

To hear us singing you'd think we were a lot of whore-mongering lechers. In fact, at least eighty per cent of us were virgin bulls. And though the barrack-room ditties that the sprinkling of old soldiers brought with them were bawdy, lewd, shamelessly ruttish, and friskily blasphemous, the singing of them in lusty chorus left us as we were before: as sexually untried as young stags with burrs in velvet.

"Go on, Shorty—start up something!"

Ah, the rude song for singing, the crude song to hear! the Old Sweat's version of "The Girl I Left Behind Me". Free beer and a crown of wild honeysuckle for the unknown poet who (when? in what barrack-room? how long ago?) hit upon the rollicking loveliness, the pure poetry of the first three lines—

> *You should see our Sue, our lilywhite Sue:*
> *You should see her in her nightie!*
> *When the moonlight flits o'er the nipples of her tits—*
> *Oh, Jesus-Christ-Almighty! . . .*

And every hour there's a ten-minute halt for urination, a sit-down on the grassy verge, a smoke for those who smoke, a swig from a waterbottle, a taking off of sweaty boots, a shaking out of grit and pebbles, an examination of blistered feet, a quiet shut-eye for a few minutes by the roadside. I remember dozing off during one of these halts—and my astonishment when we staggered to our feet at the order to "fall in".

Every man had a wild rose stuck in his cap, as though an order had been given: "Pick—*roses!* Stick roses in—*caps!*" One or two had them tucked into the tops of their puttees. So we moved off, as flower bedecked as May Day mummers, and even more outlandish.

Once a week we marched out of camp for these divisional field days. The weather held good: a perfect English summer. We marched always from lark-song to dewfall, right through the meridian heat: and at night we billeted in barns or cottages, or bivouacked, tentless, under an ambulance wagon or curled like a hedgehog in a dry ditch with the stars pinpricked overhead. This, what with pebbles, roots, and dead twigs, was hard bedding for most of the men, except for a few Irish tinkers and one or two English gypsies who were accustomed to roughing it. It didn't bother me: I was used to kipping-down in "ruffmans dark" just for the fun of it.

One tiny incident remains as clearly embedded in memory as the "fern" in a moss agate. The first shock of wartime disillusionment. We had bivouacked overnight on a poor bumpy field where the grass was strangled with bents, plantains, sheep's sorrel, and knotweed. It had rained during the night, and our blankets were damp. I took mine over to the scrawny hedge to hang them out to dry in the morning sunlight.

Through the over-arching leafage of the row of oaks and elms that stood sentinel all along the ditch, I caught a glimpse of the brilliant blue-green-mauve of the turnip-field beyond—and kneeling among the crispy-crinkled turnip-leaves, each one holding a gill of rain-water reflecting the glinting sky, was the almost Beau Brummellish khaki-clad figure of Captain ——. Praying? No, peering at an unfolded map spread across the turnip-tops. He saw me staring at him over the hedge, and called to me.

I pushed through a gap in the hedge. The cupped rain-water in the turnip-leaves spilled as I brushed past, striking ice-cold as it soaked my puttees. The captain, a good-looking youngster, blinked and grinned. I halted three paces from him, and saluted with parade-ground punctilio. How absurd it must have looked, kneeling, standing, saluting in a turnip-field!

"I'm trying to locate the position the Ambulance will have to take up in this morning's exercise," he said. "Have you any idea how to set a map, Sergeant?"

"Why yes, sir," I almost gasped, and hoped my voice hadn't carried a note of staggered astonishment.

"Well, how would you set it?" he asked.

"With the top edge to the north, sir."

"But which is the north?"

"Over there, sir." I pointed.

"How d'you know?"

"Roughly, by the sun, sir."

"Can you use one of these damn' things?" He indicated the black-enamelled W.D. prismatic compass that seemed to flash and gleam derisively in his hand. All I could say was, "I think so, sir," in a dead flat tone.

"I don't see any 'North' marked on it," he said despairingly.

"That luminous diamond at 360 degrees on the floating card points to the north—but you haven't opened back the hairline screen and the prismatic finder, and you haven't released the rotating verge. What bearing do you want, sir?"

"Bearing?" he said. "I don't know."

"What place do you want to find on the map, sir?"

"Well, we're supposed to be 500 yards south-west of Thornton's Farm by 9 a.m."

After that we set the map, found our present position, found Thornton's Farm, drew a bearing on the map from one to the other, took the angle of the bearing, worked out the road-route and mileage—and that was that.

"Thanks very much, Sergeant," he said. "Most helpful."

I went back and packed my kit, but my mind kept saying: *What is going to happen to us if, one day, our lives depend upon a map and a compass bearing? What is going to happen to us? . . .*

Impossible not to wonder about the training and efficiency of the other officers. All qualified medical men, but—could they read a map properly? . . .

No use bothering. Later that day we marched back to the camp, singing—

> *"When the bugle calls, we shall march away,*
> *And there's not one man will fear it!*
> *For we don't give a damn when the bugle calls—*
> *As long as we don't hear it!"*

Then, suddenly, the whole division was inspected on May 28 in Hackwood Park by His Majesty King George V, accompanied by Queen Mary. The cleaning and polishing for this took a whole day. A whole day devoted to "spit-and-polish"—Blanco, Brasso, blacking, and blasphemy! Yet the inspection itself has telescoped into another, three days later. The sun shone in full summer splendour. Vaguely, I recall King George perched on his charger—small, bearded, astonishingly like the Tzar Nicholas II—why do they put him on such a huge horse? —the leafy shadow-freckle from the enormous trees flows over him as he rides along the front of each corps—another man has fainted—we've been standing to attention for nearly an hour. And then the march past the saluting base. And that's all. Where is the Queen? No idea. Except for the King, the whole scene has been lost to memory—overprinted, almost obliterated by——

"Gawd-love-a-duck!—not *another* bleedin' inspection?"

"Oo is it this time?"

"K. of K."

"*Oo?*"

"Lord Kitchener."

And so, on June 1, 1915, we marched again to Hackwood Park, the demesne of Lord Curzon of Kedleston. We marched everywhere. 1914–1918 was the last of the marching-and-singing wars. No Army lorries, no P.U. vans, no jeeps, no half-tracks, no motor ambulances. We were never once transported in any motor-driven vehicle, and our heavy, lumbering Mark VI ambulance wagons (ten to each Ambulance) were all horse-drawn during this training period at Basingstoke. Magnificent black shire horses they were, four to a wagon, the near horse of the leading pair ridden postilion by an A.S.C. driver (it sounds like Agincourt now!).

The parade routine of May 28 was repeated. By 10 a.m. the divisional troops had fallen-in on their markers, and once again the long weary wait began. Those who stood under the ancient trees shivered a little, for although the sun blazed in and out on that glorious First of June, a chill bite from the north-east came sneaking into the wind.

Here and there a dazzling white line of thrown-up chalk showed where a practice trench had been dug, ripping open the smooth turf. The eye fled away from these war-wounds inflicted upon parklands and copse-dotted green rides that had not known the thudding tramp of armed men for 270 years. Not since the days of Cromwell.

It was noon before the Field-Marshal's cortège trotted on to the review ground. We were called to attention. All down the line, like stentorian cocks crowing hoarsely from farm to farm at dawn, the raucous bellowing blasted the sunlit air with mad-bull ferocity, coming nearer and nearer as battalion after battalion was brought to the salute——

"5th Battalion, The Connaught Rangers! PREE-SENT—AM!" (*click-snack-snick!*)

"6th Battalion, The Leinster Regiment! PREE-SENT—AM!" (*click-snack-snick!*)

So it went on. But there was no thundering command to "Present arms!" as the cortège came to the Field Ambulances. We had no arms to present—except scalpels, amputating saws, and surgical needles.

And then, suddenly, it seemed——

Kitchener looked me straight in the eye from a distance of

three yards as he rode slowly along the lines of the 32nd Field
Ambulance. I looked straight into his. He was 65, I was not
quite 21. That two-way glance lasted about one and a half
seconds—long enough to have *seizin* of any man's spirit.

What he saw I don't know. I was terrified. It seemed to me
that I was staring into Nothingness—a Blank—a Hole in the
Universe!

Yet there he was, a great tree-trunk of a fellow, a veritable
Richard Coeur de Lion, lacking only chain-mail and casque,
sitting his crusader's black charger as straight as a ramrod, its
bridle-buckles, bit, and snaffle-chains blinking in the mid-day
glare of that superb summer's day, in a setting as deep-rooted
in ancient verderer's lore of vert and venison as Sherwood itself.

His eyes—blue, steel-blue, and cold as ice—blazed like
oxy-acetylene blowlamps. The shock—not of the blaze, but of
the Nothing-behind-it—was shattering. *K. of K. did not exist!*
The towering beeches of Hackwood Park had more reality
than Britain's Giant War Lord. Was it possible that the war
was being directed by an Enormous No-One? The impression
came—went—in the blinding flash of a harness-buckle. No
time to think about it. Much too intent upon head up, shoulders
back, thumbs-behind-the-seams-of-the-trousers.

The next instant the great man turned to the officer on his
right, and said: "Pity they're not armed!"

I remember thinking: "He doesn't seem to want any
ambulances at all! Let the wounded bleed to death? Still,
war is war, I suppose. . . ."

By now he had passed on down the line.

None of us had the power to see a year and four days ahead—
none of us saw the cruiser *Hampshire* strike a mine west of the
Orkneys on June 5, 1916. We caught no glimpse of the sinking
ship listing in the grey heave and toss of the North Sea—nor
any fleeting prevision of K's drowned body bobbing like a cork
in the cold boil and seethe into which it sank. . . .

It hadn't happened—yet. He was out of sight, but still
there, returning now to the saluting point for the march past.
First the infantry in column of platoons, then the three Field
Ambulances, followed by the squadron of South Irish Horse,
the Artillery, Engineers, and Army Service Corps: each unit
played past by the massed drums and fifes of its own brigade

(we had no brass bands), led by the Royal Irish swinging to the lilt of "Garry Owen". The long lines of murderous bayonets stabbed and glittered against the fresh green foliage like animated packets of pins.

The satin-flanked horses, the quick-wheeling gun-limbers with their jolting ammunition-boxes, the baggage wagons clinking their tailboard chains, and the white canvas-sided, one-ton ambulance wagons with their high-perched, hooded box-seats for the drivers, and huge red crosses painted on their sides—De Wet and Kruger would have recognised them in 1900!—thudded and trundled past the black charger (that stood so still it might have been stuffed) on which sat the legendary figure of Field-Marshal Earl Kitchener of Khartoum, Secretary of State for War (who sat so still he might have been moulded in wax for Madame Tussaud's).

We could not know—*and he never knew*—how nearly he had come to sharing Churchill's fate only a fortnight before this divisional inspection. At the height of the Fisher crisis it had actually been decided that K. of K. should be "transferred from the War Office" to some such position as Commander-in-Chief. But within twenty-four hours the Coalition-makers realised that (in Churchill's words) "his hold on the confidence of the nation was still too great for any government to do without him".

The great day was over—(strange how June 1 outshone May 28). We marched back to camp, singing—

> *Why did I join the Medical Corps?*
> *Why did I join the Army?*
> *Why did I want to go to war?*
> *I must have been bloody-well barmy!*

June dawdled into July. Then, suddenly, we were issued with light khaki drill uniforms and clumsy-looking pith helmets. The old soldiers in our ranks were all agog. They began talking about *sola topis*, and (of course) *chupattis*, and *chota hazri*, and *punka-wallahs*. A whole new crop of rumours sprang up. We were going to Egypt—to India—to Hong Kong. Never a whisper that we might be going to Gallipoli. The Dardanelles Campaign made very little impression on the public mind. The real war was in France. And up to this moment we had expected to be sent to France. Now, for a certainty, we were *not* going to France.

At last the boring old sweats from Karachi, Lahore, and Peshawar, came into their own. They were able to show us how to pleat and fix the khaki cloth *pagris* round the mushroom brims of our *sola topis*—"'Ere, give it 'ere! you'll never do it that way, not in a thousand years, you won't! Gives me the willies watchin' you windin' it round all kak-handed like that!"

Suddenly, the weather broke. Blazing summer turned away and wept. We packed everything ready for a move. No one knew where. On July 11, at 11 p.m., we paraded in the wet empty darkness of Viable's field. No lights allowed. Our boots slid on the wet, grass-trampled mud-patches.

We marched away leaving our empty tents standing in the teeming rain—dark and deserted in the dismal, cloud-smothered night. It was like leaving home. There was no singing, no talking. We were glad to be wearing our ordinary khaki serge, with the new issue of khaki drill packed in our kitbags.

The massed clump-clump-clump of our army boots echoing through the streets of Basingstoke roused no sign of life. No one pulled aside a curtain to see us go by. No one opened a bedroom window to shout "Good luck!" We were dead men already. Just another lot of troops marching to the station, another lot going to the front.

Of course we didn't know that the Heavy Battery, Royal Garrison Artillery, the 57th (Howitzer) Brigade, Royal Field Artillery, and the squadron of South Irish Horse had been left behind, and would be transferred to other divisions earmarked for France. We didn't know that all our divisional and regimental transport had been left behind. We didn't know that all regimental officers' chargers had been handed over to the Remount Department.

We knew that the huge glossy black shire horses for our ambulance wagons had been taken from us and replaced by mule-teams (six mules to each wagon), because we saw the transport lines crammed with these obstinate crossbred "Jerusalem-birds", and heard the cussing-and-blinding of our Army Service Corps drivers and farriers. But we didn't hear the profanities that sprang from the lips of the men of the machine-gun detachments when they realised that the loss of transport would mean lugging their guns, tripods, and ammunition-belts everywhere by hand.

About midnight we tumbled into the dreary-looking, blind-drawn railway carriages, and sat packed together in a warm damp fug, blissfully ignorant and doltishly incurious (as soldiers learn to be), while the wearisome train carried us on what seemed to be a journey into endless night. Endless because we didn't know our destination, and because the bogies running over the rail-sections kept repeating—"nobody-knows! nobody-knows! nobody-knows! . . ."

At 8.30 a.m. we detrained at Devonport, unloaded our kit, and marched up to the rest-camp at Bull Point. And far away on Imbros Island, our unknown Commander-in-Chief was writing in his diary—"July 12th. Imbros. Had meant to start for Helles an hour before daylight . . . . But am too bad with the universal complaint to venture many yards from camp."

The "universal complaint" was, of course, dysentery. Within a fortnight most of the men of the New Army divisions were down with it.

Although there was nothing in particular for us to do, reveille was sounded at 4.30 a.m. on July 13. But it was not until 5.30 p.m. that we fell in and marched down to the docks for embarkation. Thirteen hours of heel-kicking idleness! That's the way to take the heart out of a volunteer army.

At 5.50 p.m. on July 14 we sailed from Devonport in the s.s. *Canada*, a White Star-Dominion liner of about 9,000 tons.

As our troopship sidled away from the quay, the fife band of the Irish Fusiliers shrilled "The Wearin' o' the Green", thinly, wildly, sadly, with such a high, windy whistling that when they puffed the last wry-necked squeal of ear-piercing melancholy—

> They're killin' men and women for
> The wearin' o' the green!

—a Cockney sailor standing by the bow of a coastal sloop cupped his hands and bellowed across the water: "Are we downhearted?"

There was time to count seven before a few Irishmen shouted "No!" At this rather half-hearted response, the cheery

Cockney grinned a Seven Dials grin and bellowed: "Wotcher lookin' so glum abaht?"

To which no answer came. Before a month was out there was no fife band. It had perished to a man at Suvla Bay.

Soon we slipped out of the Sound, heading for the open sea with two destroyers zig-zagging ahead. And still we watched as, little by little, the last green headland of England shrank and faded, and sank below the skyline.

3

UNDER SEALED ORDERS

We sighted Malta at 4.30 a.m. on July 21, and at six o'clock anchored in Valetta harbour for coaling. All sun-dazzle and pandemonium, dancing sparkle-tipped wavelets, white gulls wheeling, blue, white, green, red bumboats bobbing all around us, rocking to and fro, and half-naked Maltese waving and yelling: "Cee-gar-ette! cee-gar-ette!—tomart! tomart!—me dive for bullybeef! me dive for bullybeef!"

We put to sea again at 6 a.m. next day, with the breakfast margarine a pool of warm yellow oil awash in a pudding basin on the trestle table down below. By mid-day the pitch was bubbling in the seams on deck, and the wind-scoops slung to the port-holes merely added a hot breath to the stifling heat in the cabins.

July 23 was just as sweltering. And every day Sir Ian Hamilton on Imbros island—at least 1,000 miles away—was writing one grumble after another in that amazing diary of his. On this day he wrote a whole catalogue:

> "July 23. Imbros. There are not launches enough to enable people to get about. There are not lighters enough to work the daily transhipment of 300 tons. But the worst trouble lies in the bills of lading. Sometimes they arrive a week after their ships. Usually cargo shipped at Malta or Alexandria is omitted. Half the time we can't lay hands on a vital plant, tackle, supplies, munitions, because we have no means of knowing what is, or is not, on board some ship in the harbour. The trouble is of old date but has reached its climax owing to the shortage of rounds for our 18-pounders.
>
> "We were notified a new fuse key would be required for the new shells on June 12. The shells arrived but the keys were not dispatched till July 15!"

Even if we had known who he was and what he was writing,
it would have left us just as bullcalf-vacant. We were knocked
half-silly by ultra-violet glare.

Saturday, July 24: Alexandria, where we stood in the outer
harbour until 6 p.m., then eased in dead-slow to dock, passing
a troopship outward bound carrying the 6th Inniskillings (on
their way to Gallipoli, though no one knew it) with their pipe
band skirling the same sob-throbbing lament, the same bog-
curlew keening of "The Wearin' o' the Green", as we slid
slowly past each other in the sudden blue-velvet nightfall. We
let up a cheer, but somehow it seemed to blend with the sorrow-
ing plaint of the pipe-music.

Our first sight of Egypt was naval-dockyard-English to the
last tin roof. A wilderness of ghoulish coalyards, grey trucks
standing idle in dirty sidings, dingy quays and deserted wharfs
lit by lonely arc-lamps. It might have been Portsmouth,
Chatham, Devonport, or Birkenhead.

They took us the next morning for a route march through the
town. Once outside the dock zone we marched to attention via
the Rue des Soeurs ("Sister Street", as the Australians called it),
the Gardens, past the Main Guard, back to the ship. All strange
and shifty in the sparkling sunshine: a brightly-coloured scrap-
book dream.

That night, July 25, we sailed north-north-west, once more
for an unknown destination. Next day the heat increased. No
shade on deck. Suffocating below. Eyeballs ached in a glass-
blower's Mediterranean blue furnace. Each eyelid-blink a
blood-red shutter. You can't talk inside a burning sapphire.
Besides, there's nothing to say. The thousand-times-told
barrack-room jokes evaporated. Even the funny men, the Irish
wits and Cockney wags, fell silent.

The pontoon schools still dealt their cards hidden away in
the bowels of the ship. Others played "housey-housey" in
various odd corners, and their strange ritual-cries of—"Eyes
down, look in"—"Kelly's eye"—"Legs eleven"—"Sweatin' on
the top line"—and "Top of the house"—seemed to be the only
form of verbal communication. Once there was a whispered
rumour—

"We're going to make a new landing!"

"Where?"

"Might be the Dardanelles."

"Who said?"

"One of the sailors."

"Ach, to hell! Come on!—Eyes down, look in! . . ."

The card-players and bingo-boys down below were "eyes down" all the way. They saw nothing by day of the sweeping colour-change from aquamarine to fathomless peacock, with the curious milky wash hanging like a cloud below the surface— nor at night the phosphorescent shapes glowing in the dark sea like bits of broken moonlight. They heard "Slipper" Morton shouting "Pay twenties!"—but caught no silver-flashing leap of flying-fish trying to clear the tarpaulin-hooded machine-gun mounted astern. Oblivious to every sight and sound except a greasy pack, numbered lotto-cards, and the cryptic passwords of the game, as—"Clicketty-click" (66), or "Two little ducks" (22).

Who would not rather see the Isles of Greece as they come up one after the other, pink, mauve and dragonfly-green, like phantom submarine monsters slowly surfacing to blow and bask, drifting by on either hand in the pearly haze of the morning? Of all earthly enchantments the most unearthly: the most tremulously iridescent, begat of fire-and-dew, as yet (it seemed) unsmirched by bull's-blood and the beastly fertility-cult-slayings and Minotaurian ritual-rapings of the Greek Heroic Age.

Kos, Naxos, Leros, Samos, Khios, Skyros, Mytilene (Lesbos) —"Where burning Sappho clicketty-click!"—all nameless islands to us, because we didn't know one from another, and only guessed we were threading our way through the Greek archipelago. Knew nothing, in fact, except that we were part of the Mediterranean Expeditionary Force.

All day long on the 26th the unknown islands rose out of the gentian-blue, swung round, changed shape and colour, drifted astern, and slowly sank . . . while others lifted a humped back, a peaked barbican, a terraced outwork: all aflame—all carved in shimmering rose quartz, porphyry, amethyst, chalcedony, chrysoprase, topaz. Shoal after shoal of floating jewels; and the sea *"an undulating carpet of blue velvet outspread for Aphrodite . . ."*

Who wrote that? One guess. Yes—in that diary. Wiser not to look, not to see—"Eyes down, look in". Wiser not to hear the honied phrase. Words are Sirens: the islands Siren-haunted, chanting a fatal music.

Poetry was to be the death of thousands of us before long . . . .

At 3.30 p.m. on July 27 the volcanic peaks of Lemnos—where the Argonauts put in on their way to the Hellespont (and got all the Lemnian women with child at their urgently amorous request)—loomed upon us and closed around us as we needled slowly through the bottleneck of the all-but-landlocked harbour.

This, then, was the base of operations for the rumoured "new landing": the rendezvous, store-dump, and assemblage-point. A desert island the colour of strawboard, that gave off a heavy reek of herbal exhalations arising from sun-scorched juniper, camel-thorn, wild thyme, saltbush, myrtle, peppermint, and decaying stubble. A sickly-soporific fumigation that was to envelop us from now to the end of the campaign, it produced, within twenty-four hours, a strangely enervating malaise that made you wonder whether you were ill or malingering without meaning to. To begin with, just listlessness and an on-and-off looseness of the large intestine, with slight nausea.

Up to now we had been as fit as fighting-cocks, but the island was full of curiously rotten-sweet pestilential breaths, aromatic decay, and a vague contagion floating in the air.

The deep-water harbour, giving soundings of from five to seven fathoms—deep enough to berth such giant ocean-going liners as the *Mauretania* and *Aquitania*, then in use as troopships— opened before us as we inched our way in through the anti-submarine boom that was quickly closed again behind us by a little puffing fusspot of a tug.

And there we lay at anchor in that great still-as-a-millpond pool of deep-dyed cornflower blue, close alongside a dirty cattle-boat, the s.s. *Karroo*, carrying sheep and cows that stank to high heaven all night long.

A hellish burnt-out lunar landscape surrounded us. Ringed by sharp-pointed hills of barren igneous rock, the almost circular harbour might have been an extinct crater filled by the sea. And here the transports crowded like an incongruous convergence of whales, sharks, and minnows waiting for some vast oceanic upheaval.

5. Lord Kitchener inspecting the Xth (Irish) Division, Hackwood Park, June 1, 1915

6. Sir Ian Hamilton's Headquarters on Imbros Island

Unknown to us, our Divisional Commander, General Sir Bryan Mahon, had landed the same day on Imbros island, Hamilton's G.H.Q., about thirty miles north-east of Lemnos.

Sir Ian wrote in his diary:

> "July 27th, Imbros. Mahon arrived at mid-day. Very cheery, but he feels that he is the only Lieut. General executively employed with troops who has so small a command as a division."

That division was the Xth (Irish). Already the status-and-seniority trouble had set in. In less than three weeks it was to rankle and fester. Who was it said: "Lemnos, Imbros, and Chaos"?

The following morning, July 28, we were taken ashore in ships' boats roped together and towed by a launch, under the direction of men of the Naval Division: sunburnt giants in white ducks and wide-brimmed straw hats. I asked one of the straw-hatted sailormen, as he cast off the painter, what the place was like. He grinned and said: "There's nothink 'ere, only sand and flies, flies and sand."

Again and again the towline of boats plied back and forth from the s.s. *Canada* to what was called the "Turk's Head Pier", a tiny wooden jetty built by the Engineers.

No sooner did we step ashore and sink almost ankle-deep in the yellow sand, than the swarms of wicked green-and-black flies swept upon us. And never again, except at blessed nightfall under the dew-cold stars, were we free from this torment until the campaign ended.

We trudged to our camping-place along the western shore, a steady pull up and up on a sandy track tufted with myrtle, stunted ilex, peppermint, and wild thyme. The sweat poured from us. Two or three wizened-looking Greeks followed us with melons to sell, green-rinded like a vegetable marrow. Parched and choked with dust, we bought them for two or three *leptas* (about a ½d. or a 1d. each), slashed them open with jack-knives, and slaked our thirst on the Mediterranean sunset of their brilliant crimson flesh studded with black pips: all dripping with cool, sweet water—utterly tasteless. But water—*water!*—in a waterless waste of khaki sand and dust and heat. Many of the men gorged themselves on these water-melons. No one warned them of the consequences.

E

The toil of manhandling our stores and equipment began: hauling it up the dusty slope from the beach. Medical panniers, operating marquee, tents, tent-poles, cookhouse dixies, picks, shovels, bully and biscuit boxes: all the paraphernalia of a Field Ambulance on active service, from lumbering field-kitchens and spare mule-harness to surgical needles, hypodermic syringes, splints, and tourniquets.

When night fell we were deadbeat. Within moments the stars burst and hung white-hot from a black velvet sky, and our sweat-soaked uniform struck chill. Then a heavy dew drenched us from without. We shivered, drew our blankets, and lay down to sleep.

But sleep was impossible. The crystal-cold dewfall released all the reek of the island at double strength—and everywhere the loud insect-ticking of field crickets and grasshoppers turned the night into a madhouse of ten thousand watches and clocks racing against time, while a myriad cicadas over-topped the clockwork chorus with their thin tin-whistle tunelessness.

If Field Marshal Liman von Sanders had paid those few skink-eyed Greek vendors to hang around our encampment with their baskets of water-melons they could not have done a better job. One day on that accursed island was enough. The diarrhoea set in. I didn't suffer from it myself at this time, but all around were men doubled-up in the throes of the most agonising stomach-pains. Many of them were forced to sleep close to the latrines. The dawn-breeze soon sifted away the covering of sand—and then the flies settled. The diarrhoea increased. Dysentery developed.

Young Lomas, of my own section, went down with it, and was dead in a day or two—our first casualty. We were already an army of sick men. Instead of becoming acclimatised, we were being steadily devitalised. There were no letters from home.

One evening we were paraded behind the camp, told that poison-gas might be used by the enemy, and issued with the most fantastic anti-gas apparatus ever invented: a pink oblong pad of some kind of chemically-treated gauze to be worn over nose and mouth, and tied behind the back of the head by four tapes. These things were called "respirators": the first and most primitive gas-masks. Having been dished out with a pink pad apiece, we were commanded to put them on. But as it was next to impossible to tie your own tapes, each man had to help his neighbour. Instantly the parade broke into a pantomine of horseplay and helpless laughter—

"Hode your head up, Nolan, while I tie your bib on."

"Not so tight, by the holy!—would you be afther chokin' me?"

"What the hell is this contraption, anyway—a baby's nappy?"

Later, N.C.O.s were issued with maps. Would you believe it?—*maps!* I have mine before me as I write. It is marked "TURKEY—GALLIPOLI" at the top, and measures $22 \times 14\frac{1}{2}$ inches, printed on canvas-backed paper, with the imprint: *"Geographical Section, General Staff, No.* 2097: *War Office* 1908. *Reprinted at the Survey Dept. Egypt* 1915, *by permission of the War Office."*

A map! why this was better than a gallon of fresh water! But when I spread it out and looked at it, the gleam of excitement faded. It shows the whole of the Gallipoli Peninsula, the whole of the Dardanelles, and most of the Sea of Marmara! In other words it would be—and was—utterly useless wherever we might land. Why bother to issue it? I stuffed the wretched thing into my haversack with a disgusted grunt.

At 9.20 p.m. on July 31 we paraded on a parched and scabby tableland overlooking Mudros harbour for a divisional route march, or night manœuvre, during which our officers were to find the way by the stars. The stars were there all right: all the old familiar constellations blazing overhead. Otherwise the night was velvet-black.

We marched to attention in full marching order, and only the regular thudding shuffle of our boots on the sandy soil, the clink and rattle of equipment, and the shrill fifing of cicadas broke the oppressive silence. We marched inland along a dusty road that was almost impossible to see. The brilliant starlight seemed to be absorbed before it hit the ground, so that everything merged into a dim monotone. Soon we lost the road—perhaps it gave out—and found ourselves plodding across hard, stinking stubble.

We moved in column of route, with the Colonel a few paces ahead, followed by my own captain and two lieutenants. I followed two paces behind at the head of A Section, with B and C Sections in the rear. Though our boots were soaked with dew, the night air was curiously breathless—almost steamy. The reek of rotting stubble, thyme, and peppermint followed us all the way. We began to sweat. We marched the night through entirely on our own. Hour after hour went by. Even when we had trudged the clock round, we made no rendezvous, came upon no other troops.

At first we marched with confident precision, at a good even pace, all in step, in a direction that appeared to be unhesitatingly sensed by the Colonel striding jauntily ahead. But now we began to move forward joltingly, by stops and starts, with twenty-yard shuffles in between sudden halts that telescoped those in the rear like trucks being shunted in a goods siding. This erratic shambling became ludicrous, exasperating, finally exhausting.

We were still on high ground somewhere in the hinterland of the island. The stars wheeled above us like a glittering planetarium. Again we changed direction, and trudged on. Six paces ahead the ground looked as black as bitumen, with a muslin-thin wisp of white ground-mist floating a foot above it. Three seconds later the Colonel and the other officers in the lead sloshed into ten inches of water, and came to a halt. We had walked into a shallow upland tarn.

Again the column was brought to a sudden standstill. The Colonel came stomping back in high dudgeon, and went into a huddle with the adjutant and other officers. They craned their necks and stared at the stars. The adjutant pointed at the stellar wastes with his swagger-stick. The Colonel jabbed at the canopy of heaven with his Malacca cane—but in quite a different part of the hemisphere. Captain —— turned about and seemed to prod Orion's Belt. It was impossible to hear what was said, but clearly some astronomical divergence of opinion had developed. And, just as certainly, we were lost. As lost as Lost Atlantis.

Meantime many of the rank and file, thankful for this long respite, sat themselves down and, footsore and fed up, dozed off. After a time my own captain came across and said: "Sergeant, do you know which is the Pole Star?"

I said, "Yes, sir", and no more. I had enough experience as an N.C.O. to know that it is a mistake to volunteer more information than is asked for. It usually leads to trouble. And this, I could see, was the kind of situation that could be very tricky indeed. The Colonel had not forgiven me for that caricature.

"Can you point to it?" said the Captain.

"Yes, sir." But I didn't.

"Which is it?"

I pointed.

"You're certain?"

"Yes, sir."

He swung round as he moved away, and said: "Why are you so certain that's the Pole Star up there?"

"I've done a good deal of cross-country tramping at night, sir."

"I see."

He went off to tell the Colonel, and I knew the Colonel would scowl, as much as to say: "What the devil does that young puppy know about the Pole Star, or any other damn thing? I detest these non-commissioned gentlemen-ranker types!"

There was more pointing at the stars, and a further conference in the field. By this time more than half the men of A Section were either asleep on the ground, or nodding in a heavy stupor where they stood. I heard the Colonel say, in his testy-petulant tone: "It's no use now, dammit! it's too late—much too late!"

Then the column was called to attention, and we set off on the long march back to camp. Striking the dusty road at last, we staggered into camp deadbeat as dawn was breaking. The 32nd Field Ambulance had taken no part in that divisional night manœuvre, and we never heard another thing about it.

This demonstration of incompetence—together with the useless map—filled me with a kind of baffled anger mixed with dismay and dread. It was terrifying. . . .

Neither Lemnos nor any other island in the archipelago could hold the vast assemblage of troops and supplies now being mustered for the final attempt on the peninsula. Therefore the cohorts were scattered, some on one island, some on another: or, worse still, units were torn asunder and the dismembered parts banished to different islands.

The Xth (Irish) Division had already suffered such dismemberment by being split in two at the outset, one part being
sent to Lemnos and the other to Mitylene, some seventy miles
away.

Now, at 3.30 p.m. on August 5, our 29th Brigade embarked,
and, all unknown to the rest of us, sailed for Anzac Cove as
dusk fell. There they were to reinforce General Birdwood's
Australian and New Zealand Army Corps in their coming
attack on the Sari Bair heights. Thus four battalions (3,100
men) were taken from us—the Hampshires, Royal Irish,
Connaught Rangers, and Leinsters. The first Irish division ever
to take the field in war had been split in two and broken up
before going into action. In Force Orders issued from G.H.Q.
it was now listed as "Xth Division (less 29th Brigade)".

Apart from the fact that no one island could accommodate
the army required for the "new landing", another and more
serious consideration compelled the General Staff, M.E.F., to
take from one to give to another on a skimp-and-share basis.
"Old K." kept Hamilton on such a tight string for men and
guns that there was nothing for it but to dole them out as best
he could, here a little and there a little, like an old widow-
woman trying to feed a large family on half a stale loaf and a
cheese-rind. And all because Kitchener was still dithering
between a Passchendaele slaughterhouse on the Western Front
and a knock-out blow in Gallipoli to be achieved by poor
Hamilton—even at this final attempt—"on the cheap".

As Birdwood would need four more battalions in corps
reserve for the diversionary attack at Lone Pine and the assault
of Chunuk Bair on August 6, they would have to be taken from
the Xth (Irish) Division. That would leave us a brigade short
for the Suvla landing.

We were up at dawn on Friday, August 6. Orders were given
to manhandle all stores and equipment down to the beach
ready for re-embarkation. We were on the move at last.

It took all day to pack up, haul the stuff down to the landing-
jetty, and strike camp. All through the sweltering afternoon we
lifted and lugged our stores down to the harbour's edge, and
toiled slowly up the dusty slope again for more. And while we
were thus toiling up and down—at exactly 4.30 p.m.—a heavy

and continuous bombardment began on the deeply entrenched Turkish position at Lone Pine, some seventy miles away on the peninsula.

The last phase of the Gallipoli Campaign, in which we were soon to be engulfed, had opened up in a thunderous barrage, of which we heard not a sound.

At 5.30 p.m., while we were humping and dragging our last loads to the beach, the 1st Australian Brigade at Anzac began the attack on Lone Pine—a dash across the open in a hail of shell and enfilading rifle-fire to the absurd battlecry of "Come on, Australia—*Imshi Yalla!*" It was a flesh-ripping smash through barbed wire entanglements, a hand-to-hand death-struggle in the crowded trenches, with bombs, bayonets, rifle-butts, fist-fighting—even garrotting.

By 5.50 p.m. the Australians had driven out, killed, or captured the Turks holding Lone Pine, and made good the whole rabbit-warren of trenches. In twenty minutes one under-strength brigade from "down under" had carried the position under the very noses of a whole enemy division. So fierce was the trench-fight and so tightly packed, that when, later, 1,000 corpses were dragged out for burial, eight Turks and six Australians were found lying in the position in which they had bayonetted each other: a stiffening huddle locked together in death.

To think we didn't even know the name Lone Pine, now as secure in history as Rorke's Drift, Bunker Hill, or Laing's Nek.

The quick-falling twilight was closing in on the dark blue harbour as we marched away from our camp-site for the last time. Near the beach we were lined up. An elderly staff officer stood forward. He told us, in a hard, flat voice that sounded viciously authoritative, and yet hid something wanly forlorn— as though he knew damn well what we were in for—that we should soon be taking part in a new landing on the peninsula: that there would probably be considerable resistance from the enemy: and that we must expect to come under fire getting ashore. He ended by saying: "I am sure you are glad to be going into action at last, and that every one of you will do his duty. Good luck to you—God bless you all."

Short and sharp. No more was needed. But who was this Shadowy Somebody, this Anonymous Oracle that spoke to us out of the cricket-loud dusk and vanished? No one knew. And, to tell you the honest truth, no one cared.

We went aboard the s.s. *Partridge* lying in the harbour, and sailed about 7 p.m. while there was still a fast-fading afterglow from a crimson sunset swamping behind the jagged hills. A few moments later it was dark.

And at 7 p.m. the Turks launched a determined and violent counter-attack on Lone Pine, sweeping forward in wave upon wave with fixed bayonets—as we weighed anchor and slipped silently out of the five-mile-length of the keyhole-shaped anchorage where, it may be, Agamemnon assembled his fleet of (according to the catalogue set forth in the *Iliad*), 1,177 "hollow", "dark", and "red-sided" ships for the attack on Troy: the most famous sea-borne military expedition of ancient history.

But that was all for Helen. No "face that launch'd a thousand ships" launched ours. We eased out of the narrow strait of that deep, crater-like harbour into the dim Aegean as innocent of the whole floating tanglewrack of Greek mythological hocus as a flock of sheep on the mountains of Mourne.

We were just as innocent of the fact that we now formed part of three echelons converging upon Lat. 40 degrees 18 minutes N., Long. 26 degrees 14 minutes E., composed of, approximately—

10,000 of the 11th Division from Imbros,
6,000 of the Xth (Irish) Division from Mitylene, and
4,000 of the Xth (Irish) Division from Lemnos.

As we rounded the southernmost headlead, swung to port, and held steadily on a N.E.-by-E. bearing, Hamilton, our unknown Commander-in-Chief on Imbros island, was standing on the beach at Kephalos harbour—then about forty miles ahead of us—watching the 11th Division sail away. With them went the cable ship *Levant*, paying out a submarine telegraph line all the way. They were to make the first landing at Suvla at 9.30 p.m. The Xth Division (from Lemnos and Mitylene) were to follow up at dawn.

When the Kephalos transports had vanished into the on-coming night, he went back to his hut near the signals tent. A lonely, birdlike creature, spare and slim, as thin-waisted as a sand-wasp, tough as a twist of wire, with bright, enquiring eyes,

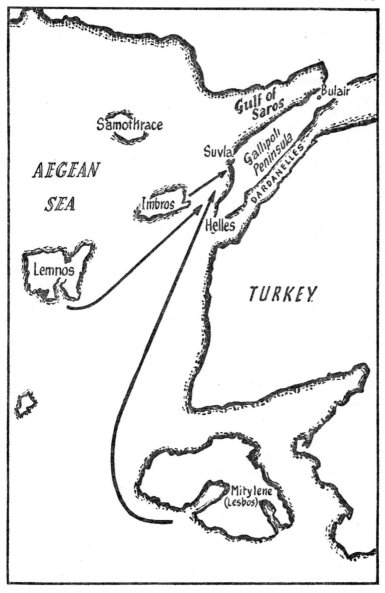

Map 1. ROUTE OF THE THREE ECHELONS

he stood always a little askew, the weight thrown lop-sidedly on one leg, never foursquare. His uniform, not exactly ill-fitting, was just not right: the pockets bulging with odds and ends, the cap set pancake-flat without the essential hint of swagger and dash. Fearless, but much too friendly: the childlike, happy-as-a-sandboy smile too wide-open, too innocently hopeful, too shy, with the head cocked aslant like a perky sparrow hesitating in front of a toastcrust. Born January 16, 1853—a true Capricornian. Too cautious, too reserved.

He sat down. His tapered Kubelik-fingers opened the diary. He wrote:

> "August 6, Imbros. O! God of Bethel, by whose hand thy people still are fed*—I am wishing the very rare wish—that it was the day after tomorrow. Men or mice we will be by then. . . .
>
> "The day before the start is the worst day for a commander. The operation overhangs him as the thought of another sort of operation troubles the mind of a sick man in hospital. . . .
>
> "These new men seem subdued when I recall the blaze of enthusiasm in which the old lot started out of Mudros harbour on that April afternoon. . . ."

He had thought of saying a few words of encouragement to each unit before they sailed—hesitated—and decided that it would not have much effect, since none of them knew him by sight.

Too late now, the men had gone. He went on with his diary—

> "Strolled back slowly along the beach, and, at 8.30, in the gathering dusk, saw the whole flotilla glide away and disappear to the northwards. The empty harbour frightens me. Nothing in legend stranger or more terrible than the silent departure of this silent army, K's new Corps, every mother's son of them, face to face with their fate.
>
> "But it will never do to begin the night's vigil in this low key. . . ."

---

* The well known hymn by Doddridge (1702–51) begins:—
"O God of Jacob, by Whose hand
Thy people still are fed," etc.
—*Hymns Ancient and Modern*, No. 512

4

THE UNKNOWN SHORE

Embarkation orders were clear and strict: no smoking, no whistling, no singing, no shouting. Even the inadvertent clink of a mess-tin against a hatchway was sharply reprimanded with a low-pitched *"s-ssh!"*

Good luck was with us. The night was dark. Sky, sea, and land groped for each other in the enormous gloom: the sea as calm as molten lead. A cool night-wind breathed upon us.

We stood crushed together on deck, as lumpy and bulging with kit as children's stockings stuffed with toys on a dark Christmas morning. Our pith helmets sat top-heavy on our heads, the pale mushroom brims totally obliterating our features. Men-without-faces standing there in the charcoal-grey of the night.

There was hardly any talking. And not a light to be seen from stem to stern. Difficult to move an arm or leg. Limbs stiffened, went numb, began to ache and tingle with pins-and-needles. Ten hours of this all-night-long waiting in full kit—some troops suffered seventeen hours of it—produced a weariness of the flesh, a mental lethargy, and a hawser-taut nervous strain that reduced us to sluggish indifference.

No seaborne army setting forth to battle ever had such propitious conjunctions, confluences, and concurrences of natural forces to aid it. And yet the whole high venture, the vast Argosy-without-a-Jason now converging north of the Hellespont, was doomed, not only from the outset, but from long ago. Certainly from as far back as the Crimean War of 1853-56.

All the defects of the old Army system (in particular, promotion by seniority) sailed with us through the night. We were under the command of men not only too old for the job, too "set" in habits of body and mind, but in poor physical condition. Sick men, in fact. Still more serious: they had no heart for the undertaking, and were more than half-convinced that it could not succeed before any one of us set foot ashore. They carried defeat with them as a mosquito carries malaria.

Mercifully we didn't know. We didn't know where we were going, nor what we were supposed to do when we got there.

Nor did they, as it turned out.

Admiral de Robeck, with the intrepid Commodore Keyes and the rest of his staff, was already sliding through the dark waters in his flagship, the light cruiser *Chatham*, on a direct bearing for Suvla.

Our corps commander, Lieutenant-General the Hon. Sir Frederick Stopford—we didn't even know his name!—had slipped that very morning and sprained his knee, and was in some pain. Just "bad luck", whatever that is. However, he had limped aboard the *Jonquil*, under the command of Rear-Admiral Christian, and was now steaming towards Suvla in the darkness. Of this we knew nothing.

Stopford was one of those stubborn, mulish men, with a big egg-shaped head that dwindled downwards into inconclusiveness. The tired, burnt-out eyes stared down a melancholy flutelike nose from which depended an obstinate upper lip bushed with a pepper-and-salt moustache. Every feature said, "No, I'm not going to!—not yet anyhow...."

He was sixty-one years of age, had been in Egypt and the Sudan in the '80s, had been General Buller's military secretary in the Boer War fifteen years ago, had seen no fighting to speak of, and had never commanded troops in war. He had left the Army in 1909, had lived in retirement until the outbreak of the First World War, and had been in poor health for some years. He was, in fact, a typical Suvla general.

This was the man who was to direct—or rather, neglect to direct—the new landing. His age, normal ill-health, lack of experience in war—and now his groggy knee—might not have mattered if his mind had been a little less mulishly hardbitten. Just as de Robeck's mind was full of floating mines (but had some good reason to be), so Stopford's was full of trenches.

There were trenches everywhere, criss-crossing in all directions like the famous "canals" on Mars.

He was not only convinced that the Turks were massed in strength at Suvla, but that they were strongly entrenched along the beaches, across the Anafarta plain, and in the hills all round—in spite of the fact that recent air reconnaissance had shown that no such entrenchments existed.

Not feeling at all well before going on board the *Jonquil*—what with the painfully swollen knee and everything—Stopford did not say goodbye to the Commander-in-Chief, but sent him a verbal message instead. "I want you to tell Sir Ian Hamilton that I am going to do my best," he said, "and that I hope to be successful. But he must realise that if the enemy proves to be holding a strong line of continuous entrenchments I shall be unable to dislodge him till more guns are landed." Then, repeating the never-ending warnings of his chief-of-staff, Brig.-General H. L. Reed, a V.C. of the South African War, he said gloomily: "All the teaching of the campaign in France proves that continuous trenches cannot be attacked without the assistance of large numbers of howitzers"—and there would be no howitzers available at Suvla.

As the *Jonquil* plowed north-east through the inky darkness, the gloomy corps commander poured out all his qualms and misgivings to the Admiral: what an impossible task had been placed upon him—with no heavy artillery, no howitzers. If there was one thing the campaign in France had demonstrated beyond the shadow of a doubt it was that continuous trenches could not be attacked without. . . . Didn't the Admiral agree?

It must have been a dreary fifty minutes run for the Admiral.

Keeping strictly to time-table a number of sea miles behind, the little *Partridge*, that used to ply between Scotland and Ireland, was heading on the same north-easterly course.

One by one we began to nod and doze, like old tired cart-horses standing asleep in their stalls. And one by one we began to lean heavily against each other, to lurch and sag and give at the knees, until at last we sank slowly down into a sprawling overlapping heap. We had been on our feet since dawn. Most of us had "gyppy tummy" and many were suffering from sandfly-fever, a mild form of dysentery. One thing to be thankful for—no flies. And no stifling peppermint-sage-juniper pungency. We could breathe at last! Cool night air sweeping over us from the wide salt-tanged sea.

Before long word was passed round: "Hot water in the cook's galley for those who want to make tea!" There was a general awakening, a slow pushing and squeezing towards the cook's galley. Each man's belt sagged with three linen bags of "iron rations" (bully-beef, biscuits, sugar, tea). At the moment of embarkation we carried two full water-bottles containing 1½ pints apiece: one reserved for the wounded, one for our own use. Those who went to the cook's galley found that they had to give up one pint of their water-ration in exchange for a pint of boiling water for tea-making. Which shows how stinted the water supply was before we set foot on the peninsula.

I decided that a pint of cold water later on might be a better asset than a pint of hot tea now. I was right—a shade too Boy-Scoutishly prudent in spirit perhaps, but eminently practical.

The tea-break over (how domestically unwarlike it all seemed), we sank once more into a semi-somnolent heap, subdued and silent.

Lemnos to Suvla is, roughly, seventy miles as the crow flies, and the little *Partridge* was making about seven miles an hour.

At 10.30 that night, while we were still chugging along, the transports bearing Major-General Hammersley and the men of his 11th Division from Imbros*—the whole flotilla that Hamilton had seen glide away to the northwards two hours before—slid noiselessly into Suvla Bay and anchored in a dead calm sea. Not a shot was fired.

Ten destroyers and ten motor lighters—three of each carrying each brigade, and one of each allotted to Divisional H.Q., signals, cyclists, engineers, and ambulances—now stood off shore in eight-to-twelve fathoms ready for disembarkation at A Beach, north of Lala Baba, and B and C Beaches below: the two landing-places being roughly two miles apart.

According to Table C, attached to Sir Ian's communication

---

* Many of these 11th Division troops had been inoculated against cholera on August 5th, the day before they sailed for Suvla. In 1915 this inoculation had a sledge-hammer effect upon the strongest constitution. These troops were up at dawn (5 a.m.) on August 6th, and must have been feeling pretty " groggy " when they were landed that night.

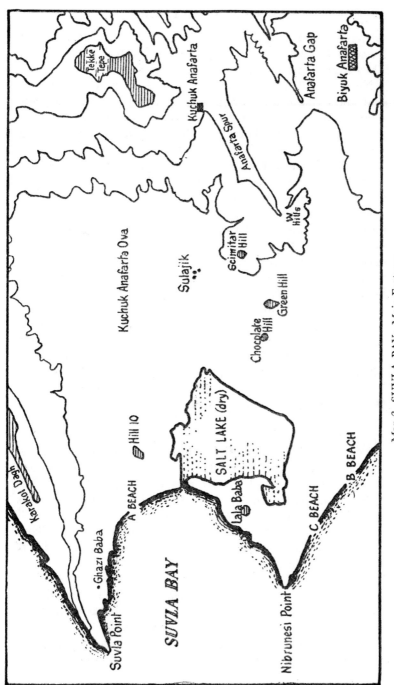

Map 2. SUVLA BAY: Main Features

to the Vice-Admiral (July 17), troops were to be landed at
B and C Beaches "beginning one hour after dark (9.30 p.m.)".
They were therefore an hour late.

Nevertheless, they were there—10,000 men, with all their
gear and equipment, waiting to go ashore—*and the Turks knew
nothing about it*. Not a cough nor a sneeze nor a lighted match
gave the show away. These men, having gone on board during
the afternoon, had already spent from six to eight hours
standing crammed together without elbow-room. Each destroyer carried from 500 to 550 men, and the congestion on the
lighters was worse than on any cattle-boat.

On embarkation each man had $1\frac{1}{2}$ pints in his water-bottle,
and was told (as we all were) not to drink it until absolutely
necessary, and then only a sip or two at a time. The lighters
carried a certain amount of reserve water, some of it in petrol
tins, "with the idea that the troops should on landing, if
necessary, refill their water-bottles" (says the Final Report of
the Dardanelles Commission, Part II, Section 142).

That may seem to be a perfectly good plan until common
sense examines it. How long would it take to fill or fill-up 500
water-bottles in pitch darkness? If two water-bottles could be
filled simultaneously in a quarter of a minute, it would take
just over an hour! And how much of the precious liquid would
be spilled upon the sand? . . . In any case, how can you wait
to fill up a water-bottle as you leap from the ramp of a landing-
lighter on a hostile shore?

Without delay, the ten lighters packed with troops made for
the beaches. As for the landing at A Beach, within the bay
itself, that same Final Report says laconically (Section 81):
"The disembarkation of the 34th Brigade did not work
smoothly. . . ." We shall come back to it later.

At B Beach, south of Lala Baba, four battalions of the 32nd
and 33rd Brigades went ashore without a casualty. There
seemed to be no one about.

So far as the lightermen were concerned, speed! speed! was
the essence of the operation. Therefore, as soon as each lighter
was empty of troops it put about and went back for the next
load—*and that reserve of water was never distributed*.

And still the Turkish outposts had not been aroused, thanks
to the coal-black night and the comparative absence of shoals

and mines on this stretch of the coast. Here the troops advanced half a mile inland before flushing a couple of Turks who fired their rifles and fled. The remaining troops to be put ashore at B and C Beaches landed without great opposition.

By this time, of course, the Turkish piquet on Lala Baba had sprung into action, and the assault on that 150-ft. knoll, carried finally by two companies of the 6th East Yorkshire at the point of the bayonet, became a clashing, thrusting, blind-man's butchery in the hateful black-out of the night, in which a third of the men were killed or wounded. Of the officers, only two junior subalterns survived.* Finding no one left to bayonet—the Turks having withdrawn from their hilltop redoubt—the remnants of the two companies, utterly deadbeat, unable to see more than a yard or two ahead, without orders, and not knowing what they were supposed to do next, flung themselves down on the harsh humpy turf and waited. They had been on their feet seventeen hours.

On the other side of Lala Baba, three companies of the 34th Brigade, under Brigadier-General Sitwell, were to have landed on the extreme left of A Beach, where they were to swing north to clear Suvla Point and secure the Kiretch Tepe ridge, while three more were to land on the extreme right, and advance due east on Hill 10.

The two destroyers carrying these troops not only managed to anchor with their positions reversed, but anchored—with a third destroyer—*nearly a thousand yards south of A Beach.†* So much for seamanship on a dark night in waters as still as a

---

* "The assault succeeded at once and without much loss, but both battalions deserve great credit for the way it was delivered in the inky darkness of the night." (Sir Ian Hamilton's dispatch of December 11, 1915.)

†The naval authorities made exactly the same kind of mistake at the Anzac Landing on April 25, 1915, when the troops were put ashore a mile to the north of the intended landing place, because the northerly current that sets along this coast was "stronger than the sailors realised", and the naval officer (steering by compass) in charge of the line of tows mistook the Ari Burnu headland for that of Gaba Tepe. The naval officer in charge of the flotilla, seeing that the covering party was likely to land two miles north of the proper place, partially corrected the error. Just before the boats grounded at daybreak, this officer shouted—"Tell the colonel that the damn' fools have taken us a mile too far north!" That error in seamanship put the whole operation of April 25 out of gear, making it impossible for the Australian and New Zealand troops to take their objectives, and costing the lives of thousands of men.

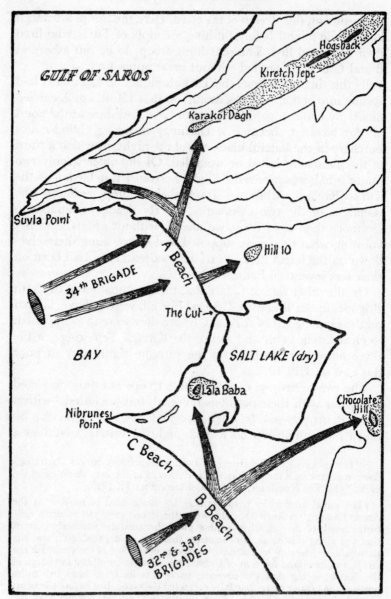

Map 3. 11th DIVISION: Intended Landing, August 6th

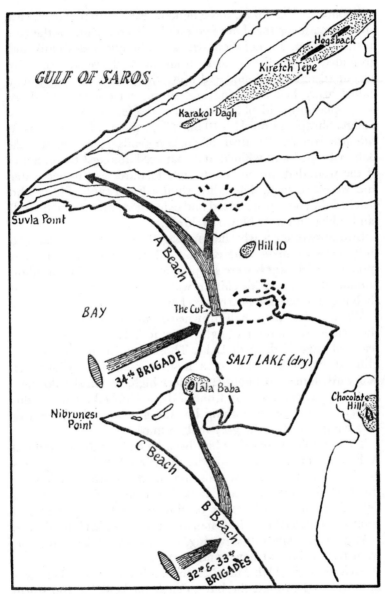

Map 4. 11th DIVISION: Actual Landing, August 6th

millpond. At 10.30 p.m. three lighters, each with 500 men, cast off and made for the shore two hundred yards south of the Cut in shoal water. Two of them struck a submerged sandbank and grounded a hundred yards from land. Here the heavily accoutred infantry floundered up to their necks in water, their nailed army boots slipping and sliding on outcrops of slimy rock, splashing and plunging into potholes bedded with thick sludge. Shrapnel from Hill 10 burst over them, while spasmodic rifle-fire from small patrols of Turkish gendarmerie below Lala Baba whipped and whined and spattered amongst them. Some of the wounded, unable to struggle forward, slid under water and were drowned. The killed slumped and sank. Those who reached the shore were dazed and exhausted: others touched-off land-mines and were blown to shreds.

Strong swimmers who had managed to land waded back to pull non-swimmers ashore. And all the time the precious moments of darkness were slipping away. One of the battalion commanders, up to his chin in water, was hauling men out of shelving shallows for nearly two hours.

When at last these half-drowned troops were formed up on the beach well after midnight, they found themselves on the seaward edge of the Salt Lake. Those detailed to advance on Hill 10—a mere pimple of a mound rising in a whaleback 300 yards long and about thirty feet high, which should have been 700 yards directly in front of them—looked about for this objective, and found nothing but the grey stretch of dry salt flats lying ahead in the grey-malkin murk.

They did not know they had been landed far to the south of A Beach, and that Hill 10 was therefore 1,300 yards north-north-east of their present position. Under scattered fire from the Turkish snipers on each flank, it was impossible to strike a light or use a torch in order to pinpoint Hill 10 by map and compass (if indeed they had map or compass, which is doubtful).

Wet to the skin and shivering, not knowing where to go or what to do, they sat down and waited.

Meantime the 11th Manchesters had been sent off on a two-mile trek right round the bay to clear Suvla Point and storm the Kiretch Tepe, in accordance with their original orders. This meant a night march of two miles trudging over soft sand, stumbling over tussocky humps—sniped at from and-dunes

and bushes all the way—before the battle began! Had they
been landed on the left of A Beach, they would have been
within 1,500 yards of the Kiretch Tepe hogsback-summit. In
fact they lost themselves and vanished into the night. . . .

The New Landing had begun. . . .

It was well past midnight, and we must have been passing
Imbros on our port side, when someone lurched forward and
said: "That was gunfire, wasn't it—somewhere over there?"

That brought us out of our fitful dreams. Those nearest the
ship's rails scrambled to their feet and peered into the darkness.
There was nothing to be seen, but once or twice we heard a
far-away *boom-boom!* on the starboard bow. Our first sound of
battle. *War became suddenly real!*

Talk died away. We slumped once more into the uneasy
nod-and-wake of restless heaviness. Somewhere not far ahead
of our transports, the third echelon of the invasion fleet—
Brigadier-General Hill's Xth Division troops. 6,000 strong, from
Mitylene—was plowing through the same waters, on the
same north-easterly course, heading for the same unknown
shore.

We didn't know a thing about that. For us there was nothing
but the darkness, and our own stiff limbs on board the *Partridge*.
We didn't know, as we slid slowly past the unseen coast of
Imbros, that, within eight miles of us, Sir Ian Hamilton, as
bright-eyed, lorn and lonely as a stilt-legged sandpiper on a
deserted estuary, was waiting, waiting, waiting—hour after
weary hour—for news from Suvla, nineteen miles away.

No news, they say, is good news. But as the hours dragged
by—9.30—10.30—11.30—12.30—1.30—without a word, suspense stretched and thinned to wiredrawn breaking-point.

By 1.30 a.m. on August 7, the original plan for a swift two-
pronged thrust inland to secure the heights north and south of
the bay had already collapsed. Not a word came through from
Suvla.

At 2 a.m. the moon came up, cold and callous, shedding a
glittering flarepath over the leaden sea, and turned us into an
unearthly green-grey herd of giant slugs slaughtered in a heap
on a ghost-ship built of verdigris and gorgonzola.

And at 2 a.m. the needle on the dial-face in the signals tent on Imbros began to dither. The telegraphist took down the message: "*A little shelling at A has now ceased. All quiet at B.*" (No signature.)

It wasn't intended for the Commander-in-Chief. It was merely the telegraphist on the cable ship *Levant* tapping out a few words to his opposite number at Imbros, just to pass the time away. Perhaps to make sure the line was working? That fragment of information did, at any rate, relieve the Commander-in-Chief's growing anxiety. A pity it did, for it set his mind at rest at the very moment when the whole situation at Suvla was floundering in a morass of inertia.

At first bedevilled by darkness—under cover of which the troops had made a surprise landing, but in which they lost touch with each other and lost their way—the position was now wide open in a flood of ghostly moonlight in which they could be picked off by the enemy.

Had the first landing parties pushed inland and taken their objectives during the hours of darkness—as they certainly could have done if they had been properly led—moonrise would have been a blessing. But three and a half hours had now elapsed, and not even the perimeter of the bay had been secured. The troops were still wandering about the sandy strip, not a thousand yards from the sea.

And so, when the protective cloak of darkness was snatched away, the ghastly lunar radiance not only lit up a sepulchral landscape of corpse-pale beaches, silver-livid salt pan, carbon-black scrub, and the glimmering catafalque of scarfaced hills, but at once revealed the wan shadow-shapes of transports and battleships in the bay, the stranded lighters, and the mass of wading, straggling, lost, and already wearied troops, some huddled for cover behind sand-dunes, some drifting in scattered groups along the sea-wet lip of the shore.

In particular, the white armlets worn as a distinguishing mark by the men of Hammersley's 11th Division became gleaming targets that the sharp-shooting Turkish outposts lurking in the scrubland seldom missed.

Sir Ian knew nothing of this perilous turn of events, and so, reassured by that telegraphist's private signal to his mate, he opened his diary and wrote: "Now, thank God, the deadliest of the perils is past. The New Army are safely ashore."

About two and a half hours later the hypnotic engine-throb, the propeller-shaft tremor, and the seethe and wash of the glassy-black water changed rhythm simultaneously, slowing by half a beat: as though the s.s. *Partridge* sensed that this wasn't the Firth of Clyde or Belfast Lough, and that she must nose her way forward cautiously. This deliberate slow-down in the quiet plunge-and-slide of hidden machinery was far more nerve-racking than the *boom-boom!* of gunfire.

Then, suddenly, a running sparkle broke out of the gloom ahead in sporadic fusillades of flickering red and orange glitter-dust, sweeping back and forth like swarms of angry fireflies. Our first sight of rifle-fire—*our first glimpse of war*.

The methodical *ting-ting* of the engine-room telegraph was followed by a distant *clang!* from a Turkish mountain battery— and a plume of water shot high into the air not ten yards away. It spouted, a towering column of feathering spray that seemed to hang for a moment, then dropped like a shattered chandelier —beautiful to see.

Again and again fantastic waterspouts foamed into the air from enemy shells that missed their mark and plunged into the bay. As we steamed slowly in, a strange armada loomed all around us. For a second or two we were back in little old rain-sodden England: back again in Tynemouth, Yarmouth, Falmouth, Plymouth Sound, Tilbury, Wapping Old Stairs, and Galleons' Reach, Gravesend.

For here, dwarfed by four grey battleships cleared for action, was that makeshift fleet of nondescripts that Britain always seems to conjure at a moment's notice for war service from every wharf, anchorage, and seaport town from Cape Wrath to Lizard Point. The same kind of rag-tag and bobtail flotilla that was to save the British army at Dunkirk twenty-five years later. Even some of the "little ships" were here at Suvla.

It was like joining a throng of old friends: North Sea trawlers and drifters, black coal-dusted colliers, yawls, sloops, ferryboats, Isle of Man paddle-steamers, lifeboats, grain barges from Rotherhithe, cargo tramps, lighters, steam yachts, Thames tugs, and seaside motor-boats. And here was our little *Partridge* that used to make the North Channel run from Greenock to Belfast. When daylight came, half an hour later,

we could read some of the names: "Kingfisher, Hartlepool"—
"Rosiland II, Bridport"—"J. Briggs, Whitehaven".

With sleek dignity ten destroyers slid up to their stations,
each towing a huge lighter lashed alongside and a picket-boat
astern. But nothing disturbed the imperturbability of the giant
battleships. What battleships they were we did not know.*
Each was H.M.S. *Blank* to us: inert, enormous, terrible, and
reassuring. Naval cutters might come and go, low-lying
monitors slide into position, cable, balloon, and hospital ships
move closer inshore, submarines surface, signal, and sneak
away: but the great grey monsters seemed to be asleep—
Admirals, Commodores, gun-crews and all. But only for a few
moments. Without warning they belched.

Livid tongues of flame spat from the gun-turrets as we eased
into shallow waters, followed by the vicious double-crack—
then another and another—as a deafening salvo shook the air,
and echoed and re-echoed and hurtled away in a screaming,
tearing crescendo.

One after the other the shells burst with a muffled crump
and a daffodil trumpet of flame—dead on the mark. Shattered
limber-wheels, earth, rocks, and human bodies soared fantastically, like small broken toys, into the air from the dark
hogsback ridge (the Kiretch Tepe) on our left. We watched
them fall and vanish in a bilious cloud of dust and smoke.
That was the end of the battery overlooking Suvla Point.

There were three more spaced at intervals along the ridge,
pounding away at us. Three more earsplitting salvos from the
naval guns blew them into the air, one after the other, with
unhurried deliberation and deadly precision. Then, for a few
moments, except for the stutter of machine-guns and the
crackle of rifle-fire, there was silence. Four puffballs of sulphurous reek rose above the ridge, unfolded, merged, and floated
away in a long, flat pancake of yellow-grey mist.

After that the battleships went to sleep again. . . .

And now, as in a dream, the mechanical heart of our own
particular little world stopped beating. It was dead! You know
how calamity of cessation dawns upon you—as when the clock

* Besides Admiral de Robeck's flagship, the light cruiser *Chatham*, the
battleships covering the landing were *Cornwallis*, *Talbot*, *Agamemnon*, and
Askold (Russian).

on the mantelpiece stops? It was like that. No tremor, no engine-throb. Suddenly we became part of this gigantic landing operation—instead of onlookers.

We heard the rattle of the anchor-chain. We weren't moving any more—our little *Partridge* was a "sitting bird".

Another shell whined overhead with a wailing wobble that showed the enemy's guns were badly worn. It dropped and burst in a snarling thunder-growl. The s.s. *Carron*, a transport riding on our starboard bow, was hit astern. Part of her after-deck broke into a running corkscrew fringe of fiery snakes that licked along the planking and sprang aloft. Soon it was a writhing inferno of tulip-bright flames crowned by a billowing coil of black smoke. We heard the relentless crackle of blazing timber. With splendid discipline the *Carron's* crew ran out the ship's firehose. The flames shrank in a hiss of steam and smother, leaving a fast-thinning smutch of smoke to join the grey smoke-laden landscape.

An inrushing tide of loneliness, helplessness, and lostness came up with the dawn wind and left us chilled and grave.

A lone Taube flew in from the sea, spotting our positions, dropped two or three small bombs as it crossed the beaches, and made off.

The sullen horseshoe of hills, as nameless to us as the mountains of the moon, came unstuck from the slow-lifting mother-o'-pearl buoyancy of the sky. The white leprous patch of the dry Salt Lake unfolded from the scumbled darkness of rock and scrub.

We watched the silvery-wet verge of the sandy shore come adrift from the grey-velvet night-gloom of the bay, and blow up, first here, then there—oh, like a wickedly marvellous bad dream!—as the tightly packed beetles touched the mine-sown shore. In the semi-darkness, and at this distance, we could not see the fiendish underwater enganglements of barbed wire reported by the naval men.

Spellbound, we watched troops leap from the landing lighters into the shallows and wade knee-deep, holding their rifles high, plunging and floundering towards the flat sandy strip under the lee of a 150-ft. hill (Lala Baba) that looked like the brown hump of a kneeling camel.

We watched them scramble ashore and form up, black against the ghost-moth pallor of the sand-dunes. And there they stood, in full view of the enemy's observation posts on the hills half-circling the bay.

At this moment my eyes were glued to a pair of binoculars that had been given to me before leaving England. Fred Boler, my unofficial batman—a huge fellow, who had been Kitchener's galloper dispatch-rider in the South African war, had done twelve years' service in India, and was a Sheffield miner, fifty years of age—stood beside me. Medical Corps sergeants in Kitchener's New Army were allowed to have unofficial batmen—or rather, it was winked at. I had a good friend as well as a batman.

With the Zeiss lenses focused on that strip of sand below Lala Baba, I mumbled something to myself in a gasping whisper: something like—"*Look at that! drilling, as though they were on a barrack square!*"

"Dekko, Sar'nt," said Boler, and took the glasses gently from me. As the close-up shrank to naked-eye dimensions, I heard him say "Sheer murder" very quietly. When he handed them back, he shook his head slowly, and said "*Sheer—bloody—murder!*" The three words meant something, because they were so deadly quiet, and because he hardly ever used barrack-room language, even when he was roaring drunk.

I had the glasses again now. Quite easily those troops could have taken cover on the western slope of the knoll facing the bay, where they would have merged into the sage-brown of dry scrub and dead grass. But no! This was the British Army on parade—with Colonel Bloodshott and Major Tyrwhitt-Toothbrush in command. Take *cover?—hide?*—in face of the enemy? No, sir! *never!*

So there they stood in the first leaden-grey streak of dawn, strictly to attention like rows of tin soldiers on a nursery floor. There seemed to be no hurry.

Then, clearly, in that crystal-sharp air, we heard them number-off—"*One!—two!—three!—four!—five!—six!*" all along the line. We watched them form fours, form two-deep, stand at ease: saw the R.S.M. salute the officer with the jerky precision of a clockwork toy.

At that moment a burst of shrapnel hurtled over the Salt

Lake and spat its load of jagged metal with a venomous-whanging clang into those ramrod ranks. Pitiful—pitiful! The dead lying so suddenly still, spreadeagled on the sand—the wounded crawling away into the bushes like injured ants. . . .

For a few seconds there was confusion. Men running—shouting—gathering together in little knots. Then, but it's beyond the frontiers of stupidity, beyond belief!—the attempt was made to re-form in exactly the same parade-ground formation.

But before this heroic imbecility could be carried out, the Turks, having got the range dead-on at the first shot, whanged-in another, and another, and another, until the beach below the little hill was a shambles, and the survivors scrambled for the cover of stunted thorn, juniper, and thick tussocky grass that they ought to have been told to seek before they were landed.

The white shrapnel-puffs hovered above them for a moment, then danced away on the dawnwind like a *corps de ballet* slowly pirouetting off stage.

Like sleepers dreamfast in a slow-motion nightmare, we had to stand and watch and wait, knowing there were men out there dying for lack of medical attention.

Our transport had arrived on time, but, despite the frantic efforts of military landing officers, beachmasters, transport officers, picket-boat cox'ns, beetle-men—harassed, grim-faced, tetchy as fly-tormented mules—all doing their damnedest to keep to time-table, everything was going slow, as it does in a nightmare when you know you must *HURRY! HURRY!*—and you can't—your feet won't move. . . .

Someone said "*Now we're for it!*" in a dead-flat whisper. He was wrong. Still we had to wait and wait for the order to go ashore. War is mostly waiting.

Then the sun came up. It was 5 a.m.

5

THE LANDING

Sunrise at Suvla on August 7, 1915, sprang out of the first streak of dawn like a slow-motion flight of flamingoes flooding up and up in a boundless oriflamme of surprise-pink. No English daybreak ever burst in such a paroxysm of Greek Fire and Turkish Delight. Death himself was taken by surprise.

And yet quite a number of Suvla survivors have no recollection of this astonishing Phoebus arise! in shell-pink, strawberry, blush-rose—changing second by second to rippling streamers of cochineal, azalea, champagne-rhubarb, and fuchsia, until the whole sky-diorama melted into a cerulean swoon high overhead.

How anyone could miss this heavenly glory I do not know. No account of the Suvla Landing that fails to mention this celestial flamboyance can be looked upon as either complete or accurate. It was the dominating feature.

No one spoke.

Imagine it: 10,000 men standing silent as the grave! About 10,000 other troops had already landed in the darkness and were now drifting hither and thither, sniped at from behind bushes and sandhills, or fighting their way inland by fits and starts.

The sounds of battle, the angry clatter sweeping round the bay, clashed and rattled—loud along the sandstone scarps, muffled in the gullies, screaming overhead. A cracking thunder-roll and recoil-rap-crump, hell-snagged and clangour split, with gaps of terrifying silence broken by machine-gun chatter. . . .

Time and time again the racketing dwindled beyond the rifted ridges, fading far away across the white glare of the Salt

Lake as though the battle-storm had blown itself out—only to break out again in swirling pockets of fury along the beaches.

How the lightermen and beetle-masters feared and hated the shallow waters of that lovely bay! Again and again during the hours of semi-darkness the heavy-laden, flat-bottomed barges fouled the sandbanks that lay submerged in three feet of water 200 yards from the shore. And now that the blazing dawn had burst upon us in all its roseate-golden swordplay, the Turkish gunners in the hills could see the boatloads coming ashore like water-beetles on a stagnant pond. Grounded in darkness on those treacherous shoals, the lighters and landing-beetles were now under shell-fire in the brilliant early morning sunshine.

More than three hours had slipped away since the telegraph-needle in the signals tent at Imbros began to spell out that unofficial message already quoted. *Not another word had reached Hamilton from Suvla.*

Sir Ian had watched "the silent departure of this silent army" from Kephalos harbour, and no official report had reached him.

Anyone might think it was a one-way cable only. But it wasn't. Yet it never seems to have crossed the Commander-in-Chief's mind that he could send a signal asking his corps commander, Stopford, to report. Not that it would have made much difference, because Stopford himself, still isolated on board the *Jonquil*, did not know the dispositions of any of his troops on any sector of the bay, nor where—if anywhere—they were attacking the enemy.

However, he did send a message to Hamilton about now (5-5.30 a.m.): *i.e.*, roughly seven hours after the landing began. It did not contain much in the way of information, for reasons already indicated. "*As you will see*", it ran, "*we have been able to advance little beyond the beach.*"

But this message was not received at G.H.Q. signals tent, Imbros, until mid-day! Thus it took seven hours to transmit a priority message from the corps commander to the Commander-in-Chief by submarine cable over a distance of nineteen miles.

So there we were, at 5.30 in the morning, still waiting to go ashore. And there was Hamilton, pacing up and down the

strip of ground between his camouflaged hut and the signals
tent, still waiting for some word from Stopford. When we
turned our heads away from the beaches and glanced south-
west, we caught sight of the mauve silhouette of Imbros riding
on the horizon like a huge humpback whale. For us it was just
another island. We hadn't a notion where our Commander-in-
Chief might be.

"The principal duty of a commander is to make decisions"—
para. 2, Sec. 5 (*The command of the military forces*), Chap. I,
Field Service Regulations, Vol. II (Operations). No one made
any decisions at Suvla. Hammersley, still at Lala Baba, had
lost touch with all his 11th Division troops and didn't know
where to find them. Stopford, with his sprained knee, lying on
a mattress on the deck of the *Jonquil*, went to sleep! No one was
sent ashore to find out what was happening, no one came from
the shore to report, and no message was sent to G.H.Q.,

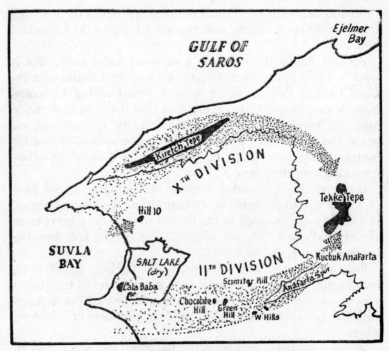

Map 5. THE SUVLA "PINCER MOVEMENT"
(as originally planned)

Imbros. Hamilton—well, Hamilton, as we know, just waited
and waited hour after hour like a cat on hot bricks. . . .

The original plan of operations at Suvla was simple, bold,
and strategically sound. The 11th Division, under Major-
General Hammersley, was to form the right wing of the attack,
and the Xth (Irish) Division, under Lieutenant-General Sir
Byron Mahon, the left. Together they were to clear the
littoral and take and hold the horseshoe of hills surrounding
the bay, while Lieutenant-General Sir William Birdwood
delivered the main assault upon the Sari Bair heights, advancing
from Anzac.

But now, at this critical moment just after sunrise, the whole
Suvla operation—and with it any chance there may have been
of securing victory in the Gallipoli Campaign—was destroyed.

It is stated that Brigadier-General Hill, the most soldierly-
looking of all the Suvla generals (but already a victim of
dysentery), had sailed into the bay with five of his six battalions
of the Xth Division from Mitylene "at daybreak". If this is
true, our transports from Lemnos carrying Sir Bryan Mahon
and his divisional staff (aboard the *Partridge*), and two battalions, one pioneer battalion, and two field ambulances,
including the 32nd, had arrived at least half an hour before-
hand. It is certain that we dropped anchor in semi-darkness
before the dawn. This question as to which arrived first is of
the utmost importance in determining the real cause of the
failure at Suvla.

When Hill arrived, with 6,000 men under his command, he
not only had no idea what the operation was in which he and
his troops were supposed to take part—*he did not even know
where he was!* He could see, as we all could, that a landing was
in progress, but it might have been at Walvis Bay or Botany
Bay for all the information he had been given. He had no map
of Suvla, had never seen a map of Suvla, did not know where
Suvla was, and had no instructions what to do now that he
was there! How could this be possible?

The explanation is given in the Final Report of the Dardanelles Commission (Part II, 1917, Section 82): "Sir Bryan
Mahon received instructions about the Suvla landing on July
28th or 29th, but having failed to obtain a vessel to convey

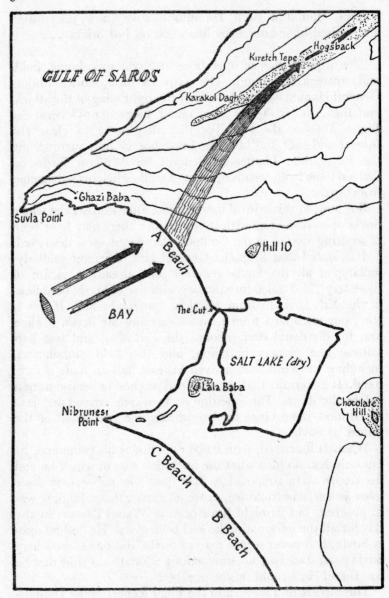

Map 6. Xth DIVISION: Intended Landing, August 7th

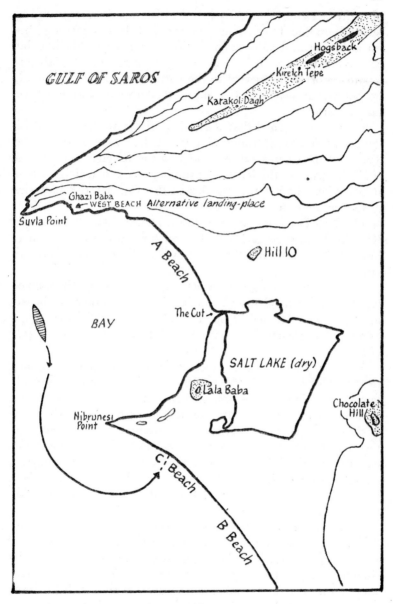

Map 7. Xth DIVISION: Actual Landing of Hill's troops, August 7th

him [from Lemnos] to Mitylene [a distance of seventy miles] he was unable to give any personal orders regarding disembarkation and subsequent action to General Hill, and his endeavour to communicate orders by cypher telegrams failed."

Hill reported his arrival to the corps commander, Stopford, on board the *Jonquil* at 6 a.m., or thereabouts, and asked for instructions.

Stopford explained that the Xth Division troops were to be landed at A Beach, from which point they were to sweep the Turks off the steep sandstone ridge of the Kiretch Tepe which could be seen on the left flank: the hogsback at which we had stared when the naval guns blasted the four Turkish batteries in the before-dawn half-gloom.

The Xth Division troops would certainly have stormed the Kiretch Tepe successfully within an hour or two of landing, but for the near-panic that now overtook the naval transport authorities.

Having had enough of A Beach, and finding themselves faced by the fearful hazards of landing troops there in broad daylight, they decided to put Hill's 6,000 Xth Division troops ashore at C Beach, below Nibrunesi Point—*on the wrong side of the bay*.

This was fatal. It is not too much to say that the decision to land Hill's 31st Brigade and the two battallions of the 30th *three miles to the south of A Beach*, when they should have been put ashore on precisely the opposite side of the bay, not only made Mahon's attack on the Kiretch Tepe impossible, but was, in the event, the chief cause of the indescribable anarchy, exhaustion, bewilderment, and procrastination that presently ensued, from which no one—not even Hamilton himself—was able to extricate us, and from which the Suvla operation never recovered.

True, the naval transport officers had wanted to avoid A Beach from the outset, because of the uncharted shoals that run out from the shore in fingers-and-thumbs and stretch in shelving ridges at depths of $1\frac{1}{4}$ ft. to 24 ft. in 600 yards. But they knew, and had known since July 17, that Xth Division troops were to be landed there, and they knew that this landing was to take place in the half-light of dawn.

The whole enterprise was set at naught and unwittingly

sabotaged an hour after dawn on August 7, when naval transport decided to abandon A Beach altogether. *It took five more hours before the landing was completed.* And all because the Navy failed to carry out any effective reconnaissance within the arms of the bay before the landing began.

A systematic search for an alternative landing-place ought to have been made on the night of August 6. Darkness was no excuse. In fact darkness was essential for such a reconnaissance. A few strong swimmers ought to have probed the indented coastline from A Beach along the northern arm of the bay until a suitable inlet was found. Any old buccaneer of the Morgan type would have had a shot at it. But de Robeck was no more of a Morgan than Carden.

The fact that a perfectly good alternative landing-place was found about half a mile east of Suvla Point within twenty minutes of making the fatal switch to C Beach reveals the position in all its tragic negligence. (See map 8, p. 108.)

The six and a half hours of precious darkness and semi-darkness (from 10.30 p.m. to 5 a.m.) had vanished for ever, and little more than half the Suvla forces had been put ashore.

Just after six in the morning, with the sun's flaming fireball climbing overhead, we were still waiting on board the *Partridge* for the order to go ashore—while the naval transport officers made ready to disembark Hill's troops at C Beach.

We at any rate were on the spot, and could see the landing operation taking place. Hamilton saw nothing, heard nothing, knew nothing. No one gave him a thought. Not a tremor of electrical impulse had passed along the submarine cable since that inadvertent oscillation at 2 a.m.

As for the two military pack W.T. stations at Suvla that were supposed to be in communication with the wagon wireless station at G.H.Q., Imbros, they were so feeble, intermittent, and decrepit as to be useless. One thing is certain: Sir Ian was clean forgotten. . . .

The Forgotten Commander-in-Chief!—could anything, in all the annals of military history, be more preposterous?

But this was nothing to what was now taking place on board the *Jonquil*. Stopford, having agreed with the naval transport officers that Hill's troops had better be got out of shell-fire as quickly as possible by diverting them to C Beach, was instructing the still bewildered brigadier to place himself under the orders of General Hammersley, and to reinforce the 11th Division—"until the arrival of his own divisional general"! (These words are from Hamilton's dispatch of December 11, 1915.)

Hill's divisional general was, of course, Sir Bryan Mahon. The Final Report of the Dardanelles Commission (Part II, Sec. 82) says: "General Hill, followed by his six* battalions, arrived at Suvla from Mitylene at daybreak [*sic?*] on August 7th, and was at once summoned to the *Jonquil*, where he saw Sir Frederick Stopford at about 6 a.m."

At this very moment Mahon and his staff were on board the *Partridge*, and had been there since before dawn, waiting with the rest of us to go ashore. Why, then, was he not "at once summoned to the *Jonquil*" to take part in the crucial briefing then taking place, in which one of his brigadiers and a brigade-and-a-half of his troops were being sent off to C Beach and placed under Hammersley's command on the wrong side of the bay?

Can it be that Stopford was unaware that Mahon had already arrived? It must have been so, otherwise he would not have instructed Hill to place himself under the orders of Hammersley "until the arrival of his own divisional general".

Can it also be that Mahon did not know that Hill and his troops had arrived from Mitylene? It looks like it. We shall probably never know exactly what happened in this Box-and-Cox affair.

The next paragraph of Section 82 of the Final Report (Part II) says that Mahon and his H.Q. staff "landed early in the morning of August 7th at New A Beach" (later called West Beach), and that: "Previous to landing Sir Bryan Mahon saw Sir Frederick Stopford, who ordered him to push on as far as possible along the ridge of Karakol Dagh and Kiretch Tepe."

It cannot have been as early as all that, because Hill's interview with Stopford not only included a conference with naval transport, and instructions about C Beach, but now—

---

* In fact there were only five. One battalion did not arrive until much later, and was landed at West Beach on the afternoon of the 7th or the morning of the 8th.

much to Hill's astonishment no doubt—a man in naval
uniform with a long upper lip, a wide tight mouth, and a
small but hellishly determined chin, broke in upon them. It
was Commodore Keyes.

Once again he was hopping mad! He had just been watching
the "leisurely proceedings" on the beaches, and could stand
it no longer. He had jumped into a pinnace and come across
from the *Chatham* "in a fever of resentment". Why all this
delay? What the devil was happening? There wasn't a moment
to lose! The Turks would have time to bring up reinforcements
before the Xth Division was ashore! Never mind a damn about
shoals, shell-fire, mines, booby-traps—! Hill ought to land his
men inside the bay—*now*—this moment—and not at C Beach.
A suitable landing-place had just been found 1,300 yards
north of A Beach, and the troops from Mitylene ought to
be landed there, since they were to operate on the northern
flank.

But the order to put them ashore at C Beach had already
been issued, and it was felt that another change of plan would
create further confusion and delay. Even so, it was not until
after 8 a.m. that Hill reported to Hammersley.

And it was only after all these problems and complications
had been settled in such a way as to nonplus the entire Suvla
operation that Stopford saw Mahon, instructed him to land
at the newly found inlet with his remaining three battalions,
ordered him to advance as far as possible up the Karakol Dagh
and Kiretch Tepe ridge forthwith, and explained that his
other five battalions (now disembarking at C Beach) would
revert to his command as soon as he got ashore. *In fact they
did not rejoin their division until another five days had elapsed!*

"These orders," says the Final Report (Part II, Sec. 82),
"were carried out so far as the small force at Sir Bryan Mahon's
disposal would permit."

The truth is that Mahon was so furious at finding himself
with a "division" consisting of no more than three battalions
that he nearly resigned his command there and then.

The fact that the instructions given to Hill left Mahon with
only a handful of troops for the assault on the gully-riven
steeps of the Kiretch Tepe does not seem to have troubled
Stopford at all. He was, by all accounts, in a curious state of

optimistic quiescence. Although not one single objective of any importance had yet been taken on either side of the bay, the gloomy forebodings that had sailed with him during the night had now miraculously evaporated. There had been some unfortunate delays, of course, but, on the whole, he felt, things were going pretty well.

We were still waiting to go ashore when, soon after the first flash of sunlight burst above the crest of the Sari Bair, the furnace-breath of day beat down upon us. The battle for the beaches was over, and the battle for the heights seemed to have lost itself in the dry water-courses intersecting the foothills.

More and more troops were landing moment by moment. More and more stores and equipment were being manhandled from lighters and piled in ever-extending dumps along the sandy flats and low-lying dunes that edged the shore. The sand at Suvla is strangely white: a kind of silver sand, finer in granulation than the yellow sands of England, and now in the morning sunshine it sheened and glittered as brightly as the silver scales of a herring catch.

We had been cooped-up on board the *Partridge* for eleven hours when the acrid, nostril-stinging reek of burning gorse reached us. It might have been the pungent smeech from a midsummer gorse-fire on Chipperfield Common in Hertfordshire! It was, in fact, the blazing gorse on Hill 10, that wretched little thirty-foot molehill of a mound held by a Turkish battery and 100 men.

Faintly, as through the earphones of a crystal-and-cat's-whisker-set, we heard shouting and sporadic rifle-fire beyond the sandhills at the centre of the bay. We were hearing (and smelling) the last phase of that disastrous landing of the 34th Brigade, under Sitwell, that had begun when they were put ashore in shoal water nearly 1,000 yards south of A Beach soon after ten-thirty the night before. The time was now between six-thirty and seven in the morning.

It was well after midnight when, you may recall, the three companies detailed to advance on Hill 10 failed to find their objective. Wandering about in the inky darkness they lost touch with each other, and came under the demoralising fire of Turkish snipers who knew every inch of the ground. Before long they were scattered in disconsolate groups north and south of the Cut. They had been on their feet for nineteen hours.

Yet at that moment there were six battalions "sitting idle" on Lala Baba, not a thousand yards away!

The colonel of the lost battalion knew nothing about that. At last the moon came up at 2 a.m., and in its spectral gleam of spookish deception he rallied his troops and advanced on what he supposed was Hill 10. In fact this was a smaller mound 400 yards to the south of it. Six platoons stormed this hillock in the chancy moonlight, only to find it undefended. As they reached the top the Turkish gunners on Hill 10 opened fire. The survivors fell back like a windblown scatter of dead leaves, and lay still amongst the scrub-belts and salty sandflats in doleful apathy. Finally, word was sent round to General Hammersley's headquarters—still situated between Lala Baba and Nibrunesi Point—asking for help.

It was not until after 3 a.m. that the two remaining battalions of the ill-fated 34th Brigade began to land under heavy fire, more than five hours after the original landing. And again there was trouble. One lighter struck a reef far out from the shore, another stuck fast on the rocks. Small boats had to be used to get these troops ashore—(why weren't they used in the first place?)—and it was after daylight before the last of them stepped on to the sticky grey saline mud below the Cut.

By this time the Turkish fire was so severe that a third lighter was forced to put about and make for B Beach, south of Nibrunesi Point, where the troops were disembarked and then had to trudge back over a mile across heavy-going sliding 'sand and shingle, under shrapnel fire most of the way.

It was not until after 4.30 a.m. that Hill 10 was located, and an attempt made to sort out the drifting confusion along the beaches north and south of the Cut, in order to muster the troops for the attack. By this time half a battalion had arrived from Lala Baba in support. But the officers who led these troops had "very little idea of what they were to do", and the attack went to pieces.

Round about 5 a.m. Hammersley ordered all the remaining troops of the 32nd Brigade, who had been sitting around on

Lala Baba for the last five hours doing nothing, to hurry to
the assistance of the 34th Brigade in the advance on Hill 10.
It took them half an hour to reach the Cut (a distance of
1,700 yards). They were now under heavy fire, with the pink
sunrise spreading overhead. Between 6.30 and 7 a.m. Hill 10
was carried, and the hundred odd Turks retired slowly eastwards across the Kuchuk Anafarta Ova, lobbing back a few
shells into their old position and setting the gorse on fire.

It had taken eight hours to locate and capture this strong-
hold: a mere pimple that, nevertheless, dominated the entire
sweep of the bay. Why wasn't it blown to dust from Lala
Baba? With what?—*no artillery had been landed.*

Having attained this objective, Sitwell decided to hold the
position at all costs—against whom? The Turks everywhere
were pulling out, fighting stubbornly in small patrols as they
fell back towards the hills, leaving skirmishers and snipers in
the bushes, but retreating steadily.

Soon after dawn Birdwood's signal corps had run a field
telephone line along the coast from Anzac to Hammersley's
headquarters, and at mid-morning a message came through
reporting that observers on the scarps above Anzac Cove
could see signs of a general Turkish retirement: guns, baggage-
carts, and troops moving back across the plain towards the
hills.

Even so Hammersley still imagined that his troops were
faced by strongly-held enemy entrenchments, and only now
began to consider the possibility of attacking Chocolate Hill.

Major Willmer, the German officer in command of the
Turkish troops at Suvla, had already sent a message to his
Commander-in-Chief, Liman von Sanders, saying that the
British marched "bolt upright", never attempted to take cover
behind scrub, and reported that: "No energetic attacks on the
enemy's part have taken place. On the contrary, the enemy is
advancing timidly." He added that this situation was unlikely
to continue, and begged that reinforcements be brought down
to Suvla from Bulair with all possible speed.

Sitwell, with true Stopfordian mulishness, not only decided
to hold on to Hill 10, but also to dig in. He was still no more
than 800 yards from the beach, but he seems to have felt that
this was all the more reason for consolidating his position.

Time enough to push on when the position was properly entrenched.

We cannot ignore the fact that his men were exhausted. However, even exhausted troops can keep going so long as they are kept on the move towards a known objective. This depends on leadership, which was entirely lacking. Sitwell himself was "looking old and haggard" and was "already worn out with worry and physical exhaustion".

Hammersley was in even worse shape. He had landed at B Beach soon after midnight, and was then feeling "rather exhausted". During the hours of darkness he tried to find out what had happened to the units of his 11th Division. No one seemed to know, and it was only when the rose-pink dawn came flooding up that he realised the position. They had done little more than secure a foothold here and there along the perimeter of the bay.

To make matters still more impossible, this old and sick man—he was in fact suffering from a "clot of blood in the leg" (phlebitis)—was quite unable to stand up to the hazards of war. When, during the morning, a shell made a direct hit on his headquarters, killing several of his staff, he was found in a state of semi-collapse with his head in his hands, weeping. Having pulled himself together, he proceeded to issue the following successive and contradictory orders:—

(1) 8 a.m.—32nd and 34th Brigades of the 11th Division to "push on vigorously" to Chocolate Hill on the arrival of Hill's Xth Division battalions, which were to protect the left flank of the two brigades advancing from Hill 10 to the W Hills.

But as Hill's troops were only beginning to come ashore at C Beach at 8 a.m., this order was countermanded—

(2) 8.35 a.m.—32nd and 34th Brigades to "push on vigorously" *alone* to the Chocolate and W. Hills.

When Hill reported at Divisional H.Q., he was instructed to—

(3) 8.—a.m. (?)—march his Xth Division troops north of the Cut, join up with the two battalions of the 32nd Brigade (then holding Hill 10) and wheel south on Chocolate Hill, with these two battalions on his left flank attacking the W Hills. (*No mention of Sitwell's 34th Brigade.*)

So Hill went off with his five battalions round the seaward edge of Lala Baba. Soon after they had gone, Hammersley again changed his mind and issued the following amendment—

> (4) 9.5 a.m.—32nd Brigade commander to use his reserve—
> "whatever that might be"—in carrying out the instructions already issued. (*Again no mention of Sitwell's 34th Brigade, and no mention of Hill's troops either.*)

Such were the conflicting, confused, and confounding orders issued by the exhausted, shell-shocked, and bemused Hammersley during a period of one hour and five minutes on the morning of August 7, in a situation already dissolved in exhaustion and loitering due to no clear orders at all at the moment of landing.

The heat of the sun was now beginning to throb like the pulse-beat of a red-hot gong. Why all this toiling north to Hill 10 (after it had been taken), then south to attack the Chocolate and W Hills, a distance of over five miles? Why not a direct thrust from C Beach skirting the southern edge of the Salt Lake, a distance of less than two miles? Simply because Hammersley had it fixed in his mind that the position was strongly entrenched on the southern and western slopes, and because he never had the nous to send out half a dozen scouts to reconnoitre and report.

In fact the southern slopes of Chocolate Hill were defended by nothing more than "a few strands of rusty wire". A straight thrust from B Beach and/or Lala Baba soon after landing on the night of the 6th would in all likelihood have cleared the Turks from this 160-foot prominence, since the Suvla garrison had been ordered not to try to hold out against any determined attack by the invaders. The early capture of this position would have turned the whole operation in our favour. This was what Hamilton hoped for and expected.

We watched the Navy putting ashore the tons and tons of stores and equipment needed by 20,000 troops. It went on all day and and they did it in record time. Enormous mountains of supplies were dumped ashore haphazard and higgledy-piggledy. There was no organisation of any kind. It took two days of rummaging and sorting before the various units could find essential munitions, food, and implements. *Amongst it all*

there were no buckets or other utensils for carrying water from the
shore to the front line—and no water.

Standing there, watching all this from the s.s. *Partridge*, we
seemed to be left out of account—forgotten, unwanted—as
though we were already an army of dead men . . . the ghosts
of dead stretcher-bearers looking on.

At last a landing-beetle shouldered gently alongside, softly
buffeting its rope-coil fenders against us as it nosed-in with a
ripple-lipping caress, and a file of troops from our transport
began shuffling down the gangway into it. They were glum,
grey-faced, silent, but glad to be going into action.

Who and what were these troops? Just youngsters, lads,
most of them, as callow as Wells's Kipps—city clerks, shop
assistants, dental mechanics, medical students, office boys,
bricklayers' mates, farm labourers, under-gardeners, architec-
tural students, miners, millworkers, barrow-boys—mothers'
darlings, as untried in war as Rupert Brooke himself: mere
saplings.

This should be said for them, must be said: they went down
the gangway into the waiting beetle grimly, silently, with
steadfast determination, heroically unheroic, unled, alone
inside themselves, stoically willing to serve—to fight—to kill—
to suffer—to die—even to die in vain. As good an army as
Alexander of Macedon ever had.

The beetle cast off. The engine coughed and chuntered
quietly. How quickly the clumsy-looking craft moved towards
the shore. Soon the pith helmets of the tightly-packed troops
were no bigger than mushrooms. The bay, bottle-green in the
shallows, amethyst-and-ultramarine in the deep-water channels,
made your eyes ache and blink.

Within a minute or two—with luck—the blunt prow would
shovel nuzzlingly into the silver sand north of A Beach without
touching-off a mine. Then it would come back for another
load. Us perhaps.

It never reached the shore. A clanging clatter of shrapnel
tore a flashing hole in the sky, livid as lightning—spat a hellfire
hail of hot scrap-iron jags—and belched a black puffball of
noxious smoke that hung there like an infernal afterbirth.
We didn't realise what had happened until we saw the beetle
put about and come round on the blind side of the *Partridge*.

The wounded were taken on board. Almost all the men in that landing-party were casualties.

Our own fear increased a thousandfold. In a few seconds terror reached saturation-point and began to ebb away. An overdose of fear produces a kind of fearstricken fearlessness. We were green at the gills, but pepped-up with fear.

We were moving along now in single file, inching slowly forward, lumbered with kit: every detail dream-solid and insect-bright in the eye-screwing sunglare. Almost before we knew what was happening we found ourselves standing crammed together in the bottom of the landing-beetle, and—as in a dream—gliding towards the white ribbon-line of beach that we had watched since daybreak.

But soon our unwieldy-looking craft changed course, heading due north for Suvla Point, and, 250 yards from that rock-strewn coastline, swung round to starboard in six-and-a-half fathoms and ran east-by-north for a small horseshoe bight marked West Beach on the post-Suvla Admiralty chart. This was the alternative landing-place on the left arm of the bay that was found within twenty minutes of making the switch to C Beach.

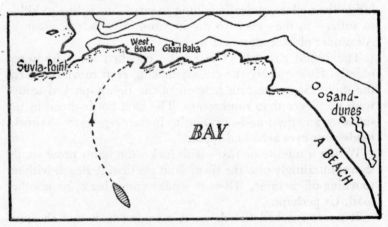

Map 8. WEST BEACH: The Alternative Landing-place

Though the main infantry attack had advanced across the Salt lake and been swallowed up in the tortuous geological jig-saw of spurs and gullies, the ear-splitting duel between the

Turkish artillery in the hills and the British battleships in the
bay screamed and hurtled overhead, burst in deafening
impacts rocketing from the Sari Bair to the Kiretch Tepe and
back again—compacting sudden, diaphragm-shuddering blast
formations of hot air that seemed to make the sunlight flicker.

Behind this over-amplification of shattering projectile-
velocity came the quick staccato of machine-guns, the hard,
snapping crackle of rifle-fire, and the murderous thud of
exploding land-mines.

As we neared the shore, enemy bullets whipped miniature
waterspouts in the glassy shallows: all dreamlike, all strangely
unreal. They looked like the skipping splashes made by
skimming pebbles flung by schoolboys playing ducks-and-
drakes. There were Turkish snipers still hidden in the dense
scrub-patches overlooking the beaches, although the tide of
battle had long since swept past them.

They could have been winkled-out without much difficulty.
No one bothered. The beachmasters were too busy: the fatigue-
parties were unarmed: the armed guards had no orders to leave
the store-dumps.

The *cuff-cuff-cuff* of the engine shut off as we ran in. We
felt the soft sand-cushioned bump and the sliding scrape as the
heavy, flat-bottomed lighter dredged to a standstill: heard the
rattle-and-creak of running tackle and rusty chains as the
iron-plated ramp at the bow lowered like a drawbridge.
We're back in the Middle Ages. And there's the moat—a
ten-foot gap of water between us and the shore. We had
grounded on a sandbank.

How limpid the water was—apple green! as clear as a
glass-alley. You could see the bas-relief of sand-ripples on the
sunlit bottom with little gleams of refracted sunlight rocking to
and fro—yes, and sharp-spined pink and mauve sea-urchins—
and your own shadow-silhouette—*ping!—splop!*—bullet—

"Get ashore, boys—quick! you'll have to jump for it!"
shouted the beetle-master. "You'll make it all right!" he
added, wiping his hands on an oily rag and plucking a Wood-
bine from behind his ear.

Some of the shorter men found themselves floundering
waist-deep. I found myself wading in two feet of water just
above the knees. So damnably *slow!*—like a diver wading at

sea-bottom. "*Still alive, anyhow*," I told myself. The moulded sand-ripples were firm underfoot. No submerged barbed-wire entanglements so far, thank God. Only the water impeded us.

We sloshed ashore, stumbling and lurching, and came out with our khaki drill uniforms turned to walnut-brown and clinging to our limbs like sopping-wet packing paper. The army biscuits in our three days' "iron rations" were soaked (but still as hard as nails). A dark stain dribbled and dripped from our tunics, because the small white linen bags (neatly tied with tapes) containing three pinches of Indian tea had been drenched, and the three precious lumps of sugar were tinctured by that sea-water tea-making.

As we staggered up the shelving sand in the strong morning sunlight, we began to steam like the steaming flanks of horses in a lather. Within ten minutes our clothing was dry!

We stood now, breathless and dishevelled, on a sandy strip dotted with prickly scrub. The 32nd Field Ambulance was safely ashore.

So began the sweating toil up and down, from the beach to the continually fluctuating front line on that fatal August 7, in the first mass attack ever made by Kitchener's New Army.

And still the pathetic figure on Imbros had no news, no report, no notion of what was happening at Suvla—and made no attempt to find out.

6

THE FATAL AUGUST 7th

Sand, the real defender of Suvla, put a drag-chain upon us, laid us by the heels. Hot sand not only baked our feet encased in hot leather, it swathed us in silence. Our clumping army boots made no sound. Men without footfalls now! Sweat poured from us. Flies smothered us. Spittle dried up. At noon it was over 90 degrees in the shade.

And at noon the telegraph needle at G.H.Q., Imbros, began to spell out the first official message Hamilton received—nearly fourteen hours after the landing began at B Beach on the night of August 6. It was the message Stopford had sent at or soon after dawn saying that his troops had been able to advance "little beyond the beach". This was bad news. However, the Commander-in-Chief noted that it had been handed in about seven hours ago, and took it for granted that Stopford's troops must have taken their objectives by now.

The very fact that the corps commander had sent no further report reinforced these wild, forlorn, and desperate hopes. Wild, forlorn, and desperate because Hamilton knew very well that Stopford and the other Suvla generals were too old and hidebound for the task: had in fact asked K. of K. for younger generals, and been refused. None could be spared from the Western Front.

Hoping against hope that all was well at Suvla, that no news must be good news (and here it was noon), this strange Don Quixote of a Commander-in-Chief did positively nothing—just went on waiting and hoping, hoping and waiting. . . .

Anxious and wistful, yet buoyed up with hope based on nothing, he waited the whole of that day without another word from anyone at Suvla.

In the meantime Feizi Bey, commanding the 7th and 12th Turkish Divisions, was bringing his troops south on a gruelling thirty-five mile forced march from Bulair.

Mustafa Kemal, the only man with any real grasp of the situation, was not yet in charge of the Anafarta battle area. He was still only a senior divisional commander with the rank of colonel, holding the position north of the Anzac front with the 19th Turkish Division. But he was on the spot with his men—alert, watching every move as he looked down on the Suvla plain from his perch on Battleship Hill, ready to spring into action—if only those damned reinforcements from Bulair would hurry, hurry!

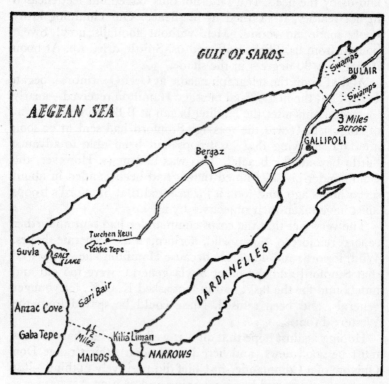

Map 9. ROUTE TAKEN BY TURKISH REINFORCEMENTS
FROM BULAIR

At the zenith of the sun's mid-day heat our stretcher-squads moved inland in extended order to what was officially called

7. Sailors coming ashore at Lemnos

8. C Beach, Suvla, showing Nibrunesi Point

9. Commodore Keyes, Admiral de Robeck, General Sir Ian Hamilton and Major-General Braithwaite on board the *Triad*

"the collecting zone", searching for wounded: a long horizontal line sweeping forward from A Beach on the right to the lower spurs of the Karakol Dagh on the left. There was no transport of any kind. Nothing but men, stretchers, and what medical supplies could be carried by hand. No water supply except the water-bottles slung over our shoulders.

The tent sub-divisions had been left on the beach to pitch the operating marquee and other tents, with the cooks and cook-house personnel near by to erect a makeshift kitchen (although there was nothing to cook), and to make gallons of tea (if the camp kettles could be located, and if water could be found).

The total lack of ambulance wagons threw an enormous extra burden of physical drudgery upon the bearer sub-divisions, who had to carry the wounded on stretchers the whole of the way back to the dressing station on the beach. Even when the wagons and mule-teams were landed, days later, the contours of the Kiretch Tepe made it impossible for them to be of any help. They could only be used along the beaches, or round the edges of the Salt Lake, where they sometimes sank up to the axle-trees in the soft sand and mud.

Moreover, the whole of the bearer sub-divisions were thrown into action at once, leaving no reserve to relieve exhausted stretcher-bearers.

Within minutes we were swallowed up in the geological convulsions of this torn and riven landscape. I remember a glimpse of a jaunty Springheeled Jack prancing ahead of us, his bandy legs skimbling at a foppishly coxcomical gait, Malacca cane and all—the only man amongst us who seemed to be highly delighted with everything, and as lively as a cricket! I was glad to see him vanish behind the ridge of a dry water-course, and thankful not to set eyes on him again during the whole of that day.

The weather suddenly took a freakish turn. Out of that blazing sky a cloud appeared, no bigger than a man's hand. Within a few moments it blotted out the sun like an enormous black tarpaulin. Then the storm broke. Impossible to tell whether the thunderclaps were thunderclaps or shell explosions, or gunfire from the ships in the bay behind us, the sounds were so alike. In seven seconds we were drenched to the skin.

During that short torrential downpour, when we stood

H

together like cattle in the corner of a field, one of our A Section bearers was saying—"That's gospel truth! Didn't you hear what he said?" Then he broke into a take-off of the Colonel's voice and mannerisms, whipping his puttees with an imaginary Malacca cane: "I want it to be a tradition in this unit that no R.A.M.C. man ever reports sick unless on a stretcher."

This was quickly translated by the rank and file as—"No Medical Corps man allowed to go sick".

"Who says?"

"Okie Mutt."

"What do we do if any of us goes down with dysentery?"

"Carry on till we drop dead. That's the order."

Later on I heard the same order, or rather exhortative direction, from my own section captain. At the time I thought it harsh, eccentric, and stupid. Long after the evacuation, when it was possible to consider the results of this peculiar homily, it struck me as a stroke of genius.

It did become a tradition that no man of the 32nd should report sick so long as he could stagger along on his two feet. Harsh it certainly was, but it kept the ambulance service going. Mad Jack's ordinance kept us toiling on. He, at any rate, understood the truth of the saying "A man can do more than he can", and acted upon it.

On this first day of our landing—"the fatal August 7 at Suvla", as Hamilton called it—we didn't realise how tired we were. Released at last from the long hours of waiting, we moved slowly inland towards the firing-line. We moved slowly because the search for wounded in that labyrinth of dry watercourses slowed us to snail's-pace, and because of the heat of the day.

Slowly, also, because we were not only carrying those heavy old-fashioned Mark II stretchers made of seasoned ash (each weighing thirty pounds *unloaded*), and three "monkey-boxes" or field medical companions (one to each section) packed with bandages, splints, and a wide range of first-aid equipment, but each one of us was loaded up with a haversack, iron rations, a surgical haversack (containing more bandages and first-aid kit), a water-bottle for the wounded, and our own personal water-bottle (both filled at Lemnos).

In spite of the injunction to take only a sip or two of water at a time in order to eke out the scanty supply, some men had emptied their own water-bottles before or soon after landing. The desire to do so was almost irresistible.

We were working now 800 yards E.-N.E. of West Beach, on the slope of the Karakol Dagh that rises at a one-in-ten gradient. Here, some 114 ft. above the shore, a goat-track led past an old stone-flagged Turkish well measuring about eight feet by seven, with a solidly built parapet of trimmed limestone blocks where the water lipped to the brim.

Water!—as clear as the crystal streams of Paradise, gallons and gallons of it!

"No man to touch that water!—pass the word along—no man to touch that water!"

As we climbed on to the grey stone kerb we saw why. This well, or rather spring, was choked with dead Turks and the carcasses of mules flung one upon the other, hideously distended by the gases of putrescence: gargantuan distortions blown-out by the heat of the sun, and now, submerged and waterlogged, decaying in a slough of dissolution.

And yet the water looked as clear as the fountain that Moses struck from the rock in the desert of Zin, and gave off no fetor.

As each man stared into this poisoned pool and caught sight of the heap of dead bodies, he moistened his lips with his tongue, and turned away downcast. Some turned away in silence. Others muttered as they trudged on—"Filthy dirty trick!"—"Bloody Turks!"—"Bastards!" For the first time hatred of the enemy became real.

Again and again we came upon little groups of lost men wandering about, dragging the butts of their rifles in the sand, their blistered lips foolishly open, their eyes burnt-out like dead cinders. They drifted slowly up and down the gullies in twos and threes, sometimes as many as half a dozen in a bunch. Always the same question-and-answer—

"Any water?"

"No"—or a shake of the head.

"Seen the 6th Munsters anywhere?" (or the 5th Royal Irish, or the 6th Dublins).

"No."

They shuffled on without another word like old foot-weary tramps looking for a haystack or the nearest dosshouse. Thirsty men waste no words.

Even more nonplussed than this near-sleepwalking army of strays, laggards, and mayhap-truants that must have numbered several thousand, were the boy-officers looking for their men. Every now and then we came across one of them—Eton, Harrow, Winchester, Charterhouse. Some of these baby-faced "sub-loots" were still in their teens. Downy-cheeked youngsters, as pathetically lost as Sealyham puppies baffled outside a warren that smells of Brer Fox instead of Brer Rabbit: "I say, Sergeant, have you seen any of my fellows anywhere?"— hoping a sergeant might turn out to be as efficient and dependable as Nannie.

You could see the spreading dismay as the ordinary Tommies recognised their own fear and hesitation in the eyes of these one-pip striplings. Men under fire—and it was never possible to get out of range of the enemy's guns at Suvla—watch each other with nerves on edge. "Blimey! even the bloody officers are lost! . . ."

Now, for the first time in our lives, we heard something for which we were, strangely enough, totally unprepared. A human cry so harrowing, so piercingly mournful, so despairingly importunate, so long-drawn-out in piteous pleading, so persistently clinging to a last hope, it brought us up sharp— halted us in our tracks.

There it was again, away to the left: a bodiless voice that seemed to come from the rocky ledge high above us—

"Stretcher-bear-e-r-s!—stretcher-bear-e-r-s! . . ."

We ran forward a few paces at a left-incline, then slowed, breathless, as the slope steepened. Prickly scrub blocked the way, forced us to zig-zag. We lost direction—halted—listened—

"Stretcher-bear-e-r-s!—stretcher-bear-e-r-s! . . ."

No cry in the whole world so woebegone, so distressfully urgent. But now it seemed to carry over to us from a different direction, more to the east, almost straight ahead. We hesitated, bewildered by the singular acoustics, cocked an ear again— shouted—listened. Nothing—not another sound, except the stutter of a distant machine-gun. We pushed on, sending one squad up the steep slope to the left, the others straight ahead.

Nothing more dreadful than that cry for help, and then— silence. . . .

During such gaps of agonising suspense, when the hell-hounding battle-rattle died out or suddenly ceased throughout the Suvla amphitheatre, we heard all the sounds of another battle being waged five miles away behind the quivering heat-haze of the Sari Bair, lost to sight among the rifts and spurs from Lone Pine to Chunuk Bair and Hill Q.

This diminutive clash of arms was in fact the main attack north-east from Anzac: Birdwood's desperate attempt to seize the heights south of Suvla—the assault that had begun at 4.30 p.m. on August 6, at Lone Pine, and was still raging.

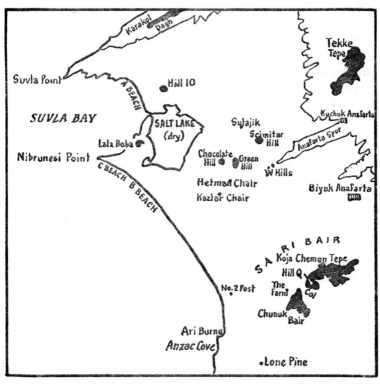

Map 10. SUVLA IN RELATION TO THE ANZAC BATTLE
FOR THE SARI BAIR

Not knowing that Anzac was only three and a quarter miles south from C Beach, we thought the far-off clangour must be our own Suvla troops storming up the Aghyl Dere to the 850 ft. Chunuk Bair summit from the low-lying scrublands and

isolated trees of the Kazlar Chair plain. Not that we knew any
of these map-names. We could hear the distant fighting on our
right, and see the puffs of smoke and dust drifting across the
burnt ochre, cinnamon, tan, and liver-coloured uplands, hazing
the buffs, lavenders, apricots, and brickdust-pinks of the wadis
and scars of the Sari Bair from which the sounds of midget
combat came.

And so it seemed to us that things were going well.

By now the chain of command had broken down completely.
We had all lost touch with each other. Some of us may have
been no farther apart than ten or fifteen yards, yet, in this
surrealist landscape*, knurled and crossgrained by an endless
confusion of ravines, ledges, and spurs, once out of sight you
might wander about for hours and never come across one of
your own unit.

Thus, within an hour of starting, we were all separated.
Officers, N.C.O.s and squads were compelled, by the geography
of the place, to work on their own, and were only able to co-
operate by some chance meeting.

By sweeping across country "in line by the right", like beaters
at a shoot, we were all scattered, alone or in little groups: some
searching one gully, some another, some plodding heavyladen
back to the dressing station on the beach, others returning sun-
staggered and deadbeat for another load—without orders,
without direction, each man doing what he felt had to be done
in a kind of semi-conscious daze. How many wounded died
before we reached them no one will ever know.

It was now about 1 p.m., and although it was my job to
direct and supervise the operations of A Section bearer sub-
division in the field, there was nothing to be done but trudge
on alone, attend to any wounded I found on the way, and hope
to fall in with stretcher-squads still moving up towards the
firing line, or coming back from the beach.

Sudden and prolonged shrapnel-fire across the bay, bursting
somewhere below Lala Baba, that blotted out the fainter
battle-sounds from the Sari Bair, made me turn half right.

* Hamilton wrote in his diary, September 21, 1915: "Memories of the
Khyber, Chitral and Tirah can hardly yield samples of a country so tangled
and broken."

Turks still shelling the beaches? One after the other the small white puffs were born out of the aching blue, hung for a moment, lifted, drifted, and faded quickly into the cloudless sky. As they vanished one by one, others were born. Impossible to know what was happening over there.

Within minutes I was too busy, anyhow, dressing a gunshot wound in a right forearm, to give it a thought.

This fierce noonday onslaught was in fact bursting over General Hill and his five Xth Division battalions, who had only now reached the northern flank of Lala Baba, about a mile and a half from Hammersley's headquarters. Thus it had taken them some four hours (from, roughly, 8.45 a.m. to 12.45 p.m.) to cover the 2,500 yards from C Beach.

The sun had reached its meridian an hour before they emerged from the blind side of the hill and debouched upon that narrow and ill-fated mud-strip between the Salt Lake and the sea, where the 34th Brigade had made their lamentable landing in the night-time darkness.

Four hours for five battalions to cover a mile-and-a-half to two miles from C Beach! True, in that time Feizi Bey's two divisions had trudged only another three miles on their way from Bulair to Suvla, making six in all. They were still twenty-nine miles from the Tekke Tepe (918 ft.)—*at this moment totally undefended*. How long before they would reach the summit?

Time—time—all a question of seconds, minutes, hours!

How did Hill and his Xth Division troops come to lose so much time before setting out on their roundabout route to Chocolate Hill via Hill 10? Since the employment of these troops on the wrong side of the bay dislocated the entire plan of operations at Suvla, it is essential to find out what happened between, say, 9.30 a.m.—about the time Hill rejoined his men after receiving his instructions from Hammersley at Nibrunesi Point—and 1 p.m., when they began to cross that narrow neck of sandy mud that separates the Salt Lake from the sea. In all, a period of three-and-a-half hours. (See map 11, p. 125.)

The factual record of these lost hours is as grotesquely fabulous as anything recounted by Jakob and Wilhelm Grimm from the dark forests of German folk-tale. It has the same nightmare harassment, the same manic-depressive overhang of stupid fatality.

And through it all marches the soldierly Hill, tall, clear-eyed, broad-shouldered, doing his best to understand a situation that had long since collapsed in Bedlamite confusion, but finding it almost impossible to grasp, what with the heat of the day—now well over a 100 degrees—and the fearful intestinal gripings of dysentery that racked the body and slowed the mind. Nevertheless, he stuck it out.

Bewildered by Stopford's orders, and not very sure about Hammersley's, Hill decided to tramp across to Hill 10 to get the hang of things at first hand, leaving his five battalions in the lee of Lala Baba in the meantime. This meant a trudge of about a mile and a quarter through ankle-deep sand and over tussocky sand-dunes in the blazing sun. It must have taken him at least half an hour, probably three-quarters. That brings us to ten o'clock, or a quarter past.

Arrived at Hill 10 he sought out the commander of the 32nd Brigade, whose troops were to move on the left flank in the projected attack on Chocolate Hill. The commander of the 32nd Brigade explained that he could not move without being instructed to do so by Sitwell, commanding the 34th Brigade, under whose orders he had been placed—and that Sitwell had no intention of taking any further action at all.

So Hill went off at once to see Sitwell in the hope of getting him to change his mind. But Sitwell explained that the 34th Brigade was still fighting the Turks beyond Hill 10, and therefore the 32nd Brigade could not be spared to take part in the advance on the Chocolate and W Hills.

It must have been 10.30 or 10.45 a.m. when Hill "started plodding back through the heavy sand" to divisional headquarters to make sure that he understood Hammersley's instructions. This involved a trudge of nearly two miles, and it must have been 11.15 or 11.30 a.m. before he got back to Nibrunesi Point. Some accounts say twelve noon.

To give the whole situation its final twist of ironic fatuity, Hill was informed that Hammersley had gone to the top of Lala Baba to watch the attack on the Chocolate and W Hills. So the O.C. 31st Brigade, Xth (Irish) Division, retraced his steps for 1,000 yards and "toiled up the hill". Here he was told that Colonel Malcolm, Hammersley's senior staff officer, had been sent across to 34th Brigade headquarters on Hill 10 to "explain everything", and that the advance was to begin "at once".

So down the hill came the weary brigadier-general, glad to know that everything was being straightened out. It was about 12.30 when he gave orders to form up for the advance.

While these preparations were taking place, Colonel Malcolm was having a heated argument with General Sitwell at Hill 10. Nothing the senior staff officer said could budge Sitwell from his determination to stay where he was. His troops were too tired to move—they must dig in—must have water—were badly disorganised—were still attacking strong enemy forces to the north-east, on the Kuchuk Anafarta Ova— must hold Hill 10 at all costs—were not fit to launch another attack—must have time to recuperate—had suffered many casualties—would have to be regrouped. . . .

Sitwell himself was played out, worried to death, physically ready to drop. The colonel urged the extreme urgency of the situation: Chocolate Hill must be taken without further delay. The W Hills must also be secured. These were General Hammersley's orders. It was essential that Sitwell's troops should co-operate with Hill's battalions which would be arriving before long.

Malcolm and Sitwell were still arguing when a young officer of the 34th Brigade came up to report that he and a party of men had just returned from reconnaissance. They had pushed forward due east across the Kuchuk Anafarta Ova (ova = plain) for a considerable distance, and were convinced that there were very few Turks anywhere in the neighbourhood. "The proof is," he said, "that I have been out for nearly three hours. I took thirty men with me, and I have brought them all back."

In fact, except for snipers, the Suvla plain was empty. Little more than 1,500 Turks, helped by an intimate knowledge of every goat-track and gully, by heat, sand, thirst, flies, dysentery—and, of course, by that imaginary "system of continuous entrenchments"—were able to keep an army of over 20,000 British pinned to the beaches.

Just as the hopelessly inconclusive argument was nearing its end, Hill's troops could be seen moving across the spit towards the Cut, the sky blossomed with floating white smoke-balls, and the vicious whanging-clang of the shrapnel barrage stung the ears.

Hill, fagged-out and footsore after tramping up and down on sleeveless errands, led his men in person to Hill 10. So close-plastered was the Turkish shrapnel-fire and so accurately registered upon that strip of sandy mud that the only way of getting across was by rushing it and trusting to luck. There was no cover of any kind. Therefore the leading battalions, the 6th Inniskillings, the 5th Royal Irish, and the 7th Dublins, were instructed to split up and make a dash for it, section by section. But, of course, these heavily booted, heavily accoutred troops, no matter how they attempted to rush across, were only able to break into a carthorse trot. There were a good many casualties.

To enhearten these young and untried troops, Colonel Downing, commanding the 7th Dublins—a veritable giant in height and girth—stood calmly twirling his stick in the midst of the shrapnel-swept zone as though he were watching a trot-past of yearlings on the Curragh racecourse.

The "dash" across the neck, the crossing of the Cut, and the final 900 yards to the low cover of Hill 10 took nearly two hours. Here the troops formed up and "stood easy", while Hill went over to Sitwell's dug-out. He was exasperated to find that nothing had been done.

At 3 p.m. Hill complained to Hammersley's headquarters that the 32nd and 34th Brigades had made no move to operate on his left flank for the attack on the Chocolate and W Hills, which had been ordered six hours earlier. He was furious.

In the meantime, things had taken another leisurely turn, another slow-up. Without modifying any of the four curiously conflicting orders issued between eight o'clock and 9.5 that morning, Hammersley again changed his mind. At 1.40 p.m.— while Hill's troops were making their "dash" across the neck— *he decided to postpone the attack until later.* In pursuance of his "attack-at-once—but-not-yet!" tactics, he now called up two battalions of his 33rd Brigade—who, since the evening of the 6th, had been busy digging a trench from the sea near C Beach to the verge of the Salt Lake, and were now waiting in the belt of low scrub south of Lala Baba—and ordered them to move to the northern side of the lake. Here, under General Sitwell, they were to join up with the 32nd and 34th Brigades, and, together with Hill's battalions, advance south-east to attack the Chocolate and W Hills—at 5.30 p.m.

Before any word of this new arrangement was known at Hill 10, Sitwell had reluctantly agreed to support Hill in the forthcoming attack, and the long-overdue preparations for this combined operation were rather grudgingly set in motion. By the time all units were ready to move off, Hammersley's orders postponing the attack had arrived.

The patch of dry grass, sand, and stones, on which Hamilton had pitched his G.H.Q. camp at Imbros, was just as scorching in the afternoon sun as the Suvla plain. The hours dragged on without another word from Stopford. The Commander-in-Chief became increasingly anxious. Surely they must be storming the heights by now—the Kiretch Tepe to the north, the Tekke Tepe (key to the whole position) in the centre, and the Chocolate and W Hills to the south?

Soon after 4 p.m. he sent a signal to Stopford urging him to push on. There was no reply.

At last the delayed attack got under way.* For the first thousand yards the troops marched (no, trudged is the only word) due east across the Kuchuk Anafarta Ova, with their backs to the bay. From this low ground little could be seen but prickly scrub, undulating stretches of dead grass, the semi-circle of hills palsy-stricken in the heat-haze, and the slender minaret of Kuchuk Anafarta (Little Anafarta village), a solitary white candle startlingly sunlit, with four windmills on the right standing like four pepper-pots in a row.

If the advancing troops had trudged steadily forward in the same easterly direction, bearing away E.-N.E. and a point

---

* "None of the three Brigadier-Generals concerned in the attack on Chocolate Hill, Generals Sitwell, Hill, and Maxwell, accompanied the troops. They established their report centres to the south of Hill 10, about two miles distant from Chocolate Hill, and remained there . . . and evidence discloses the confusion and delay which resulted from this cause." (Final Report, Dardanelles Commission, Part II, Section 86.)

to the E. for three and a half miles as the crow flies, they would have found themselves on the summit of the still undefended Tekke Tepe — and Hamilton could have cabled K. of K.: "*Peninsula taken.*"

Alas, the vital importance of taking this key position before the Turks could bring up reinforcements from Bulair had never sunk into poor Hammersley's distraught and wavering mind.

And so, after crossing the dry bed of the Azmak Dere (*dere* = valley with stream), Hill's three leading battalions wheeled south-south-east on a direct bearing for Chocolate Hill. Up to this time their left flank had been protected by the 11th Division troops, but as these troops continued to advance due east "every yard gained to the southward tended to throw this flank more and more into the air". Thus a gap appeared, leaving the left flank of the 5th Royal Irish exposed. Turkish gunners on the Yilghin Burnu uplands were quick to put down a lambasting curtain-fire on this weak spot. Finally the gap had to be filled by two companies of the 7th Dublins.

The Fusilier battalions were now moving on a line parallel to that they had taken from Lala Baba to Hill 10 nearly six hours ago, but in the opposite direction. That is to say, they were making an enormous horseshoe-bend right round three sides of the Salt Lake: a route of more than five miles that would bring them face to face with the only "system of continuous entrenchments" at Suvla—*i.e.*, on the northern and western breasts of the features marked on the maps issued to officers as the Yilghin Burnu (that included Chocolate Hill and Green Hill), and the Ismail Oglu Tepe (known as the "W Hills") 2,000 yards farther to the east.

And all the time the Tekke Tepe looked down upon them without a man or a gun to guard the eroded havoc of its crotched and quoined massif quivering 900 feet above the plain.

Opposite Sulajik, halfway to Chocolate Hill, the eastern rim of the Salt Lake makes a double bulge. Here, on ground as flat as a counterpane, the Inniskillings suffered grievously. Many sank up to their knees in the grey, porridge-like sludge, with shrapnel bursting unceasingly above them. Landmines, shallowly buried in the thick saline mud, exploded on contact. The dead and dying littered the ground. Wounded men, left behind on the saltflats, where even the coarse beach-grass could not grow, watched their comrades plod away into the distance. The pestilent flies stayed behind to settle on their wounds, and buzz a requiem mass over the dead.

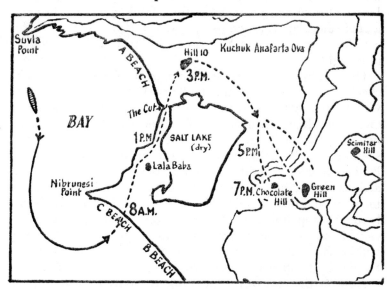

Map 11. ROUNDABOUT ROUTE TO CHOCOLATE HILL

By 5 p.m. the attackers came under raking rifle-fire 300 yards from Chocolate Hill. This molehill of a mountain, little more than 160 feet high, rose steeply out of the plain, "its sides seamed by trenches". By this time the men were spent. Unless they could be given a rest, the assault would go to pieces from sheer thirst and fatigue.

Fortunately, the battleships in the bay were due to open up on the position, and Hill's force lay down in their ranks on the sun-baked ground. In front of them they saw the chocolate-coloured earth and rocks from which the hill took its English nickname. On their left huddled the small white houses and tiled roofs of Kuchuk Anafarta, tucked, a mile and a quarter away under the precipitous southern bluffs of the Tekke Tepe. On their right the glistening sheen of the Salt Lake stretched away to the hump of Lala Baba, with the crowded bay beyond, where the naval guns slid forward, flashed, belched, slid back, double-cracked, and rent the air asunder—asunder—asunder—with the screaming speed-sound of shells overhead.

A few seconds later the hillsides quaked and threw up lumps of chocolate and chocolate powder. When the naval bombardment ceased, the field-guns on Lala Baba opened up again. Under this covering fire the leading Irish troops reached the foot of Chocolate Hill and its twin, Green Hill, 400 yards to the east. The sun's fury was cooling now in the luminous afterglow of twilight.

Here, in front of honeycombed ridges, the advance was again checked. Soon after 7 p.m. the Turkish fire slackened. They were preparing to abandon the position in accordance with the orders of Major Willmer, the Bavarian cavalry officer commanding the Suvla area. Tall, lean, with a livid duelling-scar slashing one cheek, his whole idea was to harass and delay the British, to hold on and hold out until the Bulair reinforcements arrived, defending every mound and hillock to the last possible moment, and then to retire slowly eastwards, fighting stubbornly step by step, towards the Anafarta gap. He was an extremely capable soldier who, nevertheless, would have been defeated within the first six hours but for the feeble generalship of Stopford, Hammersley, and Sitwell.

Now, in the nick of time, the 6th Lincolnshire came up to supply the long-needed extra thrust. The Irish made ready to charge. The last rays of the sun flashed along their line of bayonets as they rushed the slopes. The Turks, always doggedly resolute on the defensive, stood their ground well. But nothing could withstand the onrushing Irish—their blood was up as they made the final dash to the crest.

The sun sank beyond Samothrace as they reached it. In the oncoming dusk they pushed forward another quarter of a mile and took Green Hill (also 160 ft.). The whole position was in the hands of the British. But, in spite of the fierce fighting, most of the Turkish garrison had made good their retreat to the neighbouring W. Hills (the Ismail Oglu Tepe) a mile or more to the south-east.

As darkness closed down upon Chocolate Hill and Green Hill, the victorious troops—now on their last legs—found themselves in utter confusion, lost in a veritable rabbit-warren of trenches, communication trenches, and dug-outs, with "paths leading everywhere and nowhere". Many of the units toiled on into the night, bringing in the wounded, burying the dead.

Many more fell asleep in heaps on the hillsides. There was no food, no water.

Outposts were hurriedly posted beyond the crest, but "no scouts were sent out, and touch with the enemy was lost".

No fresh troops were sent up to keep the retreating Turks on the move. Hammersley did not know that Chocolate Hill had been captured until well after midnight. He did not hear that Green Hill had been taken until the next morning. Stopford, still on board the *Jonquil*, knew nothing. Hamilton, on Imbros, knew nothing.

After 1 a.m. the only sound from the twin hills was the vast pig-hog chorus of snoring from thousands of men drenched with dew and sweat.

The last three stretchers to come up from the beach had large patches of dark Venetian red soaked into the canvas. Dry of course. I was used to human blood by now. But I longed to see a stretcher unsmirched, unsullied. The squads had reloaded, turned about, and trudged off back to the beach. I was alone again, searching for wounded.

Somewhere in my rear, on the lower spur of the Karakol Dagh, Lieutenant-General Sir Bryan Mahon was trying to find out how and why his Xth (Irish) Division—that ought to have been storming the Kiretch Tepe—had dwindled from three brigades (= 12 battalions) to no more than three battalions before he had even landed to take command! This staggering "vanishing trick", in which more than two-thirds of the division had disappeared, was accounted for as follows:

> 29th Brigade (4 battalions) sent to Anzac from Lemnos, August 5.
>
> 31st Brigade (4 battalions), plus two battalions from 30th Brigade (6th and 7th Royal Dublin Fusiliers), from Mitylene, under General Hill. All but one battalion (5th Royal Inniskilling Fusiliers*) landed at C Beach under General Hammersley's command.

* The 5th Royal Inniskilling Fusiliers could not be landed at C Beach because of heavy Turkish fire. They had to be diverted to West Beach on the northern arm of the bay, but, owing to the general breakdown of the Navy's disembarkation programme, were not landed there until the evening of August 7.

Thus nine battalions had been landed elsewhere and were fighting under other commanders before Mahon and his staff were put ashore from the *Partridge*. Nothing remained for the assault of the Kiretch Tepe, where some 700 Turkish gendarmerie held the hogsback ridge, except—

> Two battalions of the 30th Brigade (6th and 7th Royal Munster Fusiliers), from Lemnos, under Brigadier-General Nicol, landed at West Beach.
> One battalion Divisional Pioneers (5th Royal Irish Regiment), from Lemnos, under Lieutenant-Colonel The Earl of Granard, also landed at West Beach.

A sorry check-roll for any divisional commander to contemplate. In all, less than 3,000 men: a mere handful, for one Turk on the hills was worth ten British on the plain below. To which must be added another crippling blow:

> All Divisional Artillery—54th, 55th, 56th Brigades, and 57th (Howitzer) Brigade, Royal Field Artillery, and one Heavy Battery Royal Garrison Artillery—had either been left behind in England, or were still in Egypt.

So there was Mahon, two hours after landing, with nothing but a "ghost division". No one could blame him if he felt peeved. Unfortunately, he felt both peeved and slighted. He was, after all, the senior Lieutenant-General at Suvla. As already noted, he felt very keenly the fact that he had been given "so small a command as a division"—and now even the division was not there to command.

Mahon, fifty-two years of age when he took over the Xth (Irish) Division, was a Galway man, unmistakably of the dark, longheaded, pre-Gael, neolithic (Firbolg) type, with large, aggressively-outjutting ears, and full lips enfolding a secret smile half hidden under a trim but strangely piebald grey-and-(startlingly)-saltwhite moustache. Without doubt one of the "Black Celts to the west of the Shannon", with deepset, heavy-browed, sullen-brooding eyes, as fiercely "dead" and glooming as a Fitful Head stormcloud stagnant over Inisheer. At this moment glowering in resentful fury.

He did not keep what he felt to himself. Peeved, slighted, and now deeply affronted—faced with a wellnigh impossible task—the gist of what he said reached the rank and file and

10. The " humpy ground " at A Beach, showing the Salt Lake (extreme left) and Lala Baba (centre)

11. H.M.S. *Cornwallis* firing a broadside at Turkish positions

12. Bringing wounded to the Landing-Lighters at Suvla

spread with astonishing speed. It filled us with a kind of forlorn dismay—

"General Sir Bryan Mahon's in a flamin' temper, they say. Says the Xth Division doesn't exist—says it's a damned disgrace to expect him to take over a division that's been smashed-up before he landed. Threatened to resign, they say. . . ."

All the same, he did what he could to carry out Stopford's orders. He sent the two 30th Brigade battalions, the 6th and 7th Munsters, along the crest of the Karakol Dagh (490 feet) to join up with the 11th Manchesters, the elusive battalion that lost themselves in the gullies the night before. This left Mahon with only one battalion, the 5th Royal Irish,* under his direct control, and without a single man in reserve. The 5th Inniskillings were still waiting to be landed, but Mahon of course imagined that they had already gone ashore at C Beach with the rest of Hill's troops.

And since Stopford had assured him that his Xth Division battalions from Mitylene would revert to his command as soon as possible, Mahon, having done what he could, was naturally inclined to await their arrival—little knowing that they were to be marched all-round-the-rick to attack Chocolate Hill, and would not be returned to him until five days later! So he fumed and fretted, and (hearsay had it) "threatened to resign".

In fact he fumed and fretted, and did little more than that, for he was convinced that it was impossible to advance along the Kiretch ridge without adequate artillery support. He was convinced of this because he believed there were—yes, the same old bugaboo!—"strong enemy entrenchments" in front of him.

On this I can speak with first-hand knowledge, for I covered the ground many times from August 7th to the 17th. There were it is true, some short lengths of hastily-dug transverse trenches (more in the nature of slit-trenches), but very few deeply entrenched positions, and these were not strongly held at this

---

* The 5th Royal Irish Regiment was a Pioneer Detachment, trained and armed, but intended primarily as a labour force. This was before the formation of the Pioneer Corps, later known as the Labour Corps. Without belittling the status and essential service of any such corps, it is a fact that, in effect, Mahon's command at this crucial moment was reduced to a gang of pick-and-shovel labourers.

I

time because Major Willmer, with no more—and probably less—than 1,500 men at his disposal, was hard put to it to block the Anafarta gap south of the Tekke Tepe, man the Chocolate and Green Hills in a delaying action until nightfall, and hold the Kiretch Tepe.

Moreover, the geological formation and structure of the Kiretch ridge—sheer rock throughout from Suvla Point to Ejelmer Bay (just over six miles): knife-edged where it sheers steeply down from the hogsback spine to the Gulf of Saros—consists of hard sandstone beds, showing complex erosion and faulting, with outcrops of limestone, shale, schists, and quartzite, and here and there shallow pockets of sandy soil on a bedrock base. Trench-digging on this iron-hard backbone was a Herculean task, and any effective system of trenches out of the question.

Except for the topmost ledge of naked rock, the sides of this long, whale-backed embossment, scored and studded with gullies and crags, were everywhere thickly tangled in dense holly-oak scrub. The Turks knew every inch of the ground, and, as a rule, moved only at night. Our men had to march in the broiling heat up these broken steeps "in line abreast", as you might say, each one as clearly visible and as easy to pot at as a slow-moving target on a rifle-range.

The Munsters struggled up these scrub-choked slopes under the blistering mid-day sun, and deployed for the attack about 1.30 p.m. (while, all unknown to them, their comrades from Mitylene were crossing the Cut on their way to Hill 10). In support, Mahon threw in his last remaining battalion, the 5th Royal Irish.

The fact that the Munsters, the 6th on the left, the 7th on the right, were able to push forward along the ridge in a wide sweep, establish a position astride the western spur of the hogsback itself, from sea-level on the Gulf of Saros side to the gully-grooved slopes overlooking the Salt Lake on the other, and join up with the 11th Manchesters, shows what could have been done—if these thirst-crazed troops could have got water—if they could have been reinforced without delay—if Hill's battalions had not been switched to C Beach. If—if—if—

But the troops were staggering in a daze, the rocks reeling before their eyes. . . . I recall their haggard faces, their cracked lips: for we were bringing out their wounded along with the wounded of the night before. Some of them came limping painfully towards us: unkempt, scarecrow-figures, their voices husky-low like whispering grass—"We have the heathen Turks on the run, by-the-holy!—why don't they send us up some wather?"

If there had been just half a pint of water for each man at this moment—but: "Sufficient attention was not paid by Sir Frederick Stopford and his Administrative Staff to these arrangements, which should have been more thoroughly discussed between the Administrative Staff at General Head-quarters and the Corps Administrative Staff before landing. For the absence of such adequate consultation neither Staff can be exonerated from responsibility." (Final Report, Part II, Dardanelles Commission, page 89.)

The failure of the supply of sea-borne water for the troops seems to have been due to the fact that only two of the five water-lighters arrived on August 7th, and these two grounded on a sandbank about a hundred yards from the shore. I remember seeing them out there, like a couple of stranded whales, with naval men trying to tow them off. Because of the stranding of these lighters the hosepipes provided were not long enough to reach the shore, and so "no water was available for use from them until the morning of the 8th".

The water-supply situation at Suvla can be reliably deter-mined from the following telegram sent to Stopford by Colonel Western, the Principal Military Landing Officer, at 5.30 p.m.—*note the time*—on August 7th:

> "Water for troops essential to success of undertaking. None has been landed. Can you arrange with the Admiral that this be landed at 'A' Beach?... I would add nothing has yet been landed except small arms ammunition."

And when, finally, a trickle of water was pumped ashore from the stranded lighters—no suitable receptacles could be found for carrying it up to the front line!

We see, then, why it was that Mahon's Munsters, and all the other troops at Suvla, were almost at their last gasp towards the end of the first day.

Mahon reported to Stopford that the enemy on the Kiretch

ridge in front of his present position was "strongly entrenched", and left it at that.

This, of course, did nothing but strengthen the picture of that elaborate "system of continuous entrenchments" that had been so deeply etched in Stopford's mind long before the landing took place.

And while Stopford and Reed, aboard the *Jonquil*, were considering the implications of Mahon's report, the wretched Munsters were scratching and scraping on the ridge itself, in an attempt to dig-in along the line they had just taken. We heard their entrenching-tools ringing long after dark.

At no place, even after a week of hacking and scooping, were our troops able to sink a trench deeper than waist-high: and only one of the Turkish trenches on this ridge gave breast-high cover—and this shallowed as it climbed up to the 650-foot contour of the high-striding summit, where it gave out altogether on the bare rocks. . . .

On Imbros our Commander-in-Chief, perplexed, anxious, but still hopeful, had begun his second night's vigil. "Hope on, hope ever," says the old tag. Not one word had been received from Suvla since noon.

While we lay in heavy slumber along the beaches, and only prodigious snoring could be heard on Lala Baba and Chocolate Hill, the 7th and 12th Turkish Divisions, under Feizi Bey, were tramping slowly on all through the night. By 9 p.m. they had covered a third of the way, and still had over twenty-three miles to go. They moved steadily down the neck of the peninsula, heading straight for the Tekke Tepe. There was no let-up.

7

SUNDAY—THE DAY OF REST

In the morning we were still weary and blear-eyed. The sleepy guard woke us at 3.30 with sullen north-country words from Durham and Tyneside—"Coom on, lads! it's getting-oop time now!"—laggardly words that hardly broke the slumber-drag.

Only the Suvla spiders—and Feizi Bey's troops coming down from Bulair—had toiled through the night. It was a cobweb morning, misty-thick, foretelling a steamy-hot day. Every sagebush and wild-thyme hassock festooned with spiders' webs heavy with dew.

Sunday, August 8: and all as quiet and peaceful at Suvla as any Sunday morning at Nether Stowey, or Market Deeping, or Alsop-en-le-Dale.

And there was Hamilton, on Imbros, writing in his diary:

> "August 8th. Imbros. Another night on tenterhooks. Great news: a wireless from a warship to tell us the Suvla troops are up on the foothills."

Two cables had reached him from Stopford during the early hours. The first gave the front line position of the IXth Corps as hovering north and south of the Salt Lake. The second reported (ten hours after the event!) that Chocolate Hill and Green Hill had at last been taken. Not very encouraging news, considering the extreme urgency of the situation. Yet a crumb of information radioed from a warship was hailed as "great news"! Once again we see the hopeful eagerness ready to snap up any scrap of hearsay. And perhaps the question remains whether a Commander-in-Chief ought to be scribbling his hopes and fears in the midst of a battle—no, three battles: Cape Helles, Anzac, Suvla.

Worst of all, the "great news" from that warship was inaccurate. *We had not even reached the foothills.*

Mahon, on the left, was astride the Kiretch Tepe, having pushed the Turks back nearly two miles. Hammersley, on the right, held Lala Baba, Hill 10, Chocolate Hill, and Green Hill. None of these could be called foothills. Hill 10, that outsize sand-dune in the middle of the bay's sweep—where Sitwell still sat—was over three miles from the foothills of the Tekke Tepe. From the Chocolate/Green Hill position, three and a half miles due east from Nibrunesi Point, it was another three and a half miles north-east to those foothills.

Thus, so far from being "up on the foothills", our troops on each side of the bay and at the centre were more than three miles from them. Only Mahon was up on the heights, and his Xth Division handful had been checked. There had been no further advance anywhere during the night.

That was the situation at Suvla on this cold, dark, shivery Sunday morning as we stumbled down to the wet-lipped selvage of sand for a freshener, aching in every limb, our eyelids gummed-up, our feet blistered. Soon the bay was a porpoise-splashing lido of naked men—men who had never in their lives gone naked before. All body-shyness and, more surprisingly, all barrack-room lewdery forsook them. Within seconds they were half-fish mermen sea-horsing to the manner born.

It was no more than a dip for the stretcher-bearers, for we had to start the day's work within half an hour. We dried ourselves shivering in the dawnwind, and dressed hurriedly in the lifting half-gloom. Having worn them for two days and nights, I decided not to put on puttees. They had bitten into the calf muscles, leaving red spirals where the overlap had chafed the flesh. So I left them off to give my legs a rest. It never struck me that, by doing so, I was asking for trouble.

For breakfast they dished us out with an issue of army biscuit and Tickler's apricot jam (bah!): or army biscuit and a tin of bully-beef. I always refused the jam issue. Apricot

spread with a jack-knife on a biscuit was black with flies the
next instant! Even without the flies the warm yellow syrup was
a potent purge. More diarrhoea was started at Suvla by this
sun-stewed mush than by anything else. And with diarrhoea
rampant in that temperature, dysentery was certain.

Water-bottles were replenished before starting with the same
brakish, chlorinated liquid from the meagre supplies brought
from Egypt in tanks: the tanks that had stranded on the
sandbanks the day before. Half a bottle for our own use, and a
full one for the wounded were issued to each of us.

Then we called the roll. . . .

And as we called the roll just before daybreak, Field-Marshal
Liman von Sanders, commanding the Turkish forces in
Gallipoli, rode towards the hills overlooking the Suvla
plain to watch the dawn attack he had ordered the night
before.

His hard, square face with its gimlet-sharp eyes scowled. He
looked, and was, a typical professional soldier of Kaiser
Wilhelm II's heel-clicking, goose-stepping *Offizier-Korps:* sixty
years of age, bullet-headed, thick-necked. As head of the
German Military Mission to Turkey he had trained and
equipped the Turkish army since the beginning of 1914: had
in fact taken hold of what was little more than a rabble of
ragged janissaries and shaped it into something like a modern
fighting force.

Von Sanders can be summed up as calm, steady, harsh,
terse, efficient, decisive, stubborn, and—of course—Teutonically
stupid. No imagination, and therefore no "tenterhooks". About
as much poetry in him as a *pickelhaube.* Very different
from that bright, quick, shy, all-alone-bird hopping in and out
of the signals tent at Imbros, who had, nevertheless, hood-
winked the *Feldmarschall* and caught him on the wrong foot.

At this moment the German commander faced a much more
acute dilemma than Hamilton. He had expected the British
to make a landing at the neck of the peninsula on the Gulf of
Saros coastline opposite Bulair, or at some point along the
coast of Asia Minor opposite Tenedos, and had deployed his
forces accordingly. In the event he was taken off guard by
the surprise landing at Suvla, with his only available troops—

except Willmer's handful—still miles away, while Hamilton had at least 20,000 ashore, if not "up on the foothills".*

One glance at the empty slopes of the Tekke Tepe, then at the far-off beaches crowded with British soldiers, stores, equipment, mules, wagons, was enough. The position was touch-and-go. *Where the devil were Feizi Bey's Bulair divisions?*

But scowling was no use. Suvla took no more heed of German field-marshals than it did of British generals. Von Sanders had to kick his heels for more than an hour before a staff officer

---

* The narrowest part of the peninsula is only three miles across, a little below Bulair, and thirty miles N.E. from Suvla. But there are only two landing-places: (1) a very bad one in a swamp or salt marsh to the east, and (2) in a death-trap ravine to the west. Both are dominated by high ground inland, and the swamp is commanded also from the rear. Hamilton was wise to eschew any attempt to make a landing in this sector of the Turkish defences.

Yet from the outset von Sanders felt sure that the main British attack would be made here, where the Turkish position was most vulnerable. This conviction was strongly reinforced on the morning of April 25th when he received reports of the first Allied landings at Kum Kale, Cape Helles, and north of Gaba Tepe—followed by a report that twenty Allied warships had steamed into the Bay of Saros opposite the Bulair Lines.

This last was, in fact, one of the most successful of the many ingenious stratagems devised by Hamilton and his staff to confuse the Turkish command. It had the effect of keeping von Sanders and the main body of Turkish reinforcements at Bulair, since the German Commander-in-Chief could not bring himself to believe that the landings further south were more than feints.

It was during this diversion that Lieutenant-Commander Freyberg, of the Royal Naval Division, plunged naked from a naval cutter into the ice-cold waters of the Bay of Saros and swam the two miles ashore under cover of the pitchblack night. On his back was strapped a waterproof canvas bag containing three oil flares and five calcium lights, a knife, a signal-lamp, and a revolver. He reached the Bulair beach after swimming an hour and a half, lit his first flare, swam another 300 yards towards the swampy ground to the east, landed again and lit the second flare, then hid in some bushes to see what would happen. As there was no sign of life, he crawled into the Turkish trenches. Finding no one there he crept back to the beach and lit the third flare.

Cramp-spasms overtook him, but he was determined not to be taken prisoner. He slid again into the icy sea, and was swallowed up in the night-time darkness. By sheer good luck the cutter crew spotted him about half a mile from shore and hauled him aboard.

For this exploit he was awarded the D.S.O. (and later won the V.C. in France).

came up to explain that there had been some delay. It would be several hours, he said, before the Bulair troops would arrive.

The field-marshal wasted no time. He snapped out his order —the attack was to be put in at sunset—and rode off to find out what Colonel Mustafa Kemal had to report on the Anzac front.

It was still dark when we set off in single-file towards the firing-line. Mad Jack led the way. He was in one of his taciturn moods, as tetchy as a tsetse-fly. We were all a bit glum, because of the gloom and the misty chill that hung, asthmatically thick, over the bay.

Again we passed the stone-flagged spring. There were several goat-tracks, and the one we took this morning crossed a little wilderness of the usual dry yellow grass and dead thistles. Here we halted to make sure that no stragglers at the rear of our long line of stretcher-bearers had dropped out to drink from that polluted wellspring. Waiting, hanging about, is the worst part of soldiering. Soldiers going up the line in the early hours of semi-darkness are always moody. The human spirit is at its lowest ebb just before daybreak. It needed something from the external world to shatter this overhang of sad-dog dreariness.

And there it was, standing by the edge of the track among the skeleton thistles, the scorched-up grass, and the pallid sage-clumps—a single pure white flower, sweet-scented, something like a flag*. It took our breath away! I think we all saw it. The man standing next to me at the time, Private (later Provost Corporal) R. C. Holmes, recalls it vividly to this day. It was, to those who saw it, an astonishment—a flag of wonder, a nameless *fleur-de-lis* seeded from another planet, another world: a world unsullied by war, wounds, pus, and the stench of the dead. So small a thing, this lone lily-flower, this pennon of life's joy: its slender stalk about twenty-four inches high.

---

* The Mediterranean plant *Pancratium maritimum L.* of the family *Amaryllidaceae*, commonly called "sea daffodil", which I have been able to identify thanks to the courtesy of Dr. John Hutchinson, Keeper of Museums of Botony, Royal Botanic Gardens, Kew, where some dried specimens from the Dardanelles are to be found in The Herbarium.

Worth looking at. It filled us with delight. Worth smelling too.

We were on the move again now, and, as they passed, one man after another stooped to smell the white flower: a Sunday morning genuflexion before an unconsecrated shrine.

We never came upon another white flower. Soon the sun flashed from the crest of the Sari Bair. There was no flamingo-pink sunrise to herald this second day at Suvla, nor ever again did we see such a splendour.

At last—at long last—as daylight broke over Imbros, and there was no further word from Stopford, Hamilton's doubts, fears, and anxieties began to swarm upon him like the pestering flies. The snatch of news that had seemed "great news" an hour ago no longer buoyed him up. There *must* be something wrong at Suvla? The IXth Corps had been ashore now for more than twenty-four hours. The Naval Air Service had reported that no strong Turkish forces faced them. Hamilton's G.H.Q. staff reckoned it would take the Turks about thirty-six hours to march their reinforcements from Bulair to the eastern flank of the Tekke Tepe. On this calculation they would be there in six or seven hours. If things went along at this leisurely pace the Turks would be in a position to bring the whole operation to a standstill—if they didn't swoop down and drive the British into the sea. . . .

At last he could stand it no longer. Just before 6 a.m. he sent for Colonel Aspinall-Oglander, the staff officer responsible for planning the operation, and told him to go over to Suvla and find out what was going on.

Aspinall (then aged 37) took with him Colonel Hankey (Lord Hankey, then aged 38), Secretary of the Committee of Imperial Defence, who had been sent out to report direct to the War Cabinet. Together they went down to the naval dock area at Kephalos harbour, where they expected to board a naval craft that would take them across as quickly as possible.

But they reckoned without the Suvla jinx. There wasn't even a coracle available! For three and a half hours they had to hang around before the Royal Navy managed to put a trawler at their disposal. A trawler—a slow-going, steam-driven, deep-sea fishing-boat. That was the best they could do. The fact that Aspinall's mission was of the utmost urgency—was, of course, number one top priority—made no difference at all.

It was 9.30 a.m. when they went aboard the trawler, and it took another two hours before they dropped anchor in Suvla Bay—a distance of nineteen miles that ought not to have taken more than one hour. Thus it was 11.30 a.m. when they arrived, and five and a half hours had elapsed since Aspinall had received his instructions.

One may be forgiven for wondering sometimes why Commodore Keyes was quite so hopping mad about "the ghastly inertia" at Suvla, and the "leisurely proceedings" on the beeches. The Silent Service has much to be silent about.

In the meantime, and very naturally, Hamilton was steamed-up with further anxiety and impatience. What in heaven's name had become of Aspinall? He had sent him off at six in the morning, and here it was nearly mid-day without so much as a whisper out of him!

Lack of water had been bad enough on the day of landing, but now, on this second day ashore, the position became critical. Thirst began to thrust war into the background—water became more important than killing. Even the Turks were short of water on the Kiretch Tepe.

Most of the British troops had been without a drop for nearly twenty-four hours. Not a cupful had reached Mahon's battalions straddling the ridge. Their plight was pitiful, and the fact that fighting had slackened allowed them to brood on their sufferings. They felt that they were being neglected, left in the lurch—as, indeed, they were.

And so, soon after dawn, first one and then another laid his rifle aside, grabbed two or three water-bottles, and slipped away down to the beach, where hoses long enough to reach the shore had at last been fitted to the stranded water-lighters. Here, those who were lucky managed to get a drink and fill their bottles. They probably took another swig or two as they toiled back to the firing-line, where their thirsty comrades soon gulped what was left of the scant supply. Within seconds word ran from one to another—"*There's wather down on the beach, be-Jasus!*—"

The drift-away from the front line that set in during the morning of August 8 became a serious problem over the next few days.

They passed us now in threes and fours, some with as many as eight water-bottles slung from their shoulders, and swinging two or three clinking mess-tins in each hand. Before long there were ten-yard gaps in the front line. Nothing short of a bullet will hold men driven by thirst—and Irishmen at that.

These men were in even worse shape than the legions of the "lost" still drifting aimlessly round the bay. Gaunt as shrivelled vermin nailed to a keeper's "larder", their eyes glittered. They moved down quickly with long, lurching strides, like drunken men in a hurry. They didn't speak, didn't even nod as they passed. The lips of some of them were baked black, like apples that have "caught" in an over-hot oven.

It seemed astonishing that men who had only been ashore two nights and a day could become such weatherbeaten nondescripts. Compared with these front line *loups-garous*, we were the Brigade of Guards on parade.

Although our single-file formation allowed us to keep together, and so to work methodically, it did not allow us to fan out and search for wounded who might be lying in out-of-sight gullies or on high rock ledges, and who might be too weak to cry for help.

This anxiety became more distressing as, ever and again in our winding progress towards the firing-line, we came upon casualties that we had missed yesterday in our first frantic and disorganised search: men who had crawled into dells and thickets where their feeble cries of—"*stretcher-bear-e-r-s! stretcher-bear-e-r-s!*"—could not reach our ears. Or, perhaps, they were men whose cries we had heard, faint and far away, but whom we could not find. They had lain there hour after agonising hour in the blazing sun and all through the ague-shuddering, dew-soaked night.

Some of these were still alive, their wounds flyblown. We did what we could for them. And some must have waited and waited until life ebbed away. They needed no attention except a decent burial—or at least a burial—which we had no time to give.

A burst of rifle-fire broke out ahead—with a sharp, crackling reply. We were close to the front line now. Machine-gun slugging away up there. Nasty. Shakes the diaphragm.

Suddenly we came to a halt.

Malacca cane slapping polished fieldboot. Wasp-waisted officer's tunic. Corsets—whalebone? Absurd popeyed jack-a-dandy. Little nimpy-pimpy gingerish moustache. Why's he coming back? Mad Jack coming back—something wrong? Something hellishly wrong, by the look of it. Beetroot face now—bloodshot eyeballs. Past the adjutant and the two lieutenants marching just ahead of me. What's he shouting? Apoplectic with rage—shouting at me—

"How *dare* you come on parade like that? Damned disgrace! D'you hear, Sergeant? I won't have it!—dammit! I won't have it!"

"I—don't understand, sir."

"Don't understand? Where are your puttees, dammit?"

"I didn't put them on, sir, because—"

"Go back to the beach at once—and place yourself under close arrest!"

"Place myself—?" I just couldn't believe this Mad Hatter nonsense.

"How *dare* you answer me? Improperly dressed—no puttees! Back to the beach, I say!—and place yourself under close arrest until I return! D'you hear?"

I saluted, turned about, and trudged off down the line of silent stretcher-bearers—my own section. I was stunned. So were they.

A more ridiculous situation could hardly be imagined. It meant that A Section was now not only without a sergeant in charge of stretcher-squads, but was one man short for the heavy toil of stretcher-bearing, for of course we all lent a hand when necessary, stripes or no stripes. And this at the moment when we were coming up to the firing-line!

What was it all about? Why had he waited until this moment —why hadn't he pulled me up before we started? There's no doubt about it (I said to myself, as I plodded back to the beach), I'm dreaming—I'm in a dream—I must be!

It was about 7 a.m. when I reached the beach.

And at 7 a.m., while Aspinall and Hankey were still waiting for their trawler at Imbros, Stopford signalled Mahon to entrench on the Kiretch Tepe. This was exactly what Mahon had been doing since the late afternoon of the 7th—so far as solid rock and tough holly-oak would allow his Munsters to scrape and scrabble a foot or two below the surface.

Stopford was in a good frame of mind this morning. Things were going well. No advance anywhere. In fact hardly any fighting at all. True, he had been warned that the Turkish reinforcements might be expected to reach the Tekke Tepe that afternoon, but there was nothing much to be done about that.

Commodore Keyes, driven frantic by the continued stagnation ashore, and now almost beside himself, paid another whirlwind visit to the *Jonquil*, "which", he wrote later, "nearly drove me to open mutiny." He found Stopford as perky as a cock-robin, with no intention of doing anything more just now—except entrench.

Keyes dashed back to the *Chatham* and reported to Admiral de Robeck. The Admiral at once drafted a message to the Commander-in-Chief, Imbros: a message that seethes with the urgency of the situation—"It is very important that we should meet—shall I come over to see you, or are you coming to Suvla?"

This cable was handed in during the early part of the morning. *It was never received.* No trace of it could be found in the signal logs of the only ships through which it could have passed. And there has never been any trace of it from that day to this.

It was about this time that Hammersley, having somewhat recovered from the shock and nervous breakdown of the day before, set off to consult his brigadiers. He seems to have had in mind the idea of attacking the ridge leading up to the Anafarta gap—where Willmer had now concentrated most of his troops, feeling certain that the British would deliver their main blow here.

The brigadiers explained that the men were utterly exhausted, parched with thirst, units jumbled together, without proper rations, demoralised, and with a tendency to straggle away in search of water. After hearing these reports, Hammersley gave up the idea of making an advance and went back to his headquarters below Lala Baba. Hearing nothing from Stopford, he decided to let the matter rest.

No doubt he was glad to do so, for he was still in a wretched state of health.

At 9.30 a.m. Stopford sent off a special message of congratulations to his divisional generals, Mahon and Hammersley. They had done splendidly!

At 10 a.m. Stopford sent the following cable to the Commander-in-Chief, Imbros: (and no vanishing-trick nullified this message)—"Consider Major-General Hammersley and troops under him deserve great credit for result attained against strenuous opposition and great difficulty. I must now consolidate."

The strange thing is that this eulogy had the effect of bringing a momentary reassurance to Hamilton's mind. He began to feel that perhaps things were not going too badly after all.

However, this gleam of hopefulness did not last. A glance at the map showed that the positions gained at Suvla during the thirty-six hours that had elapsed since the landing amounted to no more than two and a half miles from the beaches on each side of the bay—with the central heights still four and a half miles away. Unless something was done to forestall them, the Turkish reinforcements would reach the Tekke Tepe between 4 and 5 p.m. Yet here was Stopford saying: "I must consolidate"!

Add to this the exasperating fact that Aspinall had gone off four hours ago, and seemed to have vanished into the blue. . . .

At last—at long, long last—Hamilton decided to go over to Suvla himself. It was 11.30 a.m. when he ordered his duty destroyer *Arno*, an Italian-built Portuguese craft, to stand by ready to take him over at mid-day.

Word came back to say that the *Arno* had developed boiler trouble. Moreover, the rear-admiral in naval command at Imbros had ordered the fires to be drawn. It was this boiler trouble that had prevented Aspinall and Hankey from boarding the *Arno*, and had forced them to wait for a trawler. There wasn't even a trawler to take the Commander-in-Chief!

It made Hamilton boil. And when he read a message from the rear-admiral regretting that the breakdown should cause him any inconvenience, he blew up. There and then he sat down and wrote out a reply saying that it was "not a matter of convenience or inconvenience but one of preventing a commander-in-chief from commanding during a battle". This showed just the spirit that could have turned the tide at Suvla.

But even in this Hamilton was frustrated. His chief-of-staff, General Braithwaite, came over to say that "he had taken it upon himself to tone it down". The amended reply merely suggested that the order to draw fires should be countermanded, "as [the C-in-C was made to say] I may require her at any moment". Hamilton had *ordered* his duty destroyer "for mid-day sharp"—and no "may" about it.

He took it all like a lamb, and just waited and waited. . . .

And while he waited he sat down and drafted his reply to Stopford's panegyrical cable—in terms that could only have the effect of confirming that gentleman's congenital tranquillity. At 12 noon the Commander-in-Chief sent the following message from Imbros to the IXth Corps Commander on board the *Jonquil:* "You and your troops have indeed done splendidly. Please tell Hammersley how much we hope from his able and rapid advance.—Ian Hamilton."*

"Splendidly"—"able"—"rapid"—? It's amazing! . . . and pathetic.

Having sent off his peculiarly emphatic congratulations to Stopford, he waited hour after hour. Later, he wrote in his diary:

> "August 8th. Imbros. Rear-Admiral Nicholson, in local naval command here, had ordered the *Arno* to fill up her boilers. Some hitch arose, some d——d amphibious hitch. . . . Just as well perhaps, but here was I marooned upon an island: no other ship could be signalled."

* "With regard to this message, Sir Frederick Stopford informed us that the result of the operations on the night of the 6th and day of the 7th was not as satisfactory as he would have liked, but he gathered from Sir Ian Hamilton's congratulations that his dispositions and orders had met with the latter's approval." (Final Report, Dardanelles Commission, Part II, under Sec. 89.)

13. Lieut.-General The Hon. Sir Frederick Stopford

15. Major-General Frederick Hammersley

14. Lieut.-General Sir Bryan Mahon

16. West Beach, Suvla, before the Evacuation, showing Karakol Dagh (left)

17. Troops Landing at Suvla

Long after the event, Sir Roger Keyes, the dashing and courageous Commodore, made the suggestion that had Sir Ian's desire "been properly represented to Admiral de Robeck, without doubt one of the destroyers patrolling within a few miles could have brought him over within an hour." But Rear-Admiral Nicholson knew as early as 6 a.m. that this vessel had developed boiler trouble. It was up to *him* to see that alternative naval transport was available. He did nothing of the sort. He left Hamilton "marooned upon an island" for *four and a half hours.*

Meanwhile the trawler, with Aspinall and Hankey aboard, had made Suvla Bay at 11.30 a.m. The scene that met their eyes reminded them, they reported later, of "an August Bank Holiday in England". Hardly a sound of battle came over the quivering heat of the day. The dazzling azure and turquoise of the thirteen-fathom anchorage was crowded with shipping. According to Aspinall (in his official history of the Gallipoli Campaign): "The whole bay was at peace, and its shores fringed with bathers."

As I happened to be standing not more than twenty yards from A Beach at the time—having "placed myself under close arrest" in front of Mad Jack's dugout, in accordance with his crack-brained orders—I had a clear view of the entire sweep of the bay, from Lala Baba to Suvla Point.

Most certainly the bay was "fringed" here and there with bathers. But it is doubtful whether, on this particular day, there were more than 200 men swimming or splashing about in those warm translucent waters. Not many out of 20,000? And most of these must have been off duty: cooks, cookhouse orderlies, Army Service Corps drivers and farriers, officers' batmen, field post-office staffs, store-dump guards, fatigue parties, veterinary service personnel, and so on.

There may have been a few stragglers ("lost men") amongst them, but nearly all were men detailed for duty on the beaches, many of whom had been working continuously like galley-slaves for the past twenty-four hours or longer, without sleep, often without food, with little or no water, and under fire most of the time. Exactly the same bathing carnival was to be seen every day at Anzac.

So much for the famous Bank Holiday scene of August 8.

K

Mass bathing did not set in at Suvla until a week or ten days later. And when it did, it was not only the most natural, but also the most sensible thing in the world: the only thing that kept the troops fairly fit.

Seventeen years later, Brigadier-General Aspinall-Oglander made known his first-hand account (in the second volume of the official history of the campaign) of that noteworthy moment when he and his companion made landfall at Suvla "a little before noon on the 8th". He says they were "convinced by the holiday appearance of the place that the hills had at last been captured." Although he notes that "The enemy's guns were silent", and that "Apart from an occasional rifle-shot on Kiretch Tepe there was not a sound of war", it was "the holiday appearance" of the bay that astonished and greatly enheartened the two colonels. "In high spirits," he adds, "Aspinall at once went ashore to find corps headquarters."

No one seemed to be in any great hurry when the two colonels landed, nor particularly busy, except some men digging a trench along the shore with a staff officer near by.

"You seem to be making yourselves snug," said Hankey. To which the staff officer replied—"We expect to be here a long time." This cheery statement reinforced the impression that the troops must have pushed forward and taken the hills.

Having left Hankey on the beach, Aspinall strode off in his search for corps headquarters. He had not gone many paces when the Commander, Royal Engineers, 11th Division, came pounding along to overtake him. This officer told him that the front line was only a hundred yards ahead, and that if he pushed on too far he would find himself in front of the front line. He also said that, although the Turks appeared to have retired, there was no sign of a British advance. As for corps headquarters, the corps commander was still on board the *Jonquil* "and had not yet been ashore".

A good deal shaken by this information, Aspinall decided to make for the headquarters of the 11th Division at Nibrunesi Point, and, with Hankey, crossed the Cut and trudged round the southern arm of the bay. They found Hammersley lying full length on the ground, holding his head in his hands, still heavy-hearted because of the shelling of his headquarters and the loss of some of his staff, and seemingly unable to cope with the staggering confusion that had everywhere developed since the landing.

Hammersley's chief-of-staff told them that the troops were exhausted, and were still congregated round the shore, having made no advance since the capture of Chocolate Hill and Green Hill the night before. He seemed to be almost as dejected as the general. A message from Stopford had just been received suggesting that an advance be put in hand. It had also been sent to Mahon on the Kiretch Tepe. But it contained the following extraordinary proviso: "In view of want of adequate artillery support I do not want you to attack an entrenched position held in strength."

That, of course, settled the matter. Neither Hammersley nor Mahon felt inclined to attempt a further advance until "adequate artillery support" had arrived.

Hammersley explained that, what with the heat and the lack of water, the troops were exhausted. They had suffered heavy casualties, and all units were hopelessly mixed up and needed rest and reorganisation. It might be possible to push forward the next day. Not before.

Aghast at what he had found, Aspinall was in a hell-for-leather hurry to get across to the *Jonquil*. Nevertheless, it was about 3 p.m. before he came aboard.

He found Stopford on deck "in excellent spirits". The sprained knee was evidently less painful, for he "at once came forward to greet the new arrival". We know exactly what took place from Aspinall's own pen. It is one of those high-tension moments that teeter for ever on the edge of tragic absurdity. We can almost hear the pompous stultiloquy:

"Well, Aspinall, the men have done splendidly, they have been magnificent!"

And the colonel's quiet reply: "But they haven't reached the hills, sir."

"No," said the corps commander, "but they are ashore."

Forty-one hours after the landing the troops had not reached the hills—*but they were ashore!* The corps commander himself had not yet ventured as far as that.

Aspinall said he was "sure Sir Ian would be disappointed

that the high ground had not yet been occupied", and begged the general to "issue orders for an immediate advance before the enemy's troops from Bulair could forestall him".

That was pretty plain speaking, but it ran like water off a duck's back: "General Stopford replied that he fully realised the importance of losing no time, but that it was impossible to move till the men had rested, and till more guns were ashore. He intended to order a fresh advance next day."

There was nothing more Aspinall could do, except get a message through to Hamilton with all possible speed. This created a tricky situation. The outspoken cable he had in mind could not, of course, be transmitted from the *Jonquil's* signals office. He went off ("in despair", he tells us), and decided to go over to de Robeck's flagship, the *Chatham*, riding on the north side of the bay.

Here he found the Admiral and the Commodore tense with anxiety because of the unbelievable delay. "Hopping mad" is still the best description of the Commodore's fuming choler. The Admiral said he had sent a signal to Hamilton some hours ago, urging him to come to Suvla. As we know, that signal vanished into thin air. Aspinall now reinforced the Admiral's message by sending the following cable: "Just been ashore where I found all quiet. No rifle fire, no artillery fire, and apparently no Turks. IX Corps resting. Feel confident that golden opportunities are being lost and look upon situation as serious."

By some freak of chance this message did not vanish—it came through to the signals tent, G.H.Q., Imbros, *the following morning, August 9th!* Thus, for all the use it was, it might just as well have immaterialised like the Admiral's. . . .

No word reached Hamilton all through these sweltering hours. No ship came to take him to Suvla. No one bothered about him.

Mad Jack came prancing back to A Beach. He sent the sergeant-major to tell me to "return to duty at once"—as though I had "placed myself under close arrest" in order to "dodge the column"! The whole procedure was out of order from start to finish. But our stretcher squads were still bringing in wounded, and I was glad to be released from this senseless

pantomime and to be back at work with them. I might have
known this was not the end of the matter.

Aspinall's visit to the *Jonquil* had made Stopford a little
uneasy. But only a little. After all, he had received the Commander-in-Chief's congratulatory cable an hour or two before—
"You and your troops have indeed done splendidly." But
perhaps he ought to try to press matters forward somewhat?

He had intended to visit Hammersley at 5 p.m. in any case,
and now decided to go an hour earlier. At 4 p.m. therefore he
landed at Nibrunesi Point. This was the first time the corps
commander had been ashore at Suvla. The visit was more or
less fruitless because Hammersley was out. However, he
learned from the divisional staff that plans for an advance the
following day were going ahead. Perfectly satisfied, he stepped
into his cutter and went back to the *Jonquil*.

There he found another prod from G.H.Q. This was a
message to say that a further air reconnaissance had been
carried out showing that there were still no Turks on the Tekke
Tepe, but that formidable enemy reinforcements could be
seen on the march from Bulair heading straight for Suvla.

The leading columns of Feizi Bey's troops were, in fact, only
about ten miles from the eastern slopes. This was not known
to Stopford, but the latest cable from G.H.Q. roused him to
consider afresh the advisability of ordering a general advance
as soon as possible. It was now 4.30 p.m.

And—wonder of wonders!—at 4.30 p.m. the *Triad*, a large
yacht that once sailed along the shores of the Bosphorus on
pleasure cruises, arrived at Imbros to take Hamilton to Suvla.
Even so, it took an hour and a half to get there. Yet the sea
was calm.

Feizi Bey had held a staff conference at 2 p.m. The 7th and
12th Divisions from Bulair were exhausted after the long
forced march, and could not be thrown into action straight
away. They had been stumbling along for two nights without
sleep, and very little food or water. Many were straggling far
behind the leading columns. They still faced a long stiff climb
to the crest of the Tekke Tepe. An attack at sunset was out of
the question. It was put off until sunrise the next day, August 9.

When Liman von Sanders heard this over the telephone he snarled and snapped. The troops must attack that night. The position was critical. Willmer's handful could not hold out much longer. Unless the attack was put in at sundown the British would take the central massif. There must be no delay. (Four hours later, Hamilton was using almost the same words to Stopford.)

Feizi Bey said he would do what he could to hurry things along. He rang the field-marshal again soon afterwards, and again explained that an attack before dawn was utterly impossible. His staff as well as the commanding officers were solidly against it. No attack could be made until the following morning. (Four hours later, Stopford was using almost the same words to Hamilton.)

At this moment the Turks were hard put to it on the other two fronts: on Chunuk Bair and at Cape Helles. In the fighting for the Sari Bair their casualties had been calamitous—as they had been on the British side—and their units were just as broken up. Most of their senior officers had been killed or wounded, and everywhere on the Chunuk spurs the Turkish forces were in dire confusion. Frantic messages from junior officers were being received at G.H.Q.—"An attack has been ordered. To whom should I give it? I cannot find the battalion commanders. Everything is in a muddle...."

Nevertheless, Colonel Mustafa Kemal on Battleship Hill had smashed the Anzac attack, and was defending the position on a shoestring, holding out grimly with outstanding skill and courage. And all the time he was fretting to take command of the entire Chunuk/Suvla battlefront before it was too late. He alone of the Turco-German command had foretold the Suvla landing, but his warnings had been brushed aside. Now the whole wide mountainous sweep, from the Kiretch Tepe in the north to Battleship Hill in the south, was so thinly held that the British might storm their way up to the heights at any moment.

Things were no better at the tip of the peninsula, fourteen miles to the south. Here, on the Krithia front at Cape Helles, the German chief-of-staff with the Turkish Southern Group had lost his nerve on the morning of August 7, and had sent a panicky telegram to Liman von Sanders urging that all

troops south of Kilid Bahr be withdrawn and shipped across
The Narrows to the Asiatic shore "while there is still time to
extricate them". Von Sanders dismissed this officer instantly,
and ordered—"Not one yard of ground to be given up." That
saved the situation. The field-marshal had no imagination—
but he knew how to hold on.

Now he was faced with Commander Ahmed Feizi Bey and
the Tekke Tepe crisis at Suvla.

At 5.30 p.m., while the *Triad* was sheering through those
glittering blue waters on her way to the peaceful battle-area,
Stopford suddenly awakened from his "I-must-now-con-
solidate" serenity and issued orders. The 11th Division was to
take and hold the W Hills (Ismail Oglu Tepe) and the Anafarta
gap, while the Xth Division was to resume its advance along
the Kiretch Tepe, seize the Tekke Tepe, and then push on down
the ridge to join up with the 11th Division on the Anafarta
spur.

At last the corps commander seemed to be showing a firm
determination to grasp the encircling hills and secure the Suvla
plain. This would have enabled us to join hands with Birdwood's unrelenting attempt to storm the Sari Bair on our
right—which was the original plan of action. Successfully
carried out, it would have defeated the Turkish army and
opened The Narrows to the Fleet.

But it must not be thought that Stopford had any idea of
advancing *now*, while there was still time. He never had the
least intention of making an advance until the next day. And
as he left the time for this general advance to be fixed by poor
old Hammersley, he might as well have saved himself the
trouble of issuing any orders at all.

It is agreed by all who knew him that Lieutenant-General
the Hon. Sir Frederick Stopford, K.C.M.G., K.C.V.O., C.B.,
was "a man of great kindliness and personal charm". Alas,
these qualities are not those needed to win a battle. Apart from
the fact that he had never before commanded troops in action,
his state of health was so poor that, on leaving London for the
Aegean base of operations, he could not lift his own dispatch
case into the train. The sprained knee was no more than an
extra, and unfortunate, disability. Under his awning on board

the *Jonquil*, where he was now busy with his battle orders for the morrow, his C3 physical condition would not be noticed.

He did not dream that at this moment Hamilton was on board the *Chatham*.

De Robeck, Keyes, and Aspinall were astonished to hear from Sir Ian that he had not come to Suvla in response to the two cables: that, in fact, they had not been received up to the time he had left Imbros. The Commander-in-Chief was appalled by what the Admiral, the Commodore, and his own staff colonel told him. Appalled and infuriated.

According to Compton Mackenzie, who served with the Royal Naval Division in the Dardanelles and saw the arrival of the gaunt, slender, harassed figure from Imbros, he was now "at the mercy of the Furies" in body and mind. The position was a thousand times worse than he could have imagined.

It did not take long to grasp the facts. The impetus of a staggeringly successful surprise landing had been lost, and nothing was being done to push on. Without more ado, Hamilton dropped into a fast motor-boat and, with Keyes and Aspinall, sped across to the *Jonquil*. It was now about 6.30 p.m.

The interview with Stopford lasted just five minutes. Which shows the asperity and urgency that had taken hold of the Commander-in-Chief. In spite of this, it never broke through the crust of polite usage and good manners. Both gentlemen behaved as gentlemen, although one of them was boiling with indignation, anxiety, and dismay. This was the command crisis at Suvla—and should have been flashpoint. But Hamilton's "Furies" had clipped wings.

He asked why the troops had not yet taken the surrounding hills. Stopford had his stock reply: the men were dead-beat.

It is typical of Hamilton that he did not make the proper rejoinder, but wrote it later in his diary—that "every leader of note has had to fight that same disinclination to force men half dead with hunger, thirst, and sleeplessness to push along". He was too much of a gentleman to say even that: could not bring himself to force a commanding officer to force his troops to "push along".

Stopford explained that owing to the exhaustion of his troops, and the lack of artillery support, he had put off the attack on the Tekke Tepe until the following morning—as it "might lead to a regular battle".

And again Hamilton, noticing that the corps commander's knee seemed to be giving him some pain, refrained from making the Retort Manifest: and, instead, wrote it later in his diary— that "a regular battle is just what we are here for".

Hamilton pressed for the attack to be put in at once—now— this evening. And that evening he recorded the interchange that took place:

> "I said to Stopford, 'We must occupy the heights at once. It is imperative we get Ismail Oglu Tepe and Tekke Tepe *now!*' To this he raised objections. He doubted whether the troops had got their water yet ... there were many technical reasons against it, especially the attitude of his generals who had told him that their men were too tired."

Hammersley, it seems, was dead against a night attack. And, indeed, there was much to be said against it, since even in broad daylight officers and men were continually losing their way. But there was no choice now. The wonder was that the Turks were not already on the Tekke Tepe. They were certain to be there before daybreak.

Instead of forcing the issue with Stopford, Hamilton said he would go ashore at once and talk to Hammersley* and his brigadiers. To this Stopford agreed, the diary tells us:

> "Nothing, he said, would please him more that if I could succeed where he had failed, and would I excuse him from accompanying me: he had not been very fit: he had just returned from a visit to the shore and he wanted to give his leg a chance."

---

* It is to be noted that neither Aspinall nor Hamilton thought of having a word with Mahon. Throughout the operation he seems to have been, if not forgotten, quietly left aside. Yet (a) he was, next to Hamilton himself, the senior general at Suvla, in rank a lieutenant-general, whereas Hammersley was only a major-general: (b) his Xth Division troops had taken a leading part in the capture of Chocolate Hill and Green Hill: (c) his few remaining troops on the Kiretch Tepe were the only ones to have reached the heights, and, given the return of the missing battalions, or normal reinforcements, were in position to sweep the Turks off the northern ridge, and disrupt the entire right flank of the Turkish defence from Ejelmer Bay to the crest of the Tekke Tepe. Moreover, (d) he was, though disgruntled, physically fit and able to lead his men, which is more than can be said of poor Hammersley.

Stopford pointed out the divisional headquarters a little to the east of Nibrunesi Point, and said that Hammersley would be able to direct the Commander-in-Chief to the brigades. The diary continues—

"So I nipped down the *Jonquil's* ladder, tumbled into Roger Keyes's racing motor-boat and with him and Aspinall we simply shot across the water to Lala Baba. Every moment was priceless. I had not been five minutes on the *Jonquil* and in another two I was with Hammersley."

They landed under the low cliffs, or rocky shelf, on a small half-moon of beach, and found Hammersley at the northern end of it. "Asked to give me an idea of the situation," Hamilton writes, "he gave me much the same story as Stopford."

The same deadlock ensued. Hammersley insisted that his troops could not advance before eight o'clock the next morning. Hamilton said that "next day might be too late".

Hammersley replied that there were no troops ready for an advance that night. Hamilton countered by saying that there must be *one* battalion, somewhere, capable of getting to the top of the Tekke Tepe—a distance of about three and a half miles from Chocolate Hill, with no Turks in front of them?

Finally, after a good deal of humming and hawing, Hammersley thought it might be possible to get the 32nd Brigade to do something—he "believed it to be concentrated more or less near Sulajik" (that is, 1,600 yards north-east of Chocolate Hill).

Hamilton grabbed at this, and said quickly: "Then order at least one battalion of it to be on the top of the ridge by daylight. The presence of that one battalion on the high ground at daylight will be invaluable to the rest of the corps when they advance tomorrow morning."

Verbal orders were issued at once to the commander of the 32nd Brigade, and Hammersley's last words to Major Duncan who took the message were: "Tell him to send the pioneers."

He gave that instruction because the pioneers—the 6th East Yorkshire—had been the last battalion to move from Lala Baba, and were likely to be less exhausted than any of the other units.

Having managed to get a promise of action during the hours of darkness by at least one battalion, Hamilton went back to the *Triad*. But—and this is curiously in keeping with the whole Suvla mix-up—he did not tell Stopford that he had modified his battle orders. So Stopford spent the night without knowing that some of his troops had been ordered to advance to the crest of the Tekke Tepe before daybreak. As he still had no very clear idea of the disposition of his forces, and only wanted to be left in peace to "consolidate", it probably made very little difference. For his part, he was still of the opinion that the great thing was to avoid "a regular battle".

The tempo at Liman von Sanders's G.H.Q. was very different from that at Suvla. And the temper too. It flashed and crackled. All the difference between Sandhurst and Gross Lichterfelde, the Central Cadet School of the German Officers' Corps. As different as an old school tie from a jackboot.

11 p.m.—and still no attack? *Ach!* hopeless! The field-marshal dismissed Feizi Bey out of hand, and packed him off to Constantinople. Mustafa Kemal was given command of the whole Chunuk/Suvla area straight away. After that, even with the best of luck—and we had none—there was no chance. Kemal was a born leader.

Von Sanders had made the correct decision, and had made it swiftly at the right moment. He was dead lucky to have the chance. Even if Hamilton could have screwed up enough decisive fury to sack Stopford on the spot, there was no Mustafa Kemal to put in his place.

It is easy to see, now, that he ought to have taken command at Suvla himself, and led his troops in person to the top of the Tekke Tepe that night. That was the bold, the outrageous, the startling and unheard-of masterstroke that the three Fates, if not the three Furies, were screaming for.

Into the dark night—instead—rode Mustafa Kemal. A figure as gaunt and gaunter than Hamilton. Grim-faced, hollow-eyed from lack of sleep, more weary than any of us. His tunic and breeches soiled and crumpled. His riding-boots scratched and worn. A black astrakhan tarboosh, pulled down over his forehead to eyebrow-level and raked slightly on the right, stressed the fixed and sullen frown, intensifying the flinty glance.

As thin as a rake. Hardbitten. Grim is the word. Grim-

visaged. His cheekbones jutting. Not a left-over crease of a
smile on the stretched skin. Sun-scorched. All laughter dried
out of him. As tough as a juniper-root pickled in arrack.
Fanatical and fearless. The future Ataturk. Tough as hell,
but never fit. Now 34. Looked like a man always in pain. And
was. Pain—arrack. More pain—more arrack. Pickled in arrack.
But stone-cold sober fighting. With one idea in his head, and
one only—"Turkey for the Turks". Not like a Turk to look at.
A blond with cold blue eyes. Born in Salonika, 1881, when it
was still part of Turkey. Of mixed blood: Albanian-Turkish-
Macedonian. A born fighter. Hard as nails. Liver too—
cirrhosis. Full of bile, hatred, arrack. Full of relentless energy.
Full of drugs also. Pumped into him by his divisional medical
officer to keep him going after two days and two nights
without sleep on the Anzac front. Worn to a shred. Eyes
bloodshot. Voice a whispering-croak. Nerves shot to pieces,
and yet—and so?—no sign of nerves. Mind as cold and sharp
as a Khorassan scimitar. A splendid wreck of a man—calm
and confident. And full of fight. Riding across the hills to Suvla.

Hamilton, in the *Triad*, came on deck a little before midnight
for a breather. The whole battle area as quiet as a churchyard.
No, a mortuary. At least a thousand dead were still unburied.
They lay dew-soaked in the sand, with only the purple-black
darkness to cover them. The stench was quelled in the blessed
cucumber-cool of the night. The flies gone. The encircling
outline of jagged hills loomed against the sky, dark upon dark.
By now, somewhere over there, that battalion of East
Yorkshire pioneers must be groping its way up the skewed and
steepfaced gullies to the crestline.

8

THE RACE FOR THE TEKKE TEPE

Boler found a sandy dell in the outlet of a near-by dry water-course: a better place to sleep than the humpy ground bordering the beach. Better because it was a natural trench, with steep scrub-grown slopes ten to twelve feet high on either side, giving some protection from stray bullets, shrapnel bursts, and shellfire.

So we took our kit over to the mouth of this gully, and slept there that night without undressing. We had no blankets. They had been dumped ashore somewhere, but not yet found amidst the chaotic pile-up of stores and equipment that blocked the beaches.

And while we slept, the ill-devised and misjudged Sulajik undertaking blundered around in circles, like stumbling groups of drunken men trying to find their way home after closing-time.

Sulajik, about 1,000 yards due east of the Salt Lake and 1,600 yards north-east of Chocolate Hill, was only a name for a huddle of rough farm sheds standing on a small area of the Anafarta plain. Here the ground begins to rise from the barren saltflats towards patches of cultivation and the tree-dotted slopes that lead to the gully ridges of the Tekke Tepe, the crest of which stands about two and a half miles east-north-east of Sulajik on a line of bearing. On foot this would mean a heavy climb of some four miles over damnably broken ground.

The 32nd Brigade was moved up to Sulajik on the morning of the 8th. This was the only military movement undertaken during daylight hours on that day. The idea was to link up the "still peaceful" Chocolate Hill position with Mahon's troops on the Kiretch Tepe. But—and here we see the reason for the daylong Sulajik standstill—before the 32nd left Hill 10, Sitwell explained to Colonel Minogue, now in command of the brigade, that they were "not intended to fight". All they had to do was to "entrench a position" and wait for the arrival of the divisional pioneer battalion (the 6th East Yorkshire) from Lala Baba. And that was what they did.

Spreading like a miasma from Stopford, Reed, Hammersley, and Sitwell, the idea of not fighting had, by now, infected every senior officer at Suvla. Even stop-gap brigade commanders, like Colonel Minogue, had succumbed to it. Thus when, during the afternoon of the 8th, he received Stopford's order (suggestion, indication, hint?) that it was of vital importance to "forestall the enemy on the high ground to the east of the plain"—but with the proviso that no attack was to be made on "an entrenched position held in strength"—he reported that, as every attempt to advance drew heavy fire, he proposed to stay where he was at Sulajik "in compliance with orders received".

And there he stayed, while two of his battalions plodded off in different directions, lost touch with each other and with their headquarters, and were soon swallowed up in the tawny grasslands, dark bands of undulating scrub, and the tremulant heat-haze.

All through the blistering hours of daylight Colonel Minogue did his best to "entrench a position" north and south of Sulajik, without knowing that these two battalions (the 6th East Yorkshire and the 9th West Yorkshire) had pushed forward and were now well placed for an advance to "the high ground to the east of the plain"—without knowing where they were at all, although seven hours had elapsed since they had reached their positions!—*and without knowing that, during the afternoon, two officers and a signaller of the pioneer battalion had been right to the top of the Tekke Tepe ridge, had reconnoitred it, and found no one there but a few Turkish sentries.*

This information had been flashed to a signal station on Hill 10, and acknowledged. Nothing was done about it there. Not surprising, since Sitwell—still sitting on that whaleback-hump, less than half a mile from the beach—had decided that his troops were "not intended to fight" (even a few scattered Turkish patrols). But it is surprising that no report of this reconnaissance was sent to Colonel Minogue, commanding the 32nd Brigade. Thus, he did not know—

(a) That the 6th East Yorkshire (pioneer) battalion, under Lieutenant-Colonel Moore, was already on high ground just below the crest of the northern flank of Scimitar Hill (229 feet)—so called from a blaze of open gravel on its side—and only two and a half miles south-west from the summit of the Tekke Tepe, as the crow flies. This position was the key to the central massif, and also to the W Hills (Ismail Oglu Tepe) and the Anafarta spur.

(b) That the 9th West Yorkshire battalion was 1,000 yards north-east of Sulajik, not on high ground, but in a good position for the advance, being only two miles west-south-west from the Tekke Tepe summit, as the crow flies.

It seems likely that Major Duncan reached brigade head-quarters about 9 p.m. with instructions to "concentrate the brigade at Sulajik as soon as possible, and thence to occupy the high ground about Tekke Tepe before daylight, at least one battalion being used for the purpose—preferably the 6th East Yorkshire Regiment".

Although there were two battalions that could have been moved forward without delay, the brigade commander obeyed orders. He sent out runners to find the two missing battalions, with instructions to concentrate at Sulajik by 10.30 p.m. Thereafter, the fatal game of blind-man's-buff began.

It was not only darkness, and the fact that they were not sure which direction to take, that confused the runners in their search. They did not know the lie of the land. Moreover, these battalions were on the move.

At nightfall the 6th East Yorkshires had pushed forward to the top of Scimitar Hill, and were in an even better position than before. But it was not until 11.30 p.m. that a runner reached them with orders to fall back on Sulajik.

In the ink-black night the half-dead pioneer battalion gathered up their kit and entrenching-tools and crept away, stumbling on into the darkness, with no idea which way to go. The runner who found them was unable to find the way back. Lost . . . and Scimitar Hill lost for ever.

As soon as they discovered that the British had, for some inexplicable reason, retired, the Turks recovered the position and held it to the end. The next day the 33rd Brigade lost 1,500 men in an attempt to retake it. Twelve days later IX troops lost over 5,000 in an equally unsuccessful assault. Scimitar Hill became a Golgotha, and its name a synonym for massacre.

At one-thirty in the morning the wretched pioneers were still blundering on, and it was only by chance that, about 2 a.m., they came upon a dead Turk—skirted round it warily—and then recognised it as a "landmark" near the "foul and stinking British front-line trench at Sulajik". Even so, it was not until three o'clock in the morning that they had all assembled. Three and a half hours to cover 750 yards!—the distance from Scimitar Hill to Sulajik. This, to anyone who does not know the convulsive havoc of rockface, butte, and dry runnel north-east of Chocolate Hill, and has never had to find a way across this tumbled labyrinth at night, must seem absurd.

As these deadbeat Yorkshiremen (who were supposed to be less exhausted than any of the other units) came staggering in— a ghastly battalion of cadaverous ghosts, unkempt, unwashed, their chins bristling—they were ordered to dig in for the second time that night, on a line stretching for more than half a mile. They gripped the hafts of their entrenching-tools, and tried to hack and scoop the heavy chocolate-coloured soil—"but were so dazed with fatigue that most of them fell asleep". These were the men who were due—and long overdue—to make the dash to the crest of the Tekke Tepe.

As for the 9th West Yorkshire battalion, they had withdrawn from their well-placed forward position north-east of Sulajik, moved almost due south 1,200 yards, and at nightfall "got out of touch in the thick bush near Abrikja", where, had they but known it, they were only 500 yards from the 6th East Yorkshires on the top of Scimitar Hill. And there, lost in the dense holly-oak scrub, they stayed for nine hours, until a runner found them, after six hours of searching, at five o'clock on the morning of August 9, just as dawn was breaking.

By 3 a.m. on August 9 the Bulair divisions had not yet reached the summit.

And by 3 a.m. Colonel Minogue had gathered in all his stray sheep (except that lost battalion near Abrikja), had waited another half-hour, and then, at three-thirty, decided to advance without it.

  still dark. The race for the Tekke Tepe was on.

18. " Tea Up " as Dawn Breaks at Suvla

19. Congestion in a Gully Path

20. IRISH DIVISION TROOPS SCALING THE KIRETCH TEPE

The Manchesters attempted to take these heights during the night of August 6th, and although they lost themselves in the pitch blackness, succeeded in pushing the Turks back some distance.

Kemal lost no time. By 11.30 on the night of the 8th—half an hour after being given his new command—he was in the saddle. A lone figure riding on ahead, setting out to see for himself. The famous night-ride to reconnoitre the Suvla battlefront. Hard going over hill-tracks most of the way. His doctor and *aide-de-camp* following a few paces behind. (Significant, that doctor?)

If we could see the vice-like grip of the will holding the worn-out body upright in the saddle, it would glow like a tree made of fluorescent wire-wool shaped like a man sitting an invisible horse cut out of darkness. A dimly luminous man riding astride the night.

To the left, looking down from the high sandstone outcrops of the Sari Bair, the gloom-held plain stretched away to the thin, silver-grey streak of the Salt Lake four miles to the north-west. 20,000 British over there. Asleep? Digging-in? Moving forward under cover of the night? All as silent as the grave. . . .

Kemal had one thing in mind, and one only: to stop the British from gaining the Tekke Tepe—if there was still time.

Soon after midnight—while the pioneer battalion was still groping its way back from Scimitar Hill to Sulajik—Kemal rode up to Willmer's headquarters in the Suvla hills. Finding no one able to give him much information as to the dispositions and troop movements of the British, he rode on to Little Anafarta, and so up the steep hill-path (328–918 feet) to the crest of the Tekke Tepe—still undefended.

From there he pushed north-west, where he could see the sweep of Ejelmer Bay two and a half miles due north. And so, in a great horseshoe bend, keeping always up on the high bluffs and ridgeways, to the eastern slopes of the Kiretch Tepe. Then back along the same route, having covered a total distance of well over twelve miles, riding and walking.

It must have been about 3 a.m.—when the last of the pioneers stumbled into Sulajik—that Kemal dismounted. He had made up his mind to launch a general attack at the first crack of dawn along the entire four-mile front of the Tekke Tepe, in the centre, to the northern escarpments of the Sari Bair, in an attempt to drive the British into the sea. A bold and hazardous decision, for the weary Bulair troops were only now beginning to straggle in.

L

When, at 3.30 a.m.—*eight hours after the British Commander-in-Chief had ordered the advance*—the brigade commander decided to move forward without further delay, he sent a written order to one of the battalions that had been at Sulajik since the morning. It was instructed to lead the advance. That might have snatched us victory at the very last moment: these troops were fresher. But soon afterwards he recalled the general's final behest to "send the pioneers", quashed the original order, and told the 6th East Yorkshire to "push on at once".

This was easier said than done. Most of them were dead asleep, slumped along the half-mile stretch they had been ordered to entrench: some of them still gripping their entrenching-tools. All were worn out by long hours of trudging, waiting, digging-in. Many were down with dysentery.

It was nearly 4 a.m. before Lieutenant-Colonel Moore was able to collect seven officers and about 140 men for the attack. No more could be mustered, although there were 20,000 ashore!

One thing was certain: it wasn't Moore's fault that he could gather together no more than this remnant. Nor was it his fault that, as these poor sleep-bemused scarecrows staggered into line, the leading files of the first Turkish reinforcements from Bulair clambered to the crest of the Tekke Tepe. They were half dead with fatigue, too. So was Kemal. But he was determined to fight—and he was there on the spot with his troops. He gave them no time to rest, no time to slump.

The first grey creep of daylight lifted as Moore gave orders for the three other companies to follow on as soon as they could be assembled, and made ready to move off with his pitiful little cluster.

They had a backbreaking climb of some four miles before them, north-east-by-east, across rising uplands. All steep, wildly troubled, torn, thrawn, frantically dishevelled country. Dismaying in the shuddering dawnbreath. Packed with listening silences, and little skinky shufflings—of rock-lizards?—snipers?. . .

As Moore and his party trudged away from the cesspit-cum-charnelhouse stench at Sulajik, two Turkish battalions were toiling slowly up the slopes on the other side of the ridge, where they had one tremendous advantage: there was no thick scrub.

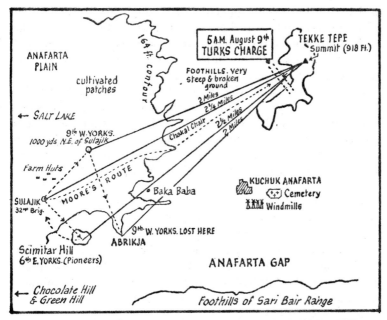

Map 12. POSITIONS IN THE RACE FOR THE TEKKE TEPE

Before the little band of Yorkshiremen had gone half a mile—
that is, before they were halfway to the gully-mouth leading
up to the crest of the Tekke Tepe—dropping shots from field
batteries near Kuchuk Anafarta had thinned them out.

Later, when they had clambered up the gully and the steep
winding goat-tracks, pushing their way between boulder-strewn
knolls and prickly thornbrakes, they came under frontal fire as
well as enfilading fire on both flanks, and were forced to scatter.
They resumed the advance in small dispersed groups to avoid
total annihilation. By the time they reached 885 feet they had
lost 110 of their number, killed and wounded.

As the thirty lionhearted survivors staggered up the last
thirty-three feet to the summit, blindingly floodlit in the golden-
quilled upthrust of dawn, they were hurled from the apex by a
bayonet charge of onrushing Turks, and swept back into the
twilight maze from which they had just emerged.

There in the shadows, trapped halfway down a snaking gully
like rats in the elbow-bend of a culvert, they were picked off—
shot one by one. Moore, seeing it was hopeless, surrendered—

and had a Turkish bayonet thrust through his back. Another
officer—wounded—was done to death where he lay, stuck like
a pig. Only four of the gallant band remained: two officers and
two men. And but for the intercession of a Moslem priest, the
two officers would have been butchered also.

No help came from the three companies that had been instructed to follow on. That was bad enough, but, for some
reason or other, Colonel Minogue had in the meantime ordered
the one remaining supporting battalion to stay at Sulajik until
the 9th West Yorkshire regiment was found! These men
were still wandering about without orders somewhere near
Abrikja.

Thus, Moore's intrepid handful went forward without support from anyone—and was wiped out. Thirty reached the
summit at about 5 a.m.*—half an hour too late.

That lost half-hour changed the course of history throughout the world.
Having pushed the British off the Tekke Tepe, the Turks
swept down the hillside in a swarming mass. Within minutes
the nearest thing to catastrophe was upon us.

At about this time, in the early morning of August 9, our
sleep-sullen, fear-silent, empty-bellied water-fatigue party came
back from the spring they had found at the edge of the Salt Lake,
below Lala Baba. The trudge of about three miles, there and
back, had taken nearly two hours.

Long before they came in sight, we heard the handle-squeak
and swinging clank of the heavy iron camp-kettles (oval, large)
from our own cookhouse stores, holding three gallons apiece,
weight (empty) eight pounds each, and each needing two men
to lift and carry when full.

Lugging them over sand and scrub was slow, back-aching
work. They came in fagged-out. And "jumpy". Because, at
Suvla, the order: "Fall in for water-fatigue!" always unleashed

---

* Most accounts give 4 a.m., or thereabouts, as the time when Colonel
Moore and his party left Sulajik, and 4.30 a.m. when the Turks swept them
off the crest. But to reach the crest of the Tekke Tepe from Sulajik in thirty
minutes would be something of a feat for fit men in full daylight. It involves
a climb from the gully-mouth of 750 feet. in a mile and a half. In the near-
dawn darkness, with exhausted troops, and under fire most of the way, it
could hardly take less than an hour.

a nasty little quick-darting fear. Fear of being picked off by a hidden sniper on the way down—or on the way back. Nothing is more demoralising.

The result of their hazardous journey was one mug (about half a pint) of tea per man, dished out by the cooks at breakfast-time. This was extra to the day's three-quarter-pint water-ration, and I felt I could spare—or rather, I had the urge to squander—about half a gill from my water-bottle for a quick shave. Others did the same. Three days' growth was bristlingly burr-like and uncomfortable.

I had just finished shaving when the sergeant-major called—"Parade at orderly room, Sergeant, in five minutes. Colonel's orders."

"*Orderly* room?" I gasped. "*What* orderly room—*where?*"—how could there be an orderly room in this howling wilderness?

"Over there, behind those bushes." He strode off.

I put my shaving kit away, made myself presentable, and pushed through those bushes. There he was—the blustering jackanapes!—sitting bolt upright on a regulation officers' green canvas camp-chair, with a large bully-beef crate (as Orderly Room table) set in front of him, on which were some papers, a pencil, and a copy of *King's Regulations*. On his right stood the adjutant, on his left the sergeant-clerk. The Colonel looked ferocious, the adjutant blankly solemn, the sergeant-clerk browbeaten. Then the sergeant-major appeared, as though from nowhere, looking both pompous and servile. Before he could say or do anything, the Colonel bellowed—"Where the devil have you been, Sergeant-Major?"

But before the sergeant-major could speak, Mad Jack turned upon me—"Take off your cap!—you're under close arrest!"

What *again?* I took off my cap. Mad Jack turned upon the wretched S.M.—"Well—dammit!—march the accused in, can't you?—march him in!"

As I was already standing facing the orderly room "table", this was a bit tricky.

"Right—*turn!*" bellowed the sergeant-major. "Quick—*march!*" Just as I was marching into the bushes, the order came—"Ab-o-u-t—*turn!*" ... "Halt!"—"Right—*turn!*"

So now I was back again, facing the "table".

"Read the charge!"

"Yes, sir!" mumbled the sergeant-clerk, and began fumbling with the papers.

"Don't say 'Yes, sir!'—*read the charge!*"

"Charge against 32819, Sergeant Hargrave, J.—coming on parade improperly dressed on the morning of August 8th, 1915."

Mad Jack glared at me. "Humph! serious charge," he muttered. "Bad example—no puttees!—anything to say?" he thundered.

I stared into his bulging watery-blue eyes for a second or two, and said very quietly, and very clearly and deliberately—"No, sir."

"Humph!—severe reprimand!"

"Cap on!—salute!—right turn!—dismiss!" bellowed the sergeant-major.

That was the end of that. All the same, a "severe rep" was a serious thing for a sergeant to have on his "crime sheet". This was only the first of a whole series of such galling harassments. It shows the kind of thing we were subjected to on the battle-field.

While this Pig-and-Pepper interlude broke in upon the work of the ambulance like a sky-wannocking of lunatics, the sun flashed down upon us from the Sari Bair—and the Turks swept Moore and his thirty valiant deadbeats from the crestline. . . .

We knew nothing about that. Neither did Hamilton. As dawn lit the bay and the horseshoe of hills, he stood watching from the deck of the *Triad*. Later he wrote in his diary:

> "August 9th.—The Officer of the Watch said that the small hours passed quietly: no firing ashore during the hours of darkness. Could not make head or tail of it!"

At this moment the Turks were pouring down from the Tekke Tepe towards Sulajik, sweeping all before them.

9

BLACK MONDAY

Thirst and heat had alarming effects. Sounds pitched off-key. Spoken words broke apart, blared, and slipped away in a glassy tinkle. The clang of shrapnel-clatter slowed-up by a fraction— you heard the mass-horseshoe stampede of a phantom cavalry charge falling out of it. Smells sharpened, changed over-poweringly from fragrance to fetor, became almost visible, danced like needle-points. Once or twice we caught a glimpse of the Salt Lake through the scrub on our right. It looked like a glittering pool of crushed diamonds shuddering to a smoky rhythm, as though about to float slowly up into the hot dark glare of the sky and vanish.

Again the throng of truculent flies rose from their death-feast in an angry roar as we skirted a deserted strongpost where ten or a dozen dead Turks still sprawled in the pitiless sunshine. An irate R.E. captain, in charge of a roadmaking party, came stamping across. And as he came, he shouted—"Why the devil don't you get these stinking dead Turks buried, for God's sake?"

I halted and saluted. "It's not our job, sir," I told him.

"Of course it's your job!—you're Medical Corps, aren't you?"

"Yes, sir—but the burial of the dead is not the work of a Field Ambulance."

"I never heard such nonsense!" he snorted.

"We're A Section bearer sub-division of the 32nd Field Ambulance, sir—ordered up the line to bring in the wounded."

"Well, I order you to bury these stinking dead Turks— they've been lying out here for days!"

"I'm sorry I can't obey your order, sir. I'll report what you say to the Colonel of the Ambulance." I saluted, and went on.

He stood there flabbergasted. "Well, I'll be damned!" I heard him exclaim. "A bloody Medical Corps sergeant!"

"Let the Divisional Sanitary Officer do his job," I muttered to myself as I hurried on to catch up with the stretcher-bearers. "It's the wounded we have to bother about—not the dead. . . ."

Two days and three nights, and not a sign of a sanitary section at work anywhere! The wonder is we didn't have an epidemic of typhus, cholera, or "yellow jack".

What with Mad Jack and his "orderly-room" circus—and now this ordering-about by some R.E. officer who didn't know that R.A.M.C. stretcher-bearers are not a gang of burying-beetles—it was a bad start to a bad day.

It was a bad start to a bad day for Hamilton too.

While we trudged steadily inland, he stood watching a head-long retreat. That night he wrote in his diary:

> "Then about 6 a.m. the whole lot seemed suddenly to collapse—including the right! Not only did they give ground but they came back—some of them—half way to the sea. But others made a stand.
>
> "Looked at from the bridge of the *Triad*—not a bad observation station—the tendency of our men to get into little groups was very noticeable: as if they had not been trained in working under fire.
>
> "My heart has grown tough amidst the struggles of the peninsula, but the misery of this scene wellnigh broke it. . . . Words are no use."

It never struck him that he and his general staff were in any way responsible for the failure to take the Tekke Tepe, and for this all-but-disastrous break-up of the front line in a headlong stream-away towards the beaches.

On the evening of the 8th, when he had seen the position with his own eyes, he wrote: "It was clear to half an eye that Tekke Tepe was the key to the whole Suvla Bay area." Yet he does not seem to have known that, in the final orders issued to Stopford by G.H.Q., *there was no mention of the Tekke Tepe.* Those orders directed that the Chocolate and W Hills were to be taken at an early period in the attack—"if possible"—and that the Kiretch Tepe was to be occupied as far as Point 156 (that is, the whole of its six-mile length)—"if possible". No time-limit was set for the gaining of these objectives.

So there he stood, his heart wellnigh breaking, compelled to watch the inevitable outcome of his own kindly and curiously quixotic nature.

Kemal, also watching, saw the British streaming away towards the beaches. Now was the moment when he might have driven us into the sea. Instead, having got the British on the run, he plastered them on the flat open ground between Sulajik and Hetman Chair with a tornado of shrapnel.

Hamilton, in his dispatch of December 11, 1915, gives an account of it:

> "At dawn on the 9th I watched General Hammersley's attack, and very soon realised, by the well-sustained artillery fire of the enemy (so silent the previous day) and by the volume of the musketry, that Turkish reinforcements had arrived; that with the renewed confidence caused by our long delay the guns had been brought back; and that, after all, we were forestalled. This was a bad moment. Our attack failed; our losses were very serious. The enemy's enfilading shrapnel fire seemed to be especially destructive and demoralising, the shells bursting low and all along our line."

He speaks of "the volume of musketry", and, indeed, this was murderous. Nevertheless, the Turks—except for snipers and small bands of skirmishers—took care not to expose themselves on the scrubless glare of the Salt Lake, and never pursued the retreating British much beyond the Ali Bey Cheshme, about 600 yards west of Sulajik, but allowed panic and the devastating storm of artillery fire to do their work. In this Kemal was wise: he knew his Bulair troops were ready to drop from fatigue.

If ever there was a moment at Suvla when the naval guns might have "spoken" to good effect, this was it. Trained on the crest of the Tekke Tepe, before the Turkish reinforcements had time to dig-in, and now, obviously, without endangering any of our own troops, they could have decimated whole battalions. But no signal was given. Not a squib was fired. The great grey battleships stood out in the bay silent and motionless.

Ashore, the Xth Division had no artillery at all—not one solitary fieldpiece—and the guns available to the 11th Division consisted of one battery of its one and only artillery brigade, with very little ammunition. There was, therefore, practically no reply to "the enemy's enfilading shrapnel fire" that "seemed to be especially destructive and demoralising".

With only one battery firing from Lala Baba, it is not surprising that the New Army troops "came back—some of them—half way to the sea". The real wonder is that we were not all swept down to the beaches into the sea and drowned. . . .

Stopford, we are told, took this setback "very philosophically". Although "our losses were very serious", he was so engrossed in his own personal affairs during the morning of the 9th that he seems to have had little time to give to this wholesale retirement of his troops almost to the water's edge.

Round about 8 a.m., two hours after the retreat began, the Turkish fire slackened, and by degrees Hammersley's troops found the heart to rally. They turned and drifted wearily back across the saltflats looking for their units along a blurred and broken "line" that straggled from the fierce swirl of fighting taking place on the western slopes of Scimitar Hill to a position north of Sulajik, where the 32nd Brigade had been forced to retire and was now making a determined stand.

The Turks, famished, thirst-stricken, ragged, and footsore, more asleep than awake, did not press their counter-attack, but stumbled slowly back up the gullies to their fastnesses in the hills to rest and lick their wounds.

Yet despite the near-stampede of the disorderly retreat, and the almost as disorderly realignment now taking place, the Turks had not been able to dislodge our main positions. We still held Lala Baba, Hill 10, Chocolate Hill and Green Hill on the right, and about two miles of the Kiretch Tepe ridge on the left. But the key position—the Tekke Tepe—had been snatched from us at the moment of victory.

Nevertheless, the fight went on, raging back and forth towards the crest of Scimitar Hill.

Stopford had gone ashore overnight. About forty-eight hours after the landing something had moved him to uproot himself from his comfortable quarters on the *Jonquil*, and to establish his corps headquarters on the northern arm of the bay. Soon after 8 o'clock Hamilton went ashore to look for him, and later wrote in his diary:

> "August 9th, Imbros.—We found Stopford about four or five hundred yards to the east of Ghazi Baba, busy with part of a Field Company of Engineers supervising the building of some splinterproof headquarters huts for himself and his staff. He was absorbed in the work, and said it would be well to make a thorough good job of the dug-outs as we should probably be here for a very long time."

At once we are carried back to the morning before, when the trench-supervising staff officer replied to Hankey's "You seem to be making yourselves snug", with the words *"We expect to be here a long time"*.

On hearing this phrase from Stopford, the Commander-in-Chief ejaculated "Devil a bit!"—(a turn of words as out of date in 1915 as Mr. Pickwick's thrice-repeated "Bless my soul!" on the way to Dingley Dell)—and assured his corps commander that he would be picking the best house in Anafarta for his billet within a day or so.

Hamilton then asked for news of the Xth (Irish) Division on the Kiretch Tepe. Stopford had no information about the position there—although Mahon's divisional headquarters was not more than half a mile away. Still the knightly chevalier, Hamilton suggested that it might be a good idea to go off on a reconnoitring stroll along the ridge. Stopford agreed, but felt he ought to stay at corps headquarters himself to deal with any messages that might come in.

So Hamilton set out with an A.D.C. to "find the Irish" for himself, and Stopford went back to the supervision of his deep-shelter dug-outs east of Ghazi Baba, about a hundred yards from the bay. However, fair's fair: we must allow some excuse for not going, since the ground over which they climbed—I think I could find my way along every gully-ridge and winding goat-track, even now—was so steep and broken that anyone still recovering from a sprained knee might easily wrick the tendons again, and be out of action for weeks.

Hamilton pushed on along the Kiretch ridge for a mile

through waist-high scrub under "a spattering of 'overs'". Later
he recorded in his diary:

> "August 9th, Imbros.—He [Mahon] is angry, and small
> wonder, at the chaos introduced somehow into the Corps.
> He is commanding some of Hammersley's men and Hammer-
> sley has the bulk of his at the far extremity of the line of
> battle."

It was a bad day for Mahon. On the morning of the 8th two
battalions of the Munsters, supported by the Royal Irish
Regiment and the 5th Royal Inniskilling Fusiliers, had attacked
the Turkish position, advancing about 800 yards. The final push
was made by a storming party of the 6th Munsters led by the
second-in-command of their battalion, Major Jephson. They
reached the western tip of the highest ridge of the hogsback
(656 feet), a rocky outcrop known thereafter as Jephson's Post.
No further advance was possible: the 350 Turks facing them
were found to be holding "a strongly entrenched position"—
one of the few in the whole Suvla area—that extended right
across the ridge. The Irish therefore dug-in on the line held.

When Mahon received Stopford's order instructing him to resume his advance along the Kiretch Tepe, seize the Tekke Tepe,
and push on down the ridge to join hands with the 11th Division
on the Anafarta spur at dawn on August 9, it was already late
afternoon on August 8, and his dark-smouldering anger "at the
chaos introduced somehow into the Corps" was spreading like
underground fire in a dry peat-bog. All he did to prepare for
the "general advance" was to tell the commander of the 30th
Brigade that he would visit his headquarters at six o'clock the
next morning "to discuss further details".

According to the corps order Mahon was to begin his attack
before or at the same time as the advance of the 11th Division:
that is, at dawn. But when dawn broke on the 9th—and Moore
with his Dauntless Thirty were flung from the crest of the
Tekke Tepe—there was no sign of an advance on the Kiretch
Tepe, and the 32nd and 33rd Brigades of the 11th Division went
into action unsupported on the left flank. Nothing was ready
on the Kiretch ridge.

There was a long delay in sending up the day's rations and
the meagre supply of water. In consequence, one of Mahon's
battalions had to march off without its water-bottles (to be

filled—or rather, partly filled—later, when the water arrived: but the men never saw them again that day), and before long "maddening thirst" reduced the fighting ability of this unit to such a degree of exhaustion that it could not stagger on.

The advance on the Kiretch Tepe did not begin until 7.30 a.m.—two and a half hours late—and although a destroyer in the Gulf of Saros shelled the crest beyond Jephson's Post, the two forward battalions were so deadbeat from lack of sleep, lack of water, and lack of food, that they could not hold that position, and were driven back—giving ground slowly, yard by yard, fighting for every inch.

Such was the situation when Hamilton decided to leave Stopford to his splinterproof dug-outs, and to go off along the ridge to see for himself. Later in the day—after he had left Suvla for Anzac—the troops were back again in their old position, about 800 yards west of Jephson's Post. A bad day indeed.

Then, to round it off with the usual Suvla quipsy-crankiness, at 4.30 p.m. Mahon received—"greatly to his surprise"—a message from Stopford congratulating him on the day's encounter. To this was added, just to keep up the habitual rôle of this *drôle de corps*—"Do not try any more today, unless the enemy gives you a favourable chance."

"Don't try any more today," said the Corps Commander.

"I wasn't thinking of trying," said Alice. . . .

During his Kiretch Tepe reconnaissance Hamilton fell in with two young Irish soldiers and had a talk with them. We do not know what was said, but the diarist tells us that it "put some new life" into him. No doubt he found these two Irish lads of the Xth Division fairly cheery in spite of everything.

They seemed to have put so much "new life" into him that, on his return to Ghazi Baba, he summoned up enough *brusquerie* to tell Stopford that "the sooner the Kiretch Tepe nettle is grasped the less it will sting". He then (according to the diary) "begged" him to make a push for it along the hogsback ridge. None of this earnest beseechment took account of the fact that the splinterproof shelters were, as yet, nowhere near deep enough.

Stopford went on with his job—nettles or no nettles. And soon after mid-day Hamilton sailed for Anzac.

There were several walking cases during the morning. I took charge of one of them, because I didn't like the glitter in his eye, and because, in spite of a rather deep buttock-wound, he was able to take a good swinging stride—and I wanted to get back to the beach as quickly as possible in order to send up more stretchers to this part of the line.

At first I thought that he had an impediment in his speech, but that was because I was examining his wound and putting on a dressing, and had not looked at his face. His first word was—"*Wather!*"—and it came from him not as a request, but more like a threat. He was a tall, gaunt, black-haired Irishman with a long flat skull. His lantern jaw was blue-black with the stubble of his beard. I could see he was a sullen, cross-grained customer by nature. His lips were cracked and blistered. That was nothing. So were mine. But his tongue was so badly swollen he couldn't close his mouth. The tip of it stuck out between his scabby lips like a dried prune—black and shiny.

"*Wather!*" he croaked again, in the same fierce, threatening tone. I couldn't help him, both my water-bottles were empty. I shook them in front of his face to prove it. All the same, he took them from me, uncorked them and tipped them up. He may have got six or seven drops from each to moisten his lips.

"What's your name?" I asked. He glared, as though I had no right to ask.

"Kelly—why?"

"We have to take the names of all wounded," I told him. (I might have known it was Kelly, I said to myself. "Kelly's eye"—glittering. . . .) As soon as I had the bandage fixed, we started off for the beach. We left the loaded stretcher-squads and the straggle of other walking cases far behind. He strode with a kind of gangling leap, like the curious loping gait of a *lung-gom-pa* lama of Tibet, neither running nor walking.

He kept half a pace ahead of me all the way, stumbling now and then, or reeling in a blind stagger. He never glanced at me, nor turned his head. And he never said more than one word until he caught sight of—but I'm running ahead of myself.

I guess he was no more than a lad of nineteen or twenty, though he looked like the shrunken mummy of Seti I.

We were still on high ground, about halfway to the beach, when a thin blue-grey smoke came wafting over the Karakol Dagh like a mist, carrying the same choking, nostril-stinging reek that had drifted across the bows of the s.s. *Partridge* on the morning of August 7. It came in long billowing drifts.

At the first of these we both stopped. I turned half-left and saw the thick coils of smoke belching from the heat-shimmering hillside two and a half miles to the south-east, on the left of Chocolate Hill. Shrapnel-puffs mingled with the coiling smeech, and a far-off crackling roar made a relentless undertone. The whole Suvla plain was enveloped in the smokedrift.

"Scrub's ablaze over there," I said. Kelly gave one quick glance.

"*Wather!*" he said, and strode on. I followed.

That smoke from the scrub-fire on Scimitar Hill fixes the time. It was twelve noon on August 9, and the tragic aftermath of the Sulajik blundering was being played out to its final holocaust.

There had been no sort of co-operation between the two divisions in the broken-winged attempt to carry out Stopford's order for a "general advance" on the morning of the 9th, and the 33rd Brigade, under General Maxwell, was the only one of the 11th Division that made any determined effort to obey that order.

The 33rd had moved overnight from Lala Baba across the Salt Lake to the assembly point for the projected dawn attack on the W Hills and the Anafarta spur, and were reinforced by two battalions of Hill's Xth Division troops (still on Chocolate Hill). When Maxwell drew up his orders for this attack he was with his brigade on Lala Baba, yet the strange thing is that he knew what Colonel Minogue at Sulajik, only 750 yards from Scimitar Hill, did not know—that the 6th East Yorkshire had taken Scimitar Hill and were still holding it.

And so, not long after dawnbreak, two battalions of the 33rd Brigade, the Lincolnshire and South Staffordshire, moved confidently from the scrubby ground near Ali Bey Cheshme, about half a mile east of the Salt Lake, to join up with the

pioneers on Scimitar Hill—and were met by a murderous hail
of rifle and machine-gun fire from the Turks on the crest.
*The East Yorkshires had left it five hours before in order to "concentrate
at Sulajik".*

To make matters worse "a stream of Turks came pouring
down the slopes of the Anafarta spur". In spite of this decimating
and nerve-racking experience the two leading battalions pressed
forward and managed to hold on to the northern slope of the
hill, but a vicious plastering of Turkish shrapnel fire had
thinned the ranks. The colonel, adjutant, second-in-command,
and all four company commanders of the South Staffordshires
were either killed or wounded. Bereft of all senior officers, the
troops became disorganised and dispirited, and "their advance
faded away".

Nevertheless, small groups of the battalion pushed on with
the Lincolnshires. More than once the line was carried to the
top and driven back again. Then, soon after sun-up (about
5 a.m.)—when Moore and his men were being butchered in
the gully below the crest of the Tekke Tepe—two more battalions
came up in support, and again the attempt was made to carry
the day on Scimitar Hill.

So the battle raged back and forth, hour after hour—bloody,
furious, and futile—with the British always outnumbered,
raked, enfiladed, and shelled by well-placed artillery—until at
last the hopeless stupidity of the situation, the bloody wounds,
heat, flies, stench, groans, sweat, and misery began to tell.
What had been good strong nerves five hours ago were now
ravelling out, thinning in a running twist to the last slowly-
twirling fibre-strand, and then—the break.

The break came about 10 a.m., when panic overtook "certain
overstrained troops on the left".

A man shouted "The Turks are on us!"—turned and fled.
Within seconds the left broke and came streaming back with the
cry *"The Turks are on us!"*—and the line had to be withdrawn
to the western slopes, where it was again restored.

A third reinforcing battalion had in the meantime swung
round the northern flank of Chocolate Hill. It belonged to the
160th Brigade of the 53rd (Welsh Territorial) Division, which
had sailed in during the night. Its officers had no maps, and no
idea of the plan of action. It had been given one definite order,

21. Field-Marshal Liman von Sanders

22. Colonel Mustafa Kemal

23. British Tommy giving water to a wounded Turk

24. Stretcher-Bearers coming back to A Beach

25. Open-Air Operating Theatre

and one only: that it must on no account "go off into the blue"
and get lost! Apart from that, it had been told to find the
33rd Brigade and "dig itself in, in a supporting position". So
it drifted around until it found itself on the western slopes of
Scimitar Hill, joined up with the general mix-up of troops there,
and with them took part in the final assault.

It was a bloody affair. Two of Hill's five Xth Division
battalions, the 6th Royal Irish Fusiliers and the 6th Royal
Dublin Fusiliers, were in the thick of it. In face of violent and
repeated Turkish counter-attacks, the line was once more
carried to the crest.

But the position was untenable, and by mid-day enemy shells
had fired the gorse and dry holly-oak scrub—even the dead
grass on the surface and the tough ilex and juniper roots
beneath it were ablaze—so that soon Scimitar Hill was a
roaring, crackling mass of flames, a raging inferno in which
"crawling figures of the wounded disappeared amidst dense
clouds of smoke".

And on the Karakol Dagh, with the reek from that fiery
furnace still drifting across, the lank-legged Kelly was still
slinging along at the same slack-jointed lope, still half a pace
ahead. Suddenly the goat-track swerved left and began to wind
downhill towards Ghazi Baba. He caught sight of the stone-
flagged pool at the bend.

Like a fool, I'd forgotten about it—we could have missed it
by taking a lower path. Too late now—the hatchet face became
wolfish. His lean tea-canister underjaw fell open, and the
swollen tongue, black as a Carlsbad plum, thrust forward
hideously. His breathing was stertorous. His small, dark, ant-
eater eyes glittered. Thirst-madness was on him.

"*Wather!*" he cried in a hoarse croak, "*Wather!* by the Holy
Mother o' God!—" and dashed down the rocky track,
his spindle legs leaping and lurching in a knock-kneed
canter.

"Don't touch it, you fool!" I yelled after him. "It's poisoned
—can't you see?"

In three strides I came up with him, and clutched his arm.
He tried to wrench himself free. "A dhrink o' wather!" he
gasped. "Let me go!"

M

I struggled with him, shouting—"*No*, you fool! *No!*
You can't drink that filth! It's poisoned, I tell you—
poisoned!"

He turned upon me. His face was no longer the face of a
human being. It was the face of a demon, a vampire, a werewolf.

"Poison be damned!" he tried to shout. "Would ye be afther
lettin' me die of thirst—and me without wather these two days?
To hell wid yez!"

With the strength of a giant he threw me off, rushed to the
stone coping of that pool of rotting carcasses—that looked so
clear and cool and quenching—and flung himself down to
drink, and drink, and drink.

I dragged him away by the legs before he had time to scoop
a drop in his cupped hands. He sprang to his feet fighting mad.
A sharp blow on the shoulder sent him sprawling. He was as
light as the hollow kex of a dead thistle. There was no stamina
in his feverish frame, and the pain from the gunshot wound in
his right buttock made him wince. That seemed to bring him
to his senses.

"Listen!" I said, close to his ear. "You'll get a drink when
we get down to the field hospital in a few minutes. Come on!"

But I still had to fight him past the pool.

"*Wather!*" he kept muttering. "*Wather!* for the love of Holy
Mary. . . ."

As we came stumbling down the track towards West Beach,
I remember catching a bird's-eye glimpse of a gang of sappers—
"part of a Field Company of Engineers"—busy on some very
deep and well-dug shelters east of Ghazi Baba.

While these building operations were going on, the blazing
Scimitar Hill had to be abandoned, and the five battalions that
took part in the attack were ordered to fall back and take up a
position south of Sulajik. They had lost 1,500 men, killed and
wounded.

A bad day, with everything gone adrift—a Black Monday
for all of us. The heavy work of stretcher-bearing left no time
to think about it, but the vague sensation of being leaderless
and lost had settled upon us. We shall see, in a moment, how
well-founded that sensation was.

At 2 p.m. that afternoon Hamilton sent a message to Stopford from No. 2 Post, Anzac, again urging him to direct his attack on the Tekke Tepe ridge.

At 4 p.m. Stopford sent a reply in which he pointed out that it was essential to keep enough troops between Kuchuk Anafarta and the W Hills—

"... as otherwise if I were to seize the high ground between Anafarta Sagir [Kuchuk Anafarta village] and Ejelmer Bay without securing the gap, I might find myself holding the heights and the Turks pouring down to the harbour behind me. . . .

I am, Sir, yours sincerely,

Fred W. Stopford."

On this Hamilton commented in his diary:

"For myself I wish the Turks would try to pour down over that flat, open country by the Salt Lake to seize the beaches under the guns of the warships."

At 5 p.m. Stopford received a letter from the chief of staff (Braithwaite) at G.H.Q., Imbros. It set forth the view that it might still be possible to take the W Hills and the Anafarta spur with an attacking force of six or eight battalions, "well commanded by a specially selected officer", and the corps commander began to work out plans for this renewed attack.

Now consider the sequence of urgent exhortations and advice that had been showered upon the unhappy Stopford at his not-yet-finished splinterproof headquarters during this day:

Round about twelve noon, Hamilton tells him to "grasp the Kiretch Tepe nettle" on the left—and the sooner the better. At 2 p.m. he tells him to go for the Tekke Tepe in the centre. At 5 p.m. Braithwaite chips in with his plan for another attempt to capture the W Hills and the Anafarta spur on the right. So Stopford is to attack everywhere—right, left, and centre! Why not tell him to take the Sari Bair range as well, and be done with it?

After midnight on the 9th, Stopford received yet another letter, this time from Hamilton. It urged him to take the Tekke Tepe ridge without fail—but only *after* the capture of the W Hills and Anafarta spur, as already suggested by the chief of staff (Braithwaite). Not a word about the Kiretch "nettle".

At nightfall Scimitar Hill was still a smouldering shoulder of ember-hot charcoal, the 33rd Brigade was still a mile west of the W Hills, and Mahon's Xth Division handful were back in the same position they had seized on the day of landing.

10

THE REAL PUSH

Hamilton at No. 2 Post, Anzac, held what he called an "impromptu council of war" with General Birdwood and General Godley at one o'clock in the afternoon of the 9th. He says they were both in "great form". The three generals ate their midday rations together as they talked things over, and there seems to have been a jolly picnic spirit about it.

And no wonder, for Birdwood and Godley were quite positive that they would have "the whip hand of The Narrows by tomorrow", as Hamilton reported in his diary. Coming from dismal Suvla, this must have cheered the Commander-in-Chief considerably. In fact all three seem to have been in high feather, if not actually cock-a-hoop. Certainly they were in cheerful mood, although there was nothing to be cheerful about at Anzac, where muddle, bad planning, and lack of energetic leadership from the top had created a situation that was—unbelievable as it may seem—worse than anything at Suvla.

This incurable top-level optimism was almost as great a danger to us as Kemal and his Turks. So here were the Three Jovial Generals munching their midday meal and chatting away in "great form"—but knowing nothing of what was happening less than 3,000 yards away on the south-western slopes of the Sari Bair, which at that very moment were "strewn with corpses in heaps, like the sheaves on a harvest field". And British corpses at that. (Have another sandwich? . . .)

Hamilton and his two chief Anzac generals were now confronted by *the* crisis of the Gallipoli Campaign, and did not know it. Events went on without them. There was no one in command at Suvla or Anzac—except Kemal.

Kemal had watched the outcome of his counter-attack at Suvla from a hill-top behind the front line. By midday it was clear that the British were checkmated, and he was free to turn his attention to the Sari Bair, from which urgent and alarming reports kept coming in: a British officer and a party of Gurkhas had reached Hill Q on the Chunuk Bair. The Turkish defence was in confusion. He therefore made ready to leave Suvla for the Sari Bair battle-front.

After enjoying their semi-alfresco lunch, the three generals at No. 2 Post talked over the Suvla situation, and between them they "composed" the message to Stopford urging him to bash away at the Tekke Tepe: which was just what he had no intention of doing, since, with the Turkish reinforcements sitting firmly astride it, such an attack was certain to "lead to a regular battle".

The renewed attack on the Sari Bair, planned to begin at dawn on the 9th, had already gone to pieces before the first streak of daylight—lost and lost again in the maze of pitch-black gullies. These gullies, lying west and south-west of the Sari Bair's main peak (Koja Chemen Tepe, "The Hill of the Great Pasture", just over 1,000 feet), present a geological jigsaw puzzle of petrified fury: a vast churn-up of the clays and soft sandstone strata that form the hill-mass. They are even deeper, narrower, steeper, more insanely serrated than those of the gully-complex of the Suvla watershed—and just as thickly throttled by waist-high holly-oak scrub.

Only three routes lead up from the Anzac coast to the heights, and these three routes—the three great gullies of the Sazli Dere, Chailak Dere, and Aghyl Dere—limit and determine any plan of attack, squeezing the troops and all supplies into these narrow, winding grooves.

Any commander who plans a night advance up these ravines for a dawn deployment in an attack on the heights is asking for trouble—for slow murder, havoc, and collapse. Yet that was the plan worked out by Birdwood, approved by Hamilton, commanded by Godley. A bad and desperate plan. It was, as Hamilton explains in his dispatch of December 11, 1915, "the real push—the step which above all others was to count—the night attack on the summits of the Sari Bair ridge."

Map 13. MAIN FEATURES OF THE SARI BAIR BATTLE AREA

It was a plan of snail-slow climbing up these gullies by 20,000 troops, most of them already worn out and sick with dysentery. Hamilton gives a vivid picture of it in the same dispatch:

> "The darkness of the night, the density of the scrub, hands and knees progress up the spurs, sheer physical fatigue, exhaustion of the spirit caused by repeated hairbreadth escapes from the hail of random bullets—all these combined to take the edge off the energies of our troops."

This "grand attack", as he calls it, began at 9.30 p.m. on August 6, and, after a brilliant opening on the flat-topped hill known as Table Top (400 feet), came to a standstill about 9.30 a.m. on August 7, in the most appalling confusion—with most of the supporting troops still straggling up the gullies and over the spurs, sniped at all the way—but with the remnants of the leading column (one unsupported battalion) "a quarter of a mile short of Chunuk Bair—i.e., of victory". The dispatch continues—

> ". . . . In spite of all their efforts their increasing exhaustion as opposed to the gathering strength of the enemy's fresh troops began to tell—they had shot their bolt. So all day they clung to what they had captured and strove to make ready for the night. . . . So ended the first phase of the fighting for the Chunuk Bair ridge. Our aims had not been fully attained, and the help we had hoped for from Suvla had not been forthcoming."

The attack was resumed at daybreak on August 8. In the "first faint glimmer of dawn" the right assaulting column, led by Lieutenant-Colonel Malone, reached the Chunuk Bair, where they saw clearly the glint of The Narrows to the south.

But Malone sited his front line trench fifteen yards behind the crest, instead of on the forward slopes, and within two hours he was bombed, shelled, and almost completely cut off. The Turks attacked again and again from the hill-crest. At last his front-line trench (only three and a half feet deep) was "so full of dead and dying that the men had to leave it and endeavour to scratch another trench immediately behind it".

They never had a chance to dig deeper than "some six inches". Towards late afternoon Malone was shot through the head, and fell mortally wounded. No help came. Before long every officer and N.C.O. was either killed or wounded, and the battalion consisted of "small groups of men commanded by junior non-commissioned officers or privates". They were all men of the New Army—civilians in uniform—but they fought on, as Hamilton reports, "from mid-day till sunset, without *any* officers".

There was no support. Alone up there, 900 ft. above sea-level, they were reduced to a mere handful. Of Malone's 760 men only seventy survived at nightfall, and the Turks were back again on the Chunuk ridge.

And still, to this day, the seabirds cry and the gully-echoes back-answer from Chakal Chair and Chailak Dere—"*Moore! Moore!—Malone! Malone!*". . . .

At dawn on that dreadful Sunday—the "day of rest" at Suvla—not more than 500 yards north-east of Malone and his men fighting their way up the Chunuk Bair, another dare-devil officer, Major Allanson, commanding the 6th Gurkhas, found himself far out ahead of the two supporting battalions, and decided to push on without them in an attempt to take the southern peak of Hill Q (918 feet) single-handed.

Hill Q is a twin-topped steep on the Sari Bair ridge, only half a mile south-east of the main Koja Chemen Tepe and joined to it by a narrow saddle-back running east and west. It was the second of the three objectives on the Anzac battlefront—Chunuk Bair, Hill Q, Koja Chemen Tepe. To hold any one of these heights in strength was to hold the peninsula.

By 9.30 a.m. Allanson and his Gurkhas had clambered to within 200 yards of what they took to be the crest of Hill Q under heavy fire. Here, from 9.30 a.m. to 6 p.m., they clung to the bare hillside under cover of the crestline, "with every conceivable shot flying overhead." Twice during the morning Allanson had gone off down to the troop-jammed gullies to beg for help, and each time had come back with only fifty officers and men. How closely this small attacking party of British and Gurkhas had to hug the rockface for eight and a half hours in the blistering heat is clear from Allanson's report that he lay all day between two British Tommies. One read the Bible the whole time—the other turned out to be a corpse. When darkness came, they climbed another fifty yards and dug-in—or rather, managed to scrape a shallow ditch 150 yards from the crest. By now Allanson had reported his position to corps head-quarters and had received orders direct from Godley. He was to hold on, and, after a dawn bombardment, make a dash for the summit.

So all night long they clung to their hard-won position. No help came from the two supporting battalions waiting in the gully-entries of the Aghyl Dere some 250 yards below, because they had instructions not to advance until Brigadier-General Baldwin's column came up. But Baldwin and his column were lost and gone astray in the eel-basket confusion of gullies leading up to the main ridge of the Chunuk Bair. This (No. 3) assaulting column was made up of five battalions, two of them—the 10th Hampshire and the 6th Royal Irish Rifles—drawn from the 29th Brigade of the Xth (Irish) Division.

It was detailed to advance up the Chailak Dere as far as Cheshire Ridge, sharp left across the ridge into the next gully (the Aghyl Dere), and from the level shelf of The Farm—marked by a small walled pound and a stone hut (an old Turkish sheepfold)—be ready to begin the assault on the Chunuk Bair at 5.15 a.m. on the 9th, and from there across the 100-yard *col* on the north-east to the assault of Hill Q. It was, in fact, to "make the main attack" on the Sari Bair heights, with the other two assaulting columns co-operating on its left and right.

Soon after nightfall on the 8th—while Allanson and his Gurkhas, with the help of a handful of 6th South Lancashire and 9th Warwickshire men (about 450 in all), were scraping their shallow ditch 150 yards from the crest—Baldwin's column set off on their long and wearisome march up the Chailak Dere in pitch darkness. "Infinite trouble had been taken to ensure that the narrow track should be kept clear", Hamilton reports. It was all to no purpose. The gully was already choked with reinforcements, fatigue parties, and pack-mules going up, and blocked by stretcher-bearers and wounded coming down. The Turks knew that this was one of the few tracks by which it was possible for men and supplies to reach the Chunuk Bair, so they shelled it systematically day and night—especially at night.

The Chailak Dere has fourteen forks branching off to the right, and twelve to the left. Some of these forks have double prongs, and a few are triple-pronged. After midnight the head of Baldwin's column lost the main track altogether in the inky blackness. So they wandered about all night—and lost the battle.

It was the failure of this column to reach its point of deployment, rather than the stagnation at Suvla, that led to the failure —the so-called "glorious" failure—of the Gallipoli Campaign.

The hours sifted away (just as they did at Suvla, where Moore and his handful were now toiling up the Tekke Tepe), and at 4.30 a.m., when the artillery and naval guns opened up a heavy bombardment on the crest of Chunuk Bair and Hill Q, Baldwin and his now worn-out assaulting column were still climbing the steep bed of the Aghyl Dere towards The Farm in the first drear-light of daybreak. Assault columns 1 and 2, on the left and right, waited and waited for them.

But events moved according to time-table, and nothing could stop them.

At 5 a.m. the sun blazed above the great square-cut summit of the Sari Bair. *This was the fatal zero-hour of the whole campaign.* Moore and his Thirty were hurled at the bayonet-point from the Tekke Tepe, five miles north-north-east of Hill Q—and at that moment Allanson crouched with his watch in his hand.

He had put the three Lancashire companies into the trenches with his Gurkhas, and had told them that the moment they saw him go forward carrying a red flag, they were to make a dash for the crest. We know what happened moment-by-moment from the report he made two days later. He wrote:

> "I had only fifteen minutes left. The roar of the artillery preparation was enormous. The hill, which was almost perpendicular, seemed to leap underneath one . . . I had my watch out—5.15. I never saw such artillery preparation." The Turkish trenches, he wrote, "were being torn to pieces. The accuracy was marvellous, as we were only just below. At 5.18 it had not stopped, and I wondered if my watch was wrong.
>
> "5.20—silence. I waited three minutes to be certain, great as the risk was. Then off we dashed, all hand in hand, a most perfect advance, and a wonderful sight. . . . At the top we met the Turks. Le Marchand was down, a bayonet through the heart. I got one through the leg, and then for about what appeared to be ten minutes, we fought hand to hand, we bit

and fisted, and used rifles and pistols as clubs. And then the Turks turned and fled, and I felt a very proud man. The key of the whole peninsula was ours, and our losses had not been so very great for such a result.

"Below I saw the Straits, motors and wheeled transport on the roads leading to Achi Baba. As I looked round I saw that we were not being supported, and thought I could help best by going after those who had retreated in front of us.* We dashed down towards Maidos, but had only gone about a hundred feet down when suddenly our own Navy put six twelve-inch monitor shells into us, and all was terrible confusion. It was a deplorable disaster. We were obviously mistaken for Turks, and had to get back. It was an appalling sight. The first shell hit a Gurkha in the face: the place was a mass of blood and limbs and screams. . ."

Pursuit of the fleeing Turks had to be broken off for fear of being wiped out by our own shells.† What were left of the Gurkha and Lancashire troops scrambled back to the crestline, and took up their old position just below.

"I remained on the crest," Allanson wrote, "with about fifteen men. It was a wonderful view. . . . We commanded Kilid Bahr, and the rear of Achi Baba and the communications to all their Army there."

Allanson, wounded, was still on top, and ready to hold on until reinforcements came up. Again there was no support. Malone and his handful shot to pieces: Moore and his handful butchered: Allanson and his handful shelled off the crest by our own guns. Three near-victories within twenty-four hours, each of which could have meant total victory—and all three thrown away because there was no support at the critical

---

*In fact they had reached the *col* or saddle at 780 feet between the main heights of the Chunuk Bair and Hill Q. This was, nevertheless, a key position in the assault of the Sari Bair range. In front of them this high *nek* dipped steeply into the narrow gully of the Kur Dere. On their right front, however, the ground fell away gently, and it was down this slope that they pursued the retreating Turks.

† The Navy flatly denied that they fired these shells, and there seems to be some doubt about it. At the same time, Allanson, an experienced regular officer, states in his report that they were naval shells and has no hesitation in identifying them as "six twelve-inch monitor shells".

moment. However, Allanson was still alive, still clinging on with fifteen men. It was now 5.45 a.m. on August 9.

"But where", Hamilton writes in his dispatch, "was the main attack—where was Baldwin?" Where indeed?

In fact it was not until 6 a.m. that the leading files of Baldwin's column began to debouch from the head of the Aghyl Dere—*three quarters of an hour late*. By this time the Turkish commander had rallied his men and was making ready to deliver a counter-charge. Nevertheless, Allanson clung to the saddle at Hill Q.

Meanwhile, Baldwin's column was closing up and getting into formation at The Farm, down below. As always in such a deployment, this entailed long waits. At last the main assault troops—that had been marched and counter-marched up and down the gullies from dusk to dawn—moved to the attack. "The men went forward", says Major Bryan Cooper (of the 29th Brigade, Xth (Irish) Division), "with splendid spirit, but the task they were called upon to perform was beyond human power. Not only did the enemy's shrapnel fire redouble its force, but the whole of the left flank was enfiladed by hostile machine-guns."

Hamilton, in his dispatch, sums up the position:

"... They had gained the high ground immediately below the commanding knoll on Chunuk Bair [that Malone had taken at dawn on the 8th], and a few minutes earlier would have joined hands with the Gurkhas and South Lancashires [on Hill Q], and, combined with them, would have carried all before them. But the Turks by this time were lining the whole of the high crest in overwhelming numbers."

The British advance was repulsed. Baldwin's troops were "flung back from the height and pressed still further down the slope", until they had to be withdrawn to their first position near The Farm. The slaughter and confusion was fantastic. The entire Sari Bair front was now a floundering mass of slow-motion disorder. The chain of command had broken down and gone to pieces utterly—if it ever really existed. Godley, whose corps headquarters at No. 2 Post was only 400 yards from the sea, was totally out of touch with the battle area, had no idea what was happening anywhere, and took no steps to find out.

Not one staff officer was sent from corps to the New Zealand Brigade headquarters at the Apex, the rocky outcrop on Rhododendron Spur*, that, facing the south-western shoulder of the Chunuk Bair, was the hub of the whole operation.

The battle was left to look after itself as best it could. The gullies were blocked with troops who were either lost or waiting for orders that never came. By now it was almost impossible to move up or down. Some of the fighting troops were so long delayed in these jams that they never reached their assembly-points at all and took no part in the battle. Many were killed and wounded in the gullies.

But at No. 2 Post "an atmosphere of confidence" prevailed, and Godley and his staff thought fit to send a message of hope and encouragement to Allanson and his Gurkhas still holding the *col* at Hill Q—"IX Corps is co-operating on our extreme left, and it is possible that developments may be entirely in our favour a little later on"—a message based upon nothing at all, for there was no sign of any co-operation by Stopford's IXth Corps at Suvla, but, on the contrary, every sign of drift and stagnation.

So there was Allanson cut off—stranded. Cut off from the beaten Turks by the deadly fire of our own guns, and left stranded after the failure of Baldwin's main attack. No reinforcements arrived. The Turks made no attempt to re-take the Hill Q saddle nor any of the nearby uplands, knowing that our naval guns and artillery had their range dead-on. They recovered their nerve a few hours later. Between 5 and 7 p.m. they made five counter-attacks, all of which were driven back by the Gurkhas.

Nothing changed at No. 2 Post. Here everyone was in high hopes. No inkling of impending disaster crept into that tiny shut-off world of brass-hats. It never struck the Commander-in-Chief (who, by now, had returned to Imbros) that his prediction of Friday, March 13—"This is going to be an unlucky show"—was about to come true.

The Tired Man was on his way. . . .

Kemal left Suvla at 3 p.m. He broke his journey at von

* So-called from the masses of brilliant crimson oleanders that blossomed there, mistaken for rhododendrons by the British.

Sanders' headquarters to report. Then he rode south up the broken steeps of the Dagh Chesme Sirte. He reached the Chunuk Bair at sundown.

This was his fourth night without sleep. Battleship Hill—then Suvla—now back to the Chunuk ridge, only a thousand yards from his old look-out on Battleship Hill. He wasted no time on food or drink, held no friendly chat with his commanders, made no mention of his success at Suvla, but at once took command of the battle.

He found his troops in confusion, many of them demoralised by the devastating British artillery fire. He was told that the British had taken the *col* at Hill Q, and had reached the summit of Chunuk Bair—for although Baldwin's main attack had been flung off the ridge and pushed back to The Farm, No. 1 assaulting column, composed mostly of New Zealanders, had managed to advance up the south-western slope of the Chunuk to the crestline where they hung on against furious counter-attacks.

In spite of the fact that a fresh Turkish regiment marching up from Helles had not yet arrived, Kemal ordered an attack at four-thirty the next morning, August 10. His staff pointed out that the men were dead beat and incapable of further effort. Kemal replied: "They will attack at four-thirty to-morrow morning", and took himself off on a hazardous personal reconnaissance along the entire Hill Q/Chunuk battle-front. The Tired Man was in command.

Next morning he led the attack in person.

In the morning I woke to find Boler pulling on his boots. I sat up. It was about four-thirty and still only half light, our usual time for "wakey-wakey". Before I had both my boots laced, the distant artillery bombardment on the Sari Bair reached crescendo, and suddenly ceased. In the strange silence a low humming sound emerged, and grew in volume.

Boler ran to the gully-mouth, and cocked an ear. I followed. "*Listen!*" he said, "*d'you hear that?*" A far-away tumult, like the swelling surge of a great wave of the sea, came rolling across from the heights, interspersed with bursts of rifle, machine-gun, and shrapnel fire. "*Men cheering, that is!*" he whispered. "*We're on the move at last, as like as not!*" The distant roar of men

shouting—cheering—yelling—increased. It sounded, now, like
the angry drone of a disturbed hornets' nest.

I ran back for my Zeiss glasses, and together we slid and
stumbled down to the beach to get a better view.

"In my opinion," said Boler, "that's the Anzacs advancing—
they've taken the hills, I shouldn't wonder!"

26. THE SUVLA PLAIN SEEN FROM THE SARI BAIR HEIGHTS

Lala Baba on the extreme left, with the Salt Lake stretching from it as a thin white line, and the Kiretch Tepe in the far distance.

27. Turks making a Bayonet Charge

11

STORM — AND LULL

Kemal had spent the night getting his troops into position on Chanuk Bair, where the British and Turkish trenches were no more than thirty yards apart. During the hours of darkness he filtered two regiments into his front line, making them creep forward noiselessly until they were as tightly-packed as pilchards in a hogshead of brine. And there they had to wait, without making a sound, until daybreak. The whole undertaking was risky, for if the British guns opened up on these densely massed troops before zero-hour, the Turkish position would be in jeopardy from Ejelmer Bay to Kilid Bahr.

Kemal moved among his men like a grey shadow, making sure they were awake and ready. Just before zero-hour he crawled forward into no-man's-land, riding-whip in hand. As he crept along on hands and knees, he called back softly to the waiting troops: "Don't hurry. Let me go first. Wait until you see me raise my whip—then all rush forward together."

So they waited, their eyes fixed on that gaunt shadow-shape out there in front of them. The British saw nothing unusual in the half-gloom, suspected nothing. Both British and Turkish were half dead with fatigue.

At four-thirty the all-night Turkish artillery barrage stopped. Kemal stood up. As he raised his riding-whip, a bullet smashed his wrist-watch. In spite of that he walked unflinchingly towards the British line on the Chunuk crest. Behind him —and then past him—the massed Turks came charging up the slope.

193

N

Turkish bombers rushed the observation posts on the summit, and the British on the reverse slope found themselves "assailed by showers of bombs". At the same time, another mass of Turks stormed over Hill Q and poured down to The Farm.

Once again the dawn broke misty-thick and dew-cold. During the night Kemal had massed six battalions of Turkish infantry for the counter-attack. And now, with the sun just topping the eastern shoulder of the Koja Chemen Tepe behind them in a blaze of light, they swept over the skyline "in eight or ten lines, shoulder to shoulder"—singing, cheering, yelling as they came on down to Rhododendron Spur (650 feet) and over its seaward scarp in full view from Suvla.

Such a charging horde on such a steep, bare, scarfaced bluff was never seen before in this world. Hamilton's dispatch describes it as "a huge column, consisting of no less than a full division plus a regiment of three battalions": a mass formation that came thundering over the crestline of the Sari Bair and down the three great gullies.

We stood dumbfounded, stupefied. . . .

Looking directly south-east from the sand-dunes at A Beach gives a frontal view up the Aghyl Dere. From its topmost drainage-sike below The Farm it tumbles into a wide cuplike flume, scrub-grown on each side, but with shelving ledges of bare sandstone and shaly screes, orange-ochre in the clear, scintillating sunshine. It was here, on these bald, precipitous ramps and slanting tongues, that we had the best view of this human avalanche: and it was here, after scanning along the heights above the Sazli Beit and Chailak gullies, that my Zeiss lenses were now focused.

Below the oncoming shoulder-to-shoulder mass, we saw little groups of men scattering, breaking down the gully-forks, taking cover behind crook-backed knolls, crossing scrub-dotted architraves from one gully-fork to another, crawling forward, firing uphill—caught in enfilading bursts of machine-gun fire—lying still—dead?—more men running down the gully-bed towards the sea—*our men*, all sickeningly antlike and far away.

Then, as the Turkish mass came full into the open, cuplike slope, about a third of the way down from the crest, every fieldpiece at Anzac and all the battleships of the Fleet opened up.* There never was such a slaughter! The Turks lay in heaps, like mounds of old clothes. And yet—there was only a momentary wavering. They came on again, wave upon wave, shoulder-to-shoulder—shouting, yelling!—as though they were fighting mad, or as though they were carried forward by sheer weight of numbers and could not stop.

"Dekko, Sar'nt," said Boler, and took the glasses from me.

The noise of gunfire was shattering. Salvo after salvo hurtled across Lala Baba and landed dead on the mark. Great clouds of yellow sandstone dust mushroomed from the Aghyl Dere. When they cleared away, the mounds of Turkish dead were higher and thicker. We saw the bayonets of the dead flashing in the sunlight: still now, immovable, like pins stuck at all angles in a pin-cushion. We saw a few wounded crawling away from the gigantic shambles: not more than a score or so out of thousands.

"They're still coming on!" said Boler. "Talk about punishment! No, they're slowing down—they're breaking up—some of them are going back—they've had enough—their officers are trying to re-form the ranks—yes, they're reforming!—they're coming on again—but there isn't many left by the look of it."

Another salvo of naval shells smashed into the gully. That was the end of it. The few that remained of Kemal's six battalions were crawling back to the heights, leaving their dead in thousands on the hillsides.

It was the end, also, of Birdwood's main assault on the Sari Bair.

The Farm was a massacre. The Turkish right wing surged down upon it *en masse*. Then it was hell let loose. Only a thousand New Army troops were holding the position and trying to dig-in. The Turks "came on again and again, covered by a very heavy shrapnel fire, and again and again they were

---

* "Once they were over the crest they became exposed not only to the full blast of the guns, naval and military, but also to a battery of ten machine-guns belonging to the New Zealand Infantry Brigade, which played upon their serried ranks at close range until the barrels were red hot. Enormous losses were inflicted, and . . . only the merest handful ever straggled back to their own side of the Chunuk Bair." (Sir Ian Hamilton's dispatch of December 11, 1915.)

driven back". The fighting became fiendishly fierce on this strange mountain ledge swept by a criss-crossing hail of machine-gun fire. Bitter back-and-forth bayonet thrusting broke out, followed by throttling hand-to-hand death-grips—(that Hamilton describes as "a series of struggles in which generals fought in the ranks and the men dropped their scientific weapons and caught each other by the throat")—with the British outnumbered forty to one, but holding on to the last. No one will ever know exactly what took place. The Turks were never able to take The Farm—now a piled-up graveyard of unburied dead—until the last exhausted defenders were ordered to give up the fight.

General Baldwin was killed just as it began to grow light. Thereafter, in quick succession, most of the senior officers were killed or badly wounded. The two Xth (Irish) Division battalions of the 29th Brigade suffered severely. By 9 a.m. they had lost nearly all their junior officers, and the rank and file casualties were so heavy that the position became untenable. Soon afterwards the British troops were ordered to withdraw. The Turks, just as worn out, and just as decimated, retreated to the Chunuk heights, and The Farm—the tiny walled-in pinfold with its shepherd's hut high-perched on its level pasture-plot at 590 feet—"forsaken by both sides, was held by the dying and the dead".

Allanson and the remnants of his 6th Gurkhas had been withdrawn from the saddle at Hill Q on the evening of the 9th, and survived. The position was taken over by the 9th Gurkha battalion. By a freak of chance, due perhaps to the early morning mist hanging in the gullies and shrouding the hillsides, they were hidden in the *col* when Kemal's counter-attack thundered over the Chunuk crest—and missed them. Otherwise they would have been wiped out to a man. Later, when twilight fell—finding themselves alone up there, except for "the dying and the dead"—they decided to come down. They and a few others were the last troops to retire from the heights of the Sari Bair. There were 240 of them. And not one British officer left.

The remainder had either been over-run, or driven—fighting stubbornly all the way, but driven—slowly back down the gullies to within half a mile of the Anzac beaches.

Of Birdwood's 20,000 assault troops for the "real push", only 8,000 were left at nightfall on August 10.

Years afterwards the gullies leading up to the Chanuk ridge were found to be white with human bones, "thigh deep".

Horrible as it was to watch those serried lines of Turks smashed against the gully-face like a swarm of flies swatted against a windowpane, it was more horrible to see them still there, silent and motionless in the bright sunlight, as though they had fallen asleep on the instant—and everything gone so suddenly quiet, it was hard to believe there had ever been any war at all, or ever would be. So quiet you could hear the almost soundless ripples lapping and overlapping along the wet-lipped margin of the bay.

It never struck me that there was any danger to us at Suvla in that massed onslaught of armed Turks, until, as we came down from the sand-dune, Boler said—"Thank God we've got a Navy! We'd all be dead as mutton by now, or else."

A five-day "lull" set in after the Scimitar Hill holocaust of August 9. But of course, at Suvla, even a lull was not a lull, but the same hopelessly confused game of hoodman-blind.

Stopford, brooding over the several urgent appeals, hints, and near-orders from Hamilton and Braithwaite, and feeling fairly secure no doubt in his new splinterproof shelter, decided on another attempt to capture the W Hills and the Anafarta spur. To lead this second attack he chose the 53rd (Welsh Territorial) Division.*

Unfortunately these reinforcements had watched the head-long retreat across the Salt Lake "like a crowd streaming away from a football match". Flung ashore without orders and without maps, the leading battalions had already had a bellyful

---

* The 53rd Division began to land at Suvla at 7 p.m. on August 8, and disembarkation went on during the night of the 8th and the morning of the 9th. The Final Report of the Dardanelles Commission (Part II, Sec. 95), states that: "It had no artillery, only one Field Company R.E. without any stores, and only one Field Ambulance. The divisional Signal Company did not arrive until five or six days after the landing of its division, and when it did arrive it was attached to another division."

of fighting on the blazing slopes of Scimitar Hill, and wanted
no more. Their morale had gone.

Altogether, nine battalions were to take part in the new
attack. The 159th Brigade of this division was to open the
assault and protect the rear by storming—yet again—the
charred and blackened hump of Scimitar Hill (229 feet) still
smouldering in smoky patches 1,200 yards north of the strongly
held jigsaw-fretted contours of the W Hills (328 feet). These
hills, like two or three old and broken teeth, guard the tip of
the long tongue of the Anafarta spur stretching south-west
from Kuchuk Anafarta village, and command the gap between
the Suvla hills and the great Sari Bair range to the south.

All clear enough on the neatly squared-up artillery maps
(Survey Dept., Egypt, 1915), but the staff of the 53rd Division
had no maps. Just an oversight, but typically Suvla.

The main difficulty, however, was that no one quite knew
where the 159th Brigade had got to. All the divisional commander could learn was that it was now under the command
of General Sitwell "somewhere in the bush near Sulajik".
Sulajik!—the very name portends trouble.

Sure enough, even when the brigade was found somewhere
north of Sulajik, two of its battalions were missing. No one
knew where they were. The brigade staff "spent a sleepless
night looking for them"—wandering about in the darkness.
All to no purpose. The two lost battalions were still missing
when the first blur of daylight oozed through the dawnmist.
(You notice there are always *two* battalions lost in or around
Sulajik? It was so on the night of August 8, and again on
the night of the 9th.) It was now the morning of the 10th.
And so, at 6 a.m., the rest of the brigade moved off without
them.

They moved off south towards Scimitar Hill at about the
time that Kemal's mass-attack on the Chunuk heights came
storming down the gullies and was smashed and halted halfway
to the sea. They knew nothing about that as they trudged past
Sulajik. Stopford had ordered the 158th Brigade, now at Lala
Baba, to move up in support. They were then to swing half-
right and secure the long tongue of the Anafarta spur that
sticks out at a more or less uniform height of 328 feet all along
its one and three quarter mile stretch.

The corps commander had also ordered the 33rd Brigade, now dug-in between Chocolate Hill and Sulajik, to co-operate by pushing south-east in an attack on the W Hills. But Maxwell, the brigadier, felt sure that if he carried out this order his brigade would be enfiladed by the Turkish batteries on Scimitar Hill and wiped out. He decided to stay where he was, and his seven battalions did not go into action at all—orders or no orders. They were strange birds, these Suvla generals: men not to be trifled with.

So that left the 11th Division out of it, and the 159th Brigade of the 53rd Division trudged sullenly on. Before long they came under fire from Turkish snipers. Nothing is more demoralising than for a body of marching troops to be picked off one by one by unseen sharpshooters, and these troops were in no heart for the battle anyhow.

As the Turkish fire increased, the leading troops faltered, turned about, and broke away in disorder. Here and there individual soldiers went on up the slopes, fighting single-handed or in twos and threes—forlorn and splendid, alone and doomed. Behind them the attack fell away.

The 158th Brigade, now coming up in support, were met by little groups in full retreat streaming back towards the Salt Lake and the beaches. The supporting battalion (also without maps) had no notion where they were supposed to go, nor what they were supposed to do. And so they, too, turned about and came drifting back with the others. The whole attack came to nothing long before the battle was joined.

Stopford had gone across the bay and had climbed Lala Baba to watch. His sprained knee must have recovered. It's a stiff climb—I know it well—nearly as steep as Silbury Hill in Wiltshire, but rougher going: all humps and tussocks. By about 10.30 a.m. the attack had collapsed, and some time later the corps commander came down and reported the failure to G.H.Q., Imbros, saying that he was ordering a renewed attack at five o'clock that evening. To this Hamilton (who had "no faith in a second attempt succeeding") replied that it would be better to rest the troops, reorganise, and consolidate. Nothing could have been more in line with Stopford's own frame of mind and general outlook, but orders for the renewed assault had already been sent out.

Now that Stopford was doing his damnedest to smash through the Anafarta gap and take the hills—Hamilton was against it! So Stopford did what he had done before. He sent out instructions modifying his battle orders, to the effect that: *if the attack was strongly opposed it was not to be pressed forward.* The true Stopfordian touch.

Result: of the eighteen battalions within two miles of Scimitar Hill on the afternoon of August 10, two companies—six officers and 240 men—went forward to the attack. They advanced 500 yards, came under fire, lost four officers and a number of other ranks, and, obeying the order not to press on if strongly opposed, were back again within half an hour at the position from which they had started. And that was all that happened. Stopford then reported to the Commander-in-Chief that the attack had been "stopped early", in accordance with instructions received.

It really did not need a Kemal to defeat us at Suvla.

Hamilton was now beginning to see that he would have to do something about Stopford. A little before dawn on this same August 10 he had received a letter from the corps commander. In it Stopford explained that he had been "*most* anxious to push on the day after landing", but was "assured by everyone that without water it was an impossibility". He said also that the Territorials would not be able to secure the hills in any circumstance, as "the attacking spirit was lacking," and he pointed out that in his opinion the failure to take the hills could not be attributed to lack of energy on the part of divisional or brigade commanders.

Next day Hamilton wrote in his diary:

"This letter has driven me very nearly to my wits' ends. Things can't be so bad! None of us have any complaint at all of the New Army troops: only of their Old Army generals. . . . The New Army and Territorials have no trained countersnipers, and are much at the mercy of the skilled Anatolian shikarris [Anglo-Indian, from the Hindu *shikar*, a hunter] who haunt the close country."

He was so bothered about Stopford's letter that, on the evening of the 10th, he again came over to Suvla and "wrestled" with him for more than an hour. In the early hours of August 11 he signalled Stopford to order the 54th (East Anglian

Territorial) Division—landed the day before* and now filling
the gap between Mahon's position on the Kiretch Tepe and
Sitwell's, still about a mile east of Hill 10—to "seize the Tekke
Tepe ridge at dawn the next morning [August 12], following
a night advance to the foothills".

That was the first definite, plain, unequivocal order Stopford
had received. And you notice that the entire Scimitar-W-Hills
and-Anafarta-spur complex, that was to be taken before
seizing the Tekke Tepe, has been left out of account altogether
—not even mentioned—as though that horribly involved
puzzle-corner of the battlefront did not exist: as though it were
now possible (with Kemal's troops astride the ridge) to storm
the Tekke Tepe by a direct head-on frontal attack! ... and
with troops, on Hamilton's own showing, quite untrained for
the task and unable to deal with "the skilled shikarris" that
infested the foothills.

To poor old Stopford it must have seemed that whatever he
did was wrong. If he rested his troops, he ought to attack. And
if he attacked, *that* was wrong—he ought to rest his troops and
consolidate.

Anyhow, it was settled now. The 54th Division was to "seize
the Tekke Tepe" at dawn on the 12th. But this was Suvla, and
somehow Stopford and Suvla were curiously *en rapport*.

Again the Commander-in-Chief interviewed the corps commander, who stated flatly that the 53rd and 54th (his two
Territorial divisions) were "sucked oranges", that their best
battalions had been sent to France, and that the dense scrub
on the Suvla side of the Tekke Tepe was "ideal ground for
skirmishers" (unknowingly using Hamilton's mitigatory argument about the "Anatolian shikarris") who, during the "night
advance to the foothills", would be certain to filter through
behind the advancing troops and harry their lines of communication.

Since there was no rebutting these objections, Hamilton
agreed to a two days' postponement: though how the "sucked
oranges" could be filled with fresh juice, and why the enemy

* The Final Report of the Dardanelles Commission (Part II, Sec. 98),
states that: "During this day [August 10] the 54th Division arrived at
Suvla and began to disembark at A Beach. It had no artillery, no divisional
signal company, no field ambulances, no ammunition, and no mules."

snipers should dematerialise in two days, is beyond understanding. However, when Hamilton promised to have a
hundred Australian sharpshooters sent from Anzac at once (in
fact they did not reach Suvla until the 14th), Stopford took
heart and agreed to launch the attack at dawn on the 13th.
As it happened, that was Friday the 13th—but any day was
"unlucky" for military operations on our side of the hills.

In the meantime the 163rd Brigade of the 54th Division
volunteered to go out and clear the foothills of snipers' nests
before the main advance began, and to give them a chance to
do this Stopford managed to talk Hamilton into granting yet
another postponement, much against his will. Yet Hamilton
cabled K. of K. saying that this preliminary anti-sniping
operation, planned for August 12, "promised well". Rather
pathetically, he added: "This morning the Xth Division
captured a trench".

An entry in his diary that evening reveals only too clearly
his outlook on Mahon's leadership:

> "Mahon . . . after sitting for three days where I left him on the
> morning of the 9th has got tired of looking at gendarmes and
> has carried their trenches by the forbidden frontal bayonet
> charge without much trouble or loss."

On the evening of the 13th he goes to the root of the trouble:

> ". . . But I feel so acutely, I seem to see so clearly, where our
> push for Constantinople first began to quit the rails, that I
> must put it down right here. The moment was when I asked
> [K. of K.] for Rawlinson or Byng, and when in reply, the
> keen, the young, the fit, the up-to-date Commanders were all
> barred, simply and solely that Mahon should not be disturbed
> in his Divisional Command. . . . Ought I to have resigned
> sooner than allow generals old and yet inexperienced to be
> foisted on to me?"

He saw the need to get rid of Stopford and appoint a new
corps commander, and hated the idea of it—

> "Still, I would harden my heart to it now—tonight—were not
> my hands tied by Mahon's seniority. Mahon is the next senior
> —in the whole force he stands next to myself."

The sniper-clearance on the 12th that "promised well"
promised nothing. First of all, most of the maps, "hurriedly
issued at the last minute, depicted another part of the

peninsula": did not show the Suvla area at all! That left the
officers commanding the brigade uncertain about their objectives.

Worst of all, this winkling-out operation must be carried out
during daylight hours. No hope of finding snipers in the blind-
fold darkness of the night. And, anyhow, these untrained
Territorial troops under untrained officers stood no chance.
What actually happened proved it.

They advanced in blazing sunlight across the Kuchuk
Anafarta Ova, trudging over flat grazing grounds and stubble-
patches of abandoned tillage, and came under heavy enfilade
fire from the Kiretch ridge on their left, and the foothills east
of Sulajik (Baka Baba and Abrikja) on their right: and "it
soon became apparent that a great mistake had been made in
attempting to cross this open plain in daylight".

Under a withering cross-fire not more than 1,000 yards from
their starting point, the advance faded out. ... One unsupported party of fifteen officers and 250 men of the 5th
Norfolk Regiment pushed on. Not one of them was ever seen
nor heard of again from that day to this.

That night, at Imbros—far removed from the actualities of
the military mare's-nest in which we were still bogged down on
the sixth day of the landing—Hamilton and his G.H.Q. staff
were busy working out plans and orders for the next attack at
Suvla. And, of course, as soon as they spread out their maps
it was obvious that there was no hope of "seizing the Tekke
Tepe ridge" without first, or simultaneously, seizing—can you
guess?—*the W Hills and the Anafarta spur*. And that involved the
capture of—*Scimitar Hill*. The same old objectives that ought
to have been taken on the 7th. Finally, orders were sent to
Stopford that the 11th and 54th Divisions were to take these
objectives at dawn on the 13th. And these orders, perhaps to
avoid treading on Stopford's corns, made no mention of the
dreaded Tekke Tepe.

But they needn't have bothered with any orders at all,
because early in the morning of the 13th Stopford cabled to
say that he doubted whether the 54th Division could be ready
for another forty-eight hours. He followed this by cabling again
a little later to say that the Turks were "inclined to be aggres-
sive". He added that his 53rd Division was in fact "only a

danger" and might "bolt at any minute"! It just about staggered Hamilton, but he was determined that the attack should go forward. He therefore left Imbros for Suvla on the 13th "to have a last look over the *band-o-bast* [Hindu = arrangement, tying and binding: he was full of these Indian Army terms] for tomorrow's twice tomorrow effort against Tekke Tepe", and to have a final interview with The Man Who Wouldn't Budge.

It was their last interview. The *band-o-bast* was hopeless, and still more so the "hopeless mood" of the corps commander. Because of this Hamilton agreed to a further delay, and told him to consolidate his present position, northwards from Green Hill to the Kiretch ridge. That evening Stopford received the following cable from the C.G.S., Imbros: "After hearing you this afternoon Chief has decided that he will not call upon your corps to make general attack at present."

And that evening Hamilton wrote in his diary—"*Something in this beats me.*"

That same evening of the 13th, Hamilton took the bull by the horns. He sent a cable to K. of K. telling him that, "in their present frame of mind", the corps commander and his divisional generals were not fit to carry out a general advance. That was tantamount to asking for permission to sack Stopford, Mahon, and Hammersley, and an oblique request for new generals to take over.

And yet, in his own mournfully tenacious, painfully secretive way, Stopford was at this very moment getting ready to make— and, without in the least knowing it, very nearly made—the one move that could, even now, have won the day. A move that, even in its slack, laggardly, don't-fight-if-the-enemy-gets-too-aggressive Stopfordian pattern, was to confront the Turco-German command with one of the three crises of the Gallipoli Campaign, and compel Liman von Sanders to call up his last reserve.

Saturday, August 14, and all quiet at Suvla. Ominously quiet. Even the Turkish snipers below the Tekke Tepe and in their hide-outs along the lower slopes of the Kiretch ridge seemed to be having a day off. A G.H.Q. staff officer saw men of the 53rd Division "standing about on the parapet and even cooking in front of the trenches". Not a shot fired. In spite of the fact that some troops in the scrub on the left of these trenches were taken for Turks. A day or two passed before they were found to be British.

And on this day—a week after the landing—the Navy discovered "a specially fitted-out steamer", the R.E. Storeship *Prah*, that had been overlooked. For seven days she had been lurking behind Suvla Point, out of range of the Turkish batteries. I remember seeing her there, when looking down at the Gulf of Saros from the steep northern slope of the Karakol Dagh on several occasions, and wondering why she was always in the same position.

The *Prah* was packed with water-tanks, motor pumps, hose, troughs, machinery for sinking wells, and "all ordnance stores requisite for the prompt development of wells and springs". (See Hamilton's dispatch of December 11, 1915.)

Though we did not know it, this was the last day of the lull.

All through the blast-furnace heat of that long, quiet, warless day Stopford remained "way down in the bowels of the earth, poring over his maps" in his splinterproof headquarters at Ghazi Baba. G.H.Q. had sent him instructions the night before to "take every opportunity to make as forward a line as possible and to make that line impregnable". He was now, therefore, considering where he could push his line forward without starting up too much of "a regular battle".

He dismissed any idea of a frontal attack on the Tekke Tepe, and was right to do so. He decided against any attempt to push forward on the Scimitar-W-Hills-Anafarta-spur jigsaw. He was right about that too. There was only one other move open to him—to grasp "the Kiretch nettle". Of the three possibilities, this was thought to be "the line of least resistance", since it was supposed that Willmer's handful was still holding the Kiretch ridge without reinforcements. Even twenty-one years later we find it stated that the original hill-garrison had not been reinforced.*

* "General Stopford was prepared to take the line that promised the least resistance, and on the morning of the fifteenth he called upon General Mahon to push forward along the Kiretch Tepe ridge—where the original Turkish garrison had not been reinforced. . . ."—*Gallipoli: The Fading Vision*, by John North (Faber, 1936).

Stopford therefore decided that tomorrow morning, August 15, he would order Mahon to push forward along the hogsback. This was the one move that could have thrown the Turks into confusion, not only at Suvla, but throughout the peninsula.

Hamilton would have been astonished to know that his IXth Corps Commander was planning even a modified attempt to grasp "the Kiretch nettle". But Stopford—perhaps because he had been rather severely gibed at for not grasping it—did not communicate his plans to the Commander-in-Chief.

While he "pored over his maps", like a mole trying to digest a particularly tough worm in his underground "fortress", Kitchener sent a reply to Hamilton's cable of the 13th. It said:

> "If you deem it necessary to replace Stopford, Mahon, and Hammersley, have you competent generals to take their place? From your report I think Stopford ought to come home."

Later that day (the 14th) he sent another cable to say that General Byng was coming over to Gallipoli from France, and added: "I hope Stopford has been relieved by you already."

Next day, August 15, the gates of hell opened.

12

THE KIRETCH NETTLE

Darkly enchanted, the battle area unfurled in a sea of vapour—
you would not believe how fresh, how newly-born, glistening,
empty of danger, ghost-white, silent. Once again a fairy-
morning, with all fairyland trooping the dawnmist to watch
the humans at war.

We emerged, shivering, into the wonder of this shuddering
honey-buzzard dawncreep, waiting for "tea-up!" and still
half-clotted in sleep. Why must they roust us out of our foxholes
at 3.30 a.m.—an hour earlier than usual? "Would the tea-dixie
be coming up before long by any chance, Corporal?"

Sunday, August 15, and "Lady-Day-in-Harvest" for the
Irish Catholics. A great Church festival. So that's why they had
us out at this hour? Mass—and Holy Communion for the
Protestants at eight-thirty. Five hours to get ready! and a big
attack starting soon. Well, there it is: the better the day the
better the deed, they say. War is war, Sunday or Monday.
Very soon it was to be a field of blood and terror for us all.
And something more than that—the most fantastic
blow-out of piqued pride that ever backfired in the midst of
a battle.

They say opportunity knocks but once. It knocked four
times during the Anzac/Suvla operation. It knocked for
Moore, Malone, Allanson, in quick succession—and now for
Mahon.

Lady-Day-in-Harvest found Mahon still smouldering-dark
in the chambered mound of his soul's resentment. He had good

reason to be, for although the Xth Division (less its 29th
Brigade, serving at Anzac) had now recovered the five battalions under Brigadier-General Hill, its fighting strength was
seriously depleted.

One by one Hill's battalions had been relieved of their posts
on Chocolate and Green Hill, and marched down to the beach
to rest. This move, begun on the 10th, was not completed
until the 13th, when the 7th Royal Dublin Fusiliers arrived
at A Beach. This was little comfort to Mahon. Death, wounds,
and sickness had thinned the ranks mercilessly. They came
back tired, dirty, "with five days' growth of stubble" on their
chins, hollow-eyed, and racked with thirst and dysentery,
like their comrades on the Kiretch Tepe.

Broken up before the landing, broken up again and sent
adrift during the landing, it remained a broken division. Yet
its fighting spirit was good. Physically, we were in no worse
shape than Kemal's troops on the hills.

The attack was ordered to begin an hour after mid-day,
when it would be ninety degrees or more in the shade, and not
in the cool of the dawn. Mahon was given little time for
planning and preparation. In fact hardly any.

So, in the heat of mid-morning, with Captain Tuke leading
just ahead of me, our stretcher-squads toiled slowly up towards
the crest of the Karakol Dagh, a pull of about a mile from the
beach to 490 feet. Heavy shrapnel burst overhead on the way
up, slowing our pace. Higher up the slopes rifle bullets moaned
and ricocheted off the rocks. As soon as we topped the shoulder
of the hill, and passed over to the seaward side, there was less
din and we felt safer. Here we stood for a moment to recover
breath, staring down the sheerdrop tilt of scree and crag into
the double-dyed hypnotically dark germander-speedwell-blue
of the Gulf of Saros far below. We looked away quickly for fear
of slipping (nailed boots on rock-slants), and dumped the
folded stretchers for a ten-minute rest. The sun-scorched rocks
struck through our paper-thin khaki drill, hot to the buttocks
like a heated griddle. We took off our *sola topis*, and wiped our
brows with dirty rags that had once been handkerchiefs.

A bearer scrambled to his feet, crying "Wad ye believe it,
by all the Saints in Heaven!" whipped off his water-bottle
before you could say "Wather", uncorked it, and held it under

28. Sazli Dere Gully leading to " Table Top "
(*See page* 184, *and Map* 13)

29. Sir Ian Hamilton being rowed ashore

30. General Birdwood's last look at Anzac

a tiny crystal dribble. Within seconds we were all standing with uncorked bottles, waiting to fill them at this spigot-sized springhead. It would have taken hours! The water, welling from some hidden crevice, collected in a small, man-made, semi-circular stone basin, or stoup, no more than eighteen inches across, and overflowed the rim in a thinly twisting rillet that trickled to waste down the hillside. It was clear, quenchingly cool, and sweet. "The most delicious water I have ever tasted," one of our bearers recalled many years later.

Most of us had drunk freely before the captain came up and stopped us. We wanted to empty out the tepid, chlorinated stuff in our bottles and fill up with this rock-cold dewdrink of the gods. He said "No" to that. Water from springs or wells, he told us, was not to be touched until it had been tested for possible pollution. Sullenly, sighingly, but without a word, we recorked our water-bottles and slung them over our shoulders.

This little incident is worth a moment's consideration, because, if anyone could get water, it was the field ambulances. They were always the first to be supplied. Yet here we were on August 15—*eight days after the first troops had landed*—still hellishly short of water, still suddenly alert at the sight of a tiny dribble of fresh water. And although we traversed the Karakol/Kiretch ridge day after day, we never came upon another crystal rill trickling from the rocks.

But now we were moving forward in single file a little below the crestline, along a rockstrewn goat-track leading up and up towards the Kiretch Tepe in the grilling downbeat of the sun's rays and the stifling upthrust of rock-reflected heat. It was 1 p.m. The attack had just begun.

Mahon, astride the ridge, but still holding his old position about 800 yards west of Jephson's Post, had made the following dispositions for the advance:

The 30th Brigade (Dublins and Munsters) on the left flank—towards which we were now trudging with our long line of stretchers—with the 7th Royal Munster Fusiliers on the extreme left, at the water's edge of the Gulf of Saros. The 30th in fact covered the whole of the northern and part of the southern slope of the Kiretch ridge.

The 31st Brigade (Inniskillings) on the right flank were to

o

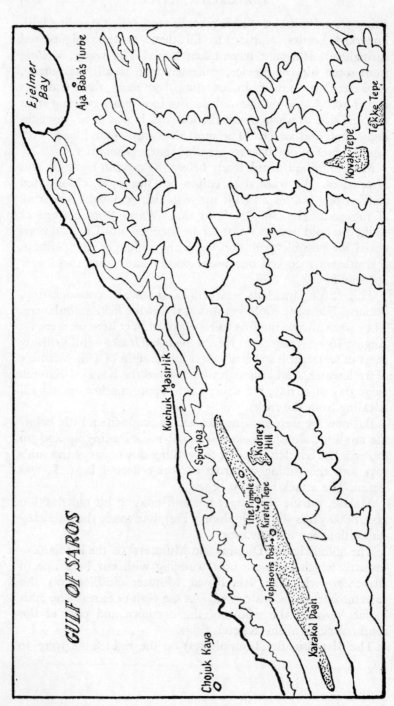

Map 14. THE KIRETCH BATTLE AREA

push through the southern gullies and foothills and across an open plain to attack a spur known as Kidney Hill (from its kidney-like shape on the map) that jutted southward from the main chain of the ridge, about halfway between Suvla Point and Ejelmer Bay. They were to be protected on their right by the 162nd Brigade of the 54th (Territorial) Division.

The guns of two destroyers* in the Gulf of Saros were to rake the high crest of the hogsback (656 feet) all along the 1,300 yards of its summit—and this they were now doing as we plodded towards the firing line.

We had come upon our first casualty, needing immediate surgical attention, and the captain stayed to deal with it. The rest of us pushed on along the steep-winding goat-track. We trod with catlike care, eyes down most of the way.

I was thinking of April in Hertfordshire—and the first milk-white spill of wild cherry blossom against the wintry woods. Then, with the salty sweat trickling into my eyes, I found myself treading on a soft, springy patch of ground that gave under my weight with a curious little "*pff!*"—and I watched, horror-stricken, as a sinewy arm rose slowly from under the loosely packed soil, with palm and fingers extended in awful warning, as though the corpse in its shallow grave wished to bar our way.

I was in fact standing on a dead man's chest with one foot, while the other had flexed his arm by treading on the whipcord-strong bicipital tendon at the elbow-joint. When I stepped away, the arm sank slowly to the ground, almost as weirdly as it had lifted. It seemed pitiful to tread with nailed boots upon those not-yet-decomposing remains.

Soon the narrow track was blocked ahead by waiting troops packed together, grim and silent. They were all Munsters. Before long we were hemmed in by more troops coming up behind, and had to pull our stretchers out of the way and flatten ourselves against the rocks to let them pass, their rifles slung, their backs bent to the steep climb, breathing hard, and sweating. As they passed, one or two said "*Any wather?*" and their split-reed voices whispered from the kingdom of the dead.

After a long wait the troops moved on, and at last we reached

* H.M.S. *Grampus* and H.M.S. *Foxhound*.

flatter ground on the high ridge. Then the day's toil began, and all the horror of it.

Hamilton, back now in his camouflaged hut at G.H.Q., Imbros, was busy most of the day making arrangements to replace Stopford as corps commander, and appears to have known nothing about the Kiretch battle. It is not vouchsafed so much as a mention in his diary. Nor did he attach any special importance to it in his dispatch of December 11, 1915, in which it is covered in one paragraph of twenty-six lines as being merely the result of the general direction given to Stopford "to confine his attention to strengthening his line across his present front", and to "straighten out the left of this line".

But soon after mid-day reports were coming in to Liman von Sanders's headquarters of a new and determined thrust along the Kiretch ridge, and before nightfall the German Commander-in-Chief was forced to give his whole attention to the threat presented by the attack of these Irish troops to the vulnerable Turkish right flank resting on Ejelmer Bay.

When you think of the total artillery support they had, it makes you want to weep. Here is the complete list (Dardanelles Report, Part II, Sec. 101, page 46): "One mountain battery, one field battery, and one heavy battery."

That was all. That, and the guns of the two destroyers in the Gulf. And even with that miserable ordnance the remnants of the Xth (Irish) Division were able to keep von Sanders—and Kemal—on tenterhooks for at least twelve hours.

Whoever got hold of the idea, either then or later, that this attack was "the line that promised the least resistance", and that the Kiretch Tepe ridge had not been reinforced and was still held by "the original small Turkish garrison", was woefully misinformed. The moment the Irish began their advance, the volume of fire that swept their ranks was "infinitely greater" than it was during the first advance on August 7. And this was confirmed later by a captured Turkish officer who stated that "they had in their firing line six fresh battalions, each possessing twelve machine-guns," says Major Bryan Cooper.

When the steep hill-track gave out, and our stretcher-squads began to move forward across a narrow neck of splintery shale the thudding rattle of these seventy-two machine-guns hit the diaphragm and throbbed like the massed kettledrums of hell. And this sweeping hail of death, with its fierce accompaniment of rifle-fire, was heavily supported by showers of shrapnel that unfolded, spat, and floated away. They might have been the discarded parachutes of a thousand invisible paratroopers—floating away and away into nothingness, but leaving behind a slaughteryard of dismemberment from which the cry of "*stretcher-bear-e-r-s!—stretcher-bear-e-r-s!*" came to us in every key and pitch of human agony, and from every direction.

For more than two hours the Turks on the hogsback kept up their hellfire resistance, and very little ground was gained. Major Jephson, leading the 6th Munsters, once more got a footing on the peak that a week earlier had been named after him—and there he was mortally wounded. But the Munsters held on. It was something to have regained Jephson's Post on the western tip of the hogsback.

We had brought up half the bearer sub-divisions of the 32nd Field Ambulance to serve the 30th Brigade (the other half served the 31st on the southern slopes), and already we were swamped with wounded. This was a day bright with the deadly nightshade of dread, glittering with the *Fata Morgana* of triumph, drooping with flowers that wither at a glance. Within those first two hours I watched our A Section bearers changing—from youth to age—turning into old men. Growing old, and worn, and haggard, without knowing it. I suppose I must have changed with them. For it was not only the heavy physical drag of stretcher-bearing that told. It was also the horror of torn limbs—the blood, pus, flies, stench, groans, and the whispered requests of the dying. No man, tough or sensitive, is proof against this. Later, of course, we recovered our youthful looks and bearing.

Most of us had got over the first mild attack of sandfly fever, and were fit enough. But it was pitiful to see men staggering along with a loaded stretcher who, in the first stages of dysentery, ought to have been carried down themselves.

From before-dawn breakfast to long after dark, we ate no food that day. Most of the time we were inextricably mixed up with the fighting troops a few yards from the front line. There was no other way of getting the wounded away. The regimental stretcher-bearers* toiled like the ancient Irish—the *Gowanree*—who were forced to drudge at the earthworks of the Rath of Cruachan, in Connaught, and are said to have finished the dyke in one day! But here, even with giant strength and staying-power, they were overwhelmed. They needed all the help we could give them.

It was now that the men of our bearer sub-divisions showed what they were made of—blind-staggered as they were. These men that I knew so well, that seemed to have shrunken into a straggle of tired troglodytes, their arms almost wrenched from their shoulders, "carried on".

They carried on through the swealing heat of that Tophet afternoon, on and on, late into the dusk, until darkness blotted out rock, scrub, goat-track, and gully. They shuffled, stooping to the weight, fire-walking like fakirs over hot shaly beds that slid and clattered. Gently, gently, descending rock ledges where the rear bearer must lower his stretcher-handles until he is squatting on his haunches, and the leading bearer must turn about facing him, straining to raise his stretcher-handles above his head, and come down backwards—slowly, slowly—feeling with his feet for a foothold, while the wounded man moans a little or cries out at each jolting lurch. Then down the familiar gullies and across the humpy ground, two long miles to the beach. And—within ten minutes—up to the ridge again.

Killing work for Agamemnon's Trojans. "Gradely lads," as Boler said, and some of them no more than lads. They took strength, somehow, out of their own dark fear. They drew new strength from the dragging ache of their own weariness. And don't forget their terrible nakedness. Naked to the storm of shrapnel and machine-gun fire that takes no heed of Red Cross

---

* These were not the original R.S.B.s, for they had all, or nearly all, become casualties themselves. These were ordinary troops of the line doing R.S.B. duties. For all practical purposes, after the first few days at Suvla, the Medical Corps did the work of the regimental stretcher-bearers. In the First World War the work of R.S.B.s was the active service duty of the bandsmen. In consequence, the world-famous Guards Bands were decimated. It took years of training at Kneller Hall to bring the Army bands back to anywhere near pre-war standard. In this matter at any rate the lesson was learnt, and during the Hitler-war the crack Army bands were preserved.

brassards. No chance to turn and fight. Nothing to fight with. No chance to run with a loaded stretcher.

We hardly spoke the whole day through. Never uttered a word that was not essential—

"Don't move his arm, for God's sake!"

"Lift him on one side a little."

"Wait till that machine-gun's finished—you'll never get across to him."

"Abdominal wound. Don't give him any water—take his bottle away if there's any in it."

Our advanced dressing station was still down below on the Kuchuk Anafarta Ova, where it had been wrongly sited from the first. So we had no advance dressing station up here on the ridge, which meant that our bearers not only had to go into the firing-line, and even into no-man's-land beyond, to fetch out the seriously wounded, but must carry them all the way to the beach—where the ambulance wagons and their mule teams stood in the soft sand, unable to help.

Men toiling down the gullies with loaded stretchers met men coming back from the beach with folded stretchers. They passed each other like sleepwalkers—without a word. . . .

And still the Turks beyond Jephson's Post kept up their fury. And still the Munsters clung to Jephson's Post. About three-thirty in the afternoon Brigadier-General Nicol, seeing no sign of slackening in the Turkish fire, and knowing that darkness would make any further advance impossible in another four hours, ordered that an attempt be made to push forward along the northern slope of the ridge without delay.

Nicol, commanding the 30th Brigade, was an oldish man, like all the Suvla generals, and, like the others, was suffering from dysentery. Again and again he had refused to go to hospital. He was determined to stay with his troops in the front line and "stick it out". And did. He was the only brigadier still holding his original command when we sailed away from Suvla. A gentle-looking creature, with grey hair and a trimly droopy white moustache, and laughter in his eyes: and though the underlip thrust forward a little with determined pugnacity, it was the pugnacity of a playful bull-pup. The rest of the face was rounded like a schoolboy's, and tended to slip away to a slightly slung-back chin. Misleading, because he had that quiet easy-going courage that always wins the devotion of troops under fire. They knew he was there with them, in the thick of it all the time.

And so, when he ordered this advance, there was no moment of hesitation. Two companies of the 6th Munster and two companies of the 6th Dublin pushed forward at once, and, thanks to a stretch of dead ground, managed to get about halfway across the 500 yards that separated Jephson's Post from the Turkish line of defence. Here they rested for some time, taking stock of their position, and making ready for a final assault.

About 6 p.m., with the blazing sun setting at their backs, they stood up—fixed bayonets—and charged! Their sudden raucous outcry, something like a hoarse cawing of rooks flapping away from a rookery, made me straighten-up and turn my head sharp left. But for that outlandish sheballahay I should have missed the only British—well, Irish—bayonet charge I have ever seen. For a split second I thought the Turks were on us!

It was uphill for the first few yards. The Irish seemed to have been shot like rocket-men out of the sun itself—their bayonets splinters from the sun's blinding rays. Most of them were great strapping fellows, and there was a fair sprinkling of redheads among them. These, with flaming carroty stubble bristling their chins, mingled with the black eight-day growth of the majority, gave the charge a ghoulish frightfulness. They stormed up and over the crest at a bull-heavy canter, heedless of the thudding torrent of hissing lead that swept them. Many fell, but there was no wavering. The thrusting bayonets flashed, blinked, and flashed again as they streamed forward along the hogsback. Few Turks stayed to meet them. Those who did, threw up their hands and surrendered. The rest were on the run.

With Major Tynte of the 6th Royal Munster Fusiliers leading, the Irish gained the position—and let go a high-croaking chanticleering cheer of breathless triumph that was taken up by all the troops on the ridge, and spread like a great sea of cheering from the Gulf of Saros to the Salt Lake—and came echoing back up the gullies! Even the wounded tried to raise themselves and cheer. There was far-off cheering from

Chocolate Hill and Green Hill and Lala Baba, and cheering down on the beaches. The first cheering heard at Suvla since the landing.

Again Hamilton was proved to be right in the scathing comment of his diary entry of August 12. Not just the taking of a trench this time. Today the Turks holding the Kiretch Tepe had been routed "by the forbidden frontal bayonet charge" and were in full retreat.

But Hamilton knew nothing about it.

Liman von Sanders knew all about it, by runner and field telephone. He knew it was touch-and-go. The Bulair reinforcements on the Kiretch were unable to hold on—could not face the "frontal bayonet charge" of the Irish. If the British pressed their attack now, the game was up. That mighty hillside massacre of Kemal's troops pouring down from the Chunuk Bair on the morning of the 10th had left the Turkish defences on the Suvla/Chunuk battlefront seriously thinned-out. The survivors were in poor fettle: they knew what naval guns could do. There were no other reinforcements to bring up from anywhere. The Turkish army was stretched to breaking-point right across the peninsula.

Von Sanders called up his last reserve.

We know now why he was so "jumpy" about this thrust along the hogsback. It caused him "very keen anxiety" because the main Turkish ammunition depot could be captured from Ejelmer Bay, and because, as he wrote after the war: "If on August 15th and 16th the British had taken the Kiretch Tepe they would have outflanked the entire Fifth Army and final success might have fallen to them."

Having raised their cheer, the Dublins and Munsters did not rest. They drove the Turks before them, back and back along the bare rock ledges and great scattered boulders that litter the high ridge. Along this rock-hackled spine rose three small prominences, the central one being marked by a cairn of stones, known to us as the "Pimple". This stood roughly halfway along the hogsback.

Soon the whole of the northern slope as far as and even beyond the "Pimple" was cleared of the enemy—and all that seemed to bother the Irish was that so few of the retreating troops would turn and fight. One Irish soldier—this is well authenticated—was heard to cry out to a fat Turk who fled before him: "I don't want to stick ye behind. Turn round now, and I'll stick ye in the belly, dacent!"

None of this lightheartedly chivalrous pigsticking was for us. The Medicals are the menials, the Mrs. Mops of war. The dead and the dying lay strewn across the ground ahead of us like the mutilated trunks of a felled forest. The cries and moans of the wounded, into which the cheering had subsided, told why Jesus wept. And now, on the edge of twilight—

No stretchers! All in use. . . .

This was a new nightmare-twist to the day's turmoil. Only a few of us remained on the ridge, mostly N.C.O.s There was nothing for it but to bring the wounded out on our backs by fireman's lift. How we managed the job I don't know. I tipped the scales at just under twelve stones at the time, and it left me with a strained heart for several years.

It meant running through an intermittent blizzard of shrapnel laced with spraying bursts of machine-gun fire, because the position was enfiladed on the right flank where the advance on Kidney Hill by the Inniskillings of the 31st Brigade, supported by the Territorials, had gone adrift in hopeless confusion.

By this time the Turks had been driven back nearly a mile from Jephson's Post, and the Dublins and Munsters had taken almost the whole of the hogsback. But the failure to take Kidney Hill on the right flank threatened their victorious advance. A halt was called in the fast-failing light in order to consolidate the position. "The soil of the ridge," writes Major Bryan Cooper, "was too stony to admit of much entrenching, and in most cases the men lay down on their arms just behind the crest on the seaward side." At one or two points they built stone *sangars* (Hindu, *sunga:* a stone breastwork used by Indian hill-tribes).

At nightfall the front line on the Kiretch Tepe ran something in the shape of a Z. The upper horizontal stroke of the letter represents a shallow line of trench running steeply uphill from the Gulf of Saros to the point on the crest reached by the bayonet charge. This trench was exposed to fire from the

Turks still holding the eastward heights of the ridge, and also from a spur known as "103" (328 feet) jutting northward and dipping almost sheerly to the Gulf. The diagonal joining the two horizontal strokes of the Z represents the line running along the seaward side of the hogsback just below the crest, where it was possible to scrape a shallow trench. The crest itself, liable to be pounded by the two destroyers, and swept by Turkish shrapnel and machine-gun fire, could not be held by anyone. The lower horizontal of the Z represents the trench running past Jephson's Post towards the southern slopes overlooking the plain and Salt Lake, down to the spurs and gullies where the Inniskillings and the Territorials had been balked and broken up in their attempt to capture Kidney Hill.

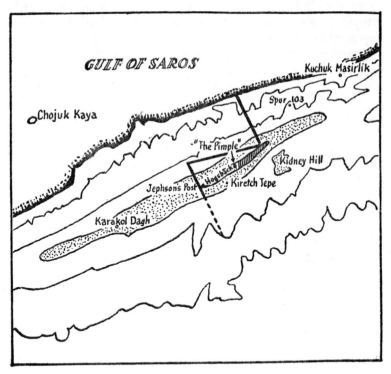

Map 15. KIRETCH TEPE: THE BATTLE OF THE HOGSBACK

I set this out in some detail because the Battle of the Hogsback was the most important of any fought at Suvla, and the only one in the whole Gallipoli Campaign that threatened the complete defeat of the Turkish Army. Yet it is usually brushed aside in a sentence or two, if it is mentioned at all.

Fantastically—for the tragic eccentricity of the Suvla situation never broke—the Kiretch battle went forward hour after hour without direction from anyone. Except, of course, the stouthearted Nicol.

And while the Irish made their successful "frontal bayonet charge" along the hogsback, the Battle of the Generals blew up in their rear.

At the very moment when the Turks were on the run, Stopford was sacked. The Final Report of the Dardanelles Commission, (Part II, Sec. 102, page 46), puts it with mordant laconism: "On the evening of August 15th Sir Frederick Stopford was relieved of the command of the IXth Corps and replaced for the time being by Major-General de Lisle."

Stopford was sacked, and—far more unexpected—Mahon had packed up and gone!

13

CHAOS IN COMMAND

All night the battle on the high ridge had snarled and grumbled. And during the night Major Holden, the D.A.D.M.S. (Deputy Assistant Director of Medical Services), had attended to many of the wounded that we could not evacuate when darkness fell. Soon we should be going up again to bring them down.

On Sunday the 15th Hamilton had cabled Mahon asking him to waive his seniority in the matter of de Lisle's temporary appointment as corps commander. To this Mahon had replied—

"I respectfully decline to waive my seniority and to serve under the officer you name. Please let me know to whom I am to hand over the Division."

There and then, "furious and disgusted with everyone and everything", he packed his traps and sailed for Lemnos, where he was left to "cool down quietly". He went in the midst of the battle he had set in motion. Even before the Dublins and Munsters fixed bayonets and charged—and their hoarse, cock-crowing cheer resounded round the bay—he had gone.

Later, Hamilton wrote in his diary:

"August 17, 1915, Imbros. A Lieutenant-General in the British Army chucking up his command whilst his division is actually under fire—is a very unhappy affair."

It had a peculiar effect upon us all. As our long line of stretcher-bearers moved off, with Captain Young leading, to bring in the wounded from the Kiretch ridge at dawn on August 16, we picked up the half-whispered news—

"Have ye heard the way it is? Sir Bryan Mahon's packed up and gone!"

"You can't blame him—the way the Division's been b——d about!"
"D'ye think we moight be sailin' home before long?"

That gives the general reaction. Leaderless and lost in the midst of a battle—and dreaming about packing up and going home. . . .

Now was gathered on the high ridge all that was left of the Xth Irish, with the Kiretch "nettle" grasped—but with their right flank hanging in the air, and no one in command.

In that shape the second day of battle sprang up, begrimed, with Sunday's stale blood tear-wet without weeping: the living and the dead bathed in night-dew. The living yawning and stretching on the bare rocks, as other men yawn and stretch in their beds at home. They'd had little sleep that night: at the most an hour or two. One here, one there, grasped his rifle and clambered up to relieve the men at the listening-posts on the crest. All along the ridge huddles of men grunted, yawned, cleared their throats, got to their feet, slung on their kit, buckled their belts, and took up their rifles.

Don't think of them as soldiers—the word conjures the wrong impression—but as fighting men. Think of them as they really were: the last remnants of a once-splendid division—an army of scrubby giants, lean and scrawny. Terrible to behold. Deadbeat and dirty, but ready to fight. Ready to push on past the dead and the wounded that littered the corpse-cold gloom at daybreak.

Again and again we had to stand aside and wait while the Indian Mule Corps climbed up the hill-track, their pack animals loaded with ammunition boxes, petrol-tins, and water-bags. At last a meagre trickle of water and other supplies was reaching the front line.

We passed little groups of "lost men" wandering about, as on the day of landing: six-foot Inniskillings trying to find their brigade headquarters, and looking like cut-throats and casta-ways. Some of these Northern Irish giants from Fermanagh and Tyrone had drifted away from the frustrated Kidney Hill battle-ground, and were fighting with the Dublins and Munsters on the hogsback.

Here and there we met weary straggles of East Anglian Territorials of the 54th Division, looking "fail", as the Irish say (peaky, as we might put it). Too young and callow for the job. Most of them were mere boys, some only sixteen or seventeen years old. From my own observation, then and later, Stopford was right about his Territorial reinforcements. They could not stand the strain. Moreover, the 54th Division was under the command of Major-General Inglefield, who at the time was sixty, much too old for this kind of soldiering.

On the 15th three battalions of these youngsters of the 162nd Brigade, then bivouacked near A Beach, were to move up in support of Hill's 31st Brigade in their advance on Kidney Hill, along the southern slopes of the Kiretch ridge. This attack on the right flank began at the same time as that of the 30th Brigade—at about 1 p.m.—with the 5th Inniskilling Fusiliers leading. But whereas the dead-on-the-mark fire of the two destroyers in the Gulf of Saros made it possible for the leading battalions of the 30th Brigade to push forward along the hogsback on the seaward side, these naval guns could not fire over the ridge.

The Turkish gunners could see "every detail of the advance over the plain", and the Inniskillings came under a heavy curtain of shrapnel interspersed with well-placed high explosive shells. And as there was no distraction elsewhere in the Suvla area, the whole force of hostile artillery was laid down on this sector.

Although the attack failed, the Inniskillings did not fall back. With almost all their officers killed or wounded, the survivors of the leading battalion hung on. They could not advance— they would not retire. All day long "little groups of men clustered in the bushes waiting for orders". After sundown Lieutenant Lyndon, of the 6th Service Battalion, the Royal Inniskilling Fusiliers, went out and rounded up most of these diehard groups, and brought them in. For this he was awarded the Military Cross.

The three Territorial battalions of the 162nd Brigade had advanced to protect the right flank in the attack on Kidney Hill, but had "no information about the probable whereabouts of the enemy". In fact these young untried troops breasted the rough and tumbled lower slopes of the Kiretch ridge, and actually advanced the left of the line to the south-western shoulder of Kidney Hill before nightfall on the 15th. But—as always—*they were unsupported*. And so, during the night, having suffered nearly 1,000 casualties, they retired to a line that extended the position held by the 31st Brigade before the attack began. No wonder these young fighters of the 54th Division were worn out and dispirited when daylight came.

It will be recalled that this division (footnote, page 201) landed with "no artillery, no divisional signal company, no field ambulances, no ammunition, and no mules". They were issued with a certain amount of ammunition before the advance on Kidney Hill, but it was in short supply. Most of these troops were now in a state of acute dejection—many seemed vacant and shell-shocked—and were unfit for further service under fire. But, of course, they had to "soldier on".

Inferno broke along the shell-torn spine of the hogsback at dawn on August 16, and there was no let-up during the whole of that day. It began its death clatter when the first stab of sunlight slashed across the topmost ridge, and the Turks made a fresh attack led by bomb-throwers.

We came up to the crest with the stretcher party soon after the listening-posts had been driven in. A strong phalanx of these bombers managed to take and hold a position on the southern slope. From there they were able to bomb the whole length of the British line. Before long they were hurling hand-grenades over the crest from the "Pimple" to Jephson's Post. They burst with deadly effect in the ranks of the Fusiliers, but the Turkish bombers took care to keep their heads well down below the crestline on their side. A few bold ones crossed the crest, and were either shot or stuck with the bayonet. Any fighting-mad Irish who tried to dash over the crest were met by a shower of bombs and blown to shreds.

Hour after hour the bombing went on. The stream of wounded (walking cases) limped and hobbled from the high ridge down the gullies to the dressing station on the beach in an unbroken single file. It seemed unending. It blocked the narrow track, slowing and holding up the stretcher-bearers, making their toil more toilsome.

At the outset the Fusiliers retaliated in kind, flinging the few bombs they had at hidden Turks across the crest. Soon there were none left, and no more were forthcoming. They were poor

31. A 32nd Field Ambulance Wagon on the edge of the Salt Lake

32. Wounded waiting to be taken aboard

33. Carrying wounded to Boats by Pick-a-Back from A Beach

rough-and-ready contraptions anyhow: a detonator pushed into a jam-tin, with a fuse that had to be lighted with a match. The Turkish hand-grenade, shaped like a cricket-ball, was "infinitely superior to that issued by the British", being "more accurately fused and easier to throw". Still, at this moment, the Irish would have been glad of a plentiful supply of jam-tins.

Rifles and bayonets were useless. The two sides were like "men sitting in the gutters of a house, fighting across the roof". Hand-grenades were the only effective weapon, and the side that lacked them was practically defenceless. We may well ask how such a situation could have come to pass. What allowed the Turks—driven beyond the "Pimple" in headlong retreat by the Munsters' bayonet charge on the 15th—to creep back and occupy the southern slopes? The answer is dreadfully simple. None of this could have happened if the Kidney Hill attack on the right flank had been properly planned and supported.

All day long on the 15th the battle raged on the hogsback and in front of Kidney Hill with no one in command. Stopford had been dismissed—de Lisle was taking over. Mahon had gone—and this morning, August 16, Hill was put in charge of the Xth Division as stop-gap commander. It made no difference. The battle, completely out of control, went rattling to its doom.

Cry havoc! and let slip the dogs of war—with no one in command. Repeat—*no one in command.* And all the Kiretch gullies echo—

"Chaos in command!"

Clinging just below the crestline, waiting to be torn asunder or limb-shattered (but still alive), left the Irish in a seething rage.

Here and there an individual officer gathered together a group of daredevils and led them over the crest in an attempt to drive the enemy back at the bayonet-point. Major Harrison, of the 7th Dublin Fusiliers, finding his line dangerously thinned by the unceasing bombing, organised such a charge. He chose a party from D Company ("The Pals") under Captain Poole Hickman.

P

They charged up the rocky slope with a wild joy. As soon as they topped the crest they were met by a storm of rifle and machine-gun bullets. Captain Poole Hickman was killed. Major Harrison dashed forward bareheaded, took his place, and led the charge across the bullet-whistling crest—right across to the Turkish line, where a hand-grenade hurled at close quarters ended his life. A shower of bombs followed. Only four men got back from that raid. Other raids elsewhere along the hogsback came to the same disastrous end. Sometimes "a whole platoon disappeared and was never heard of again".

The badly wounded, lying waiting for stretchers in the lee of the rocks on the seaward side, hindered the coming and going of the fighting men.

And all along the ridge shrapnel flashed and blossomed like magical death-flowers, budding and overblown on the instant, shedding their death-seed in a whanging clangour that rang on the hard sandstone like a thousand hammers on a giant anvil.

It's easy to build up a battle-scene: to make it sound ten times worse than it was. Old soldiers love to pile on the agony. But here the difficulty is to find the flaming words—the spattering, bullet-thudding, nightmare-dark words that crack the waiting silence and spit and wail and scream!—and the little whispering words that zip and ting and shiver like tissue-paper, and give-up-the-ghost—all the hot-metallic Hurlo-thrumbo words to make the battle writhe and rattle at the full blast of its lost and bloody-stupid butchery.

Tell me the words of searing horror! Spell me the words of weeping rage! . . .

During the morning of the 16th, when the Irish on the hogsback had no bombs left, and were running short of small arms ammunition, first one and then another "tried to catch the Turkish bombs as they were falling to throw them back into the enemy's lines before they exploded". One of them, Private Wilkin, of the 7th Dublin Fusiliers, managed this feat five times. At the sixth attempt he was blown to pieces.

It was then that, finding they had neither bombs nor ammunition, the Dublins and Munsters "took up stones and hurled them" at the Turks—"in default of anything more deadly".

After nearly five hours of stone-throwing—the ranks thin, the living in a daze of exhaustion, the mangled bodies of the dead lying beside them—Brigadier Nicol felt compelled to make an urgent appeal for reinforcements.

It reached divisional and corps headquarters at a bad moment to ask for anything. Mahon had gone—and neither Hill nor anyone else knew what to do. Stopford was busy packing up. De Lisle was busy taking over.

Nothing happened. There was, literally, *no one in command*.

Sir Beauvoir de Lisle—what a name to conjure with! it might have come out of Malory's *Morte d'Arthur*—a regular cavalry officer, then fifty-one years of age, commanding the 29th Division at Cape Helles (a regular division that Field-Marshal Sir John French, the British Commander-in-Chief, looked upon as "stolen from the West"), whose chief interest was polo, made no impression whatsoever upon the Suvla situation. Suvla swallowed him as soon as he stepped ashore.

Hamilton had telegraphed to Kitchener on August 14 "to the effect that the one man on the spot who could pull the IXth Corps together again was Major-General de Lisle", says the Dardanelles Report (Part II, Sec. 105, page 48). The telegram continued:

> "Unfortunately Mahon is senior to de Lisle, but I could not put him in command of the Corps at present, though as Divisional General he has done better than others, and I would ask him to accept the position" [in which he was to waive his seniority] ". . . I hope you will agree to this and give de Lisle the temporary rank of Lieutenant-General".

To this Kitchener had replied on the same date suggesting Byng for the corps command, and adding that it would be "better not to act definitely until he had heard what Sir John French could do".

But Hamilton had already acted. De Lisle did not "pull the IXth Corps together again", because, like Humpty-Dumpty, it had been smashed beyond repair. The more he saw of these troops, and of the generals who were supposed to command them, the more convinced he became of the hopelessness of trying to do anything. In fact Sir Beauvoir came to the conclusion that the only thing to do was to "get out"—*but he did*

not make this known to Sir Ian. This is proved by the following
entry in the famous diary:

> "August 17th, Imbros. De Lisle reports confusion throughout
> Suvla Bay area. He *must* have three or four days to pull the
> troops together before he organises a fresh offensive. The
> IXth Corps has been *un corps sans tête*."

And again the next day:

> "August 18th, Imbros. De Lisle tells me he has now been round
> every corner of Suvla and that the want of grip throughout
> the higher command has been worse than he dared to put on
> paper. To reorganise will take several weeks; but we have to
> try to act within two or three days."

De Lisle, however, gave a very different impression in his
evidence before the Dardanelles Commission, 1917. The Report
(Part II, Sec. 107, page 49) says:

> "He was in favour of the evacuation of Suvla, which he
> regarded as the only thing to do when we had the factor of
> surprise no longer in our favour, and for the same reason he
> would have evacuated Helles and Anzac and abandoned the
> enterprise in June, as by that time there was no prospect of
> ultimate success."

So Hamilton had appointed a new corps commander who
had no faith in any further offensive at Suvla, nor anywhere else
on the peninsula, and whose solution to the stalemate was—
"evacuation"! The one word that had never entered Hamilton's
thoughts: the one word that was anathema to him to the very
end. Even Poor Old Stopford, so determined not to start "a
regular battle", never had the idea of pulling out.

At this moment he was pulling out himself, but only because
he had been relieved of his command. He probably never knew
that, at the moment of his going, his Xth Division troops
were stone-throwing at the enemy within two miles of his
splinterproof dug-out.

Back to the palæolithic battle on the ridge at noon on the
16th—back to Inferno. Temperature: over 110 degrees.
Reeling confusion. Shaggy men loom and vanish. Filthy
sulphurous smoke hanging over everything.

Nothing holds together any more. All broken up. Thick
smoke again—patch of blazing scrub over there. More shaggy

men shuffling back, passing more shaggy men trudging up the line. My feet seem to be enormously swollen—boiled vegetable marrows. Who's taken the "monkey-box"? That rock seemed to bend just now (rocks don't bend—must be the heat—mirage-effect?—optical illusion, hallucination?). Face looming up—it's Captain Young. Wondered where he'd got to. He's bending over the rock—he's got the "monkey-box"—

"Hand me a scalpel, Sergeant—quick!"

He's operating—*clang!*—that shrapnel-burst was a close one. Operating under fire—

"Lion-forceps, Sergeant" (for gripping bone). There aren't any—

"All right—any forceps—quick!" Where the devil are they? I've got 'em.

More shrapnel. He doesn't turn a hair. Might be in an operating theatre.

"Pad—gauze pad—cotton-wool."

Operating with no anaesthetic—up here under fire. . . .

"Surgical needle—catgut sutures—" (for stitching wounds). No catgut.

"Wire—silk—horsehair—anything!—"

So it goes on. . . .

"Got a stretcher?"

"Three coming up now, sir."

"Right—get him away—see he doesn't roll over on his left side."

The captain's sallow, podgy face, with its small, clipped, toothbrush-moustache, loomed and faded. He was a short, stocky man, with a permanently glum expression, as though he suffered from chronic dyspepsia. He said little, seldom smiled, lacked charm, and was not particularly popular with the rank and file, although he was one of our best surgeons. He was always scrupulously fair, meticulous in his work as a Medical Corps officer, but—well—stodgy.

Now—suddenly—up here on the ridge—I had watched this stodgy little man earn ten Victoria Crosses in less than ten minutes! He got nothing. But what a man! To me he seemed a kind of god. In spite of the mortal danger and the shrapnel-clatter, he wielded the scalpel as I have seen Augustus John wield a pencil during a 1943 air-raid, with calm and swift dexterity. Stooping over the rock-slab "operating table", he worked at speed but didn't hurry. He didn't just operate—he made a beautiful job of it. Shrapnel lodged in the left side (lower thorax)—pretty tricky. He saved the man's life.

I don't know where he went after that. He loomed and vanished in the pandemonium. Everyone loomed and vanished. . . .

The Kiretch "nettle" had been grasped, but not uprooted. Instead of pushing every available man up to the high ridge, de Lisle, in his circumambulation "round every corner of Suvla" noted that the Irish were "beating themselves to pieces" on the Kiretch Tepe—and left them to get on with it. Well, there were plenty of stones up there. . . .

During the whole of the 16th, and right through the following night, no fresh troops were sent up. It has been stated that "none were available". But Hamilton's day-to-day diary shows the true position:

> "August 17th, Imbros. De Lisle has at his disposal the Xth Division, less one brigade, the 11th, 53rd and 54th Divisions: total rifles, owing to casualties, under 30,000."

If 5,000 of these troops had been sent up to the hogsback on the 16th, the fighting remnants of the Dublins, Munsters, and Inniskillings would have cleared the Kiretch Tepe of the enemy before nightfall.

The Irish did not give in. The line still held. The scruffy troops clung to the crestline, more like warmed-up corpses than living men. Many corpses lay amongst them stiffening in *rigor mortis*, and it was hard to tell the living from the dead. At one point the parapet of crenellated rocks seemed to be strongly held, but seven out of ten were dead men, their rifles still pointing towards the Turkish lines.

During the day little groups of Turkish prisoners were brought in at the bayonet-point—poor, nondescript Anatolian peasants, ragged, bewildered, thirst-stricken—and some of the gaunt Irish desperadoes with a drain left in their water-bottles gave it to them to drink. These Turks were always as parched and lip-blistered as our own troops. A point to note, for it has been stated that: "A few hundred yards in rear of the Turkish position [east of Jephson's Post] was a magnificent spring of water*, of which the British were to remain in ignorance throughout the campaign." The Turks seem to have been in ignorance of it, too.

With the westering sun scorching our backs, the ridge was lit by a crimson glare that made the scene more hellish. At the extreme forward position, the 6th Royal Irish Fusiliers, exposed in front and in flank, had been practically wiped out. Their 5th Battalion, brought up to reinforce them, had suffered the same fate. These two battalions had lost nearly all their officers, and the other regiments were in no better case. The total casualties were appalling.

The Irish felt themselves abandoned on the Kiretch ridge. What remained of the Xth Division had been shattered in a battle that was left to fight itself out.

Yet even now, with twilight falling over the fatal ridge on the 16th, left to shift for themselves—unable to strike a blow in their own defence—these tough tatterdemalions still held their ground twenty-nine hours after they had gone in to the attack.

They were all young soldiers—though they looked old and worn now—all volunteers with less than a year's training in Kitchener's much-sneered-at "civilian army". A week ago none of them had been under fire. They did not flinch. They did not budge. They used their bayonets. They flung stones. They got no help. They stayed where they were because they had been given no order to retire.

Without ammunition or reinforcements they were left up there to be bombed and shelled by the Turks for another twenty-four hours.

The Kiretch "nettle" had the sting of death. . . .

---

* *Gallipoli: The Fading Vision*, by John North (Faber, 1936), page 173. It may be noted here that on the right flank of the Suvla battle-front the meagre water-supply also affected British and Turkish troops alike. Major Bryan Cooper of the 29th Brigade, Xth (Irish) Division, serving at Anzac, states: ". . . About four hundred yards north of Damakjelik stood two wells called Kaba Kuyu. These wells were extremely valuable to the Turks, since they, too, were short of water."

14

THE LAST BATTLE

Disaster hit the 32nd Field Ambulance on Tuesday, August 17.

Up to now we had been one officer short. Lieutenant Smith had been left behind in Egypt suffering from dysentery. He rejoined the unit this very morning, and Mad Jack immediately put him in charge of the party of stretcher-bearers, about twenty-four strong, due to go up to the Kiretch ridge.

I remember him as though it were yesterday, pale and sickly, the fever still on him, his eyes burning in panda-dark sockets, his skin semi-translucent like eggshell china, his voice flat and lifeless.

As this was his first day at Suvla, and the first time he had been under fire, Captain Young, the adjutant, came up with us as far as the slope leading to Jephson's Post. The following quick briefing took place at the final rest-halt, before the squads went up to the high ridge to collect the wounded:

Young: "Do you think you'll be all right?"

Smith: "Yes, I think so."

Young: "Well, just stick here and send down the wounded as you find them. Don't go any farther along, it's too dangerous up there—you understand?"

Smith: "All right, sir."

But the young subaltern seemed to answer absentmindedly. The adjutant himself, stocky as a tree-stump, looked as though he might fall asleep where he stood. On the third day of the Kiretch battle we were all ready to drop.

As the adjutant turned to go, he said: "You'd better come down with me, Sergeant." But for that I should have stayed with Lieutenant Smith and the stretcher-party.

Alas, no one knew that, during the night, the forward troops on the left of the ridge had been withdrawn two or three hundred yards.

It was some hours before we heard that Smith and most of the stretcher-bearers had vanished.

For one reason or another, he did not obey the order to stay where he was. Thinking the ground ahead of him was still held by the British, he led the stretcher-squads into no-man's-land between the lines. Their Red Cross brassards did not save them. Lieutenant Smith was killed, and nineteen other ranks—including a sergeant, a corporal, and a lance-corporal—were either killed, wounded, or listed as missing (believed killed). Twenty casualties in one day made a serious gap in the ranks of so small a unit as a field ambulance, and the backwash down on the beach was one of dejection breaking into little swirls of anger,

"'E wasn't fit to take charge—'e was ill, you could see."

"Loike one that had the hand of Death restin' on him, God help us!"

"Never ought to've bin sent up. . . ."

As soon as we got news of the calamity the adjutant told me to fall-in half a dozen stretcher-squads, and with them we retraced our steps to the spot where we had left Smith and the ill-fated stretcher-party. We found a cook and an orderly still up there. All they could tell us was that the squads had formed up and gone off under Lieutenant Smith along the goat-track overlooking the Gulf of Saros.

We went over the ridge to the seaward side, and some way along the track. There wasn't a sign of them to be seen. We picked up a little information on the way. A machine-gun section had seen them pass. Some officers had warned them not to go forward, but they went on. One of the party—the sergeant—had been seen lying on some rocks "riddled with bullets". That was about all we could discover.

We searched for two or three hours, but it was no use. There was nothing more we could do, except attend to the wounded fighting men, now nearing breaking-point but still clinging to the ridge after fifty-three hours of it.

At 7 p.m. what remained of the three Irish battalions on the Kiretch Tepe were ordered to withdraw to their old front line:

the position they had gained on August 7, about 800 yards west of Jephson's Post. "Not a man moved until he received the order, and then slowly, deliberately, almost reluctantly, they retired." After that there was no chance of finding our lost squads.

So, at nightfall on August 17, the Kiretch battle—that might have been the turning-point in the campaign—came to an end, and the Turks regained the hogsback.

Inferno died away in fitful explosions. The blood-frenzy of war was dowsed at last in dew and darkness—the hideous wounds hidden from us in the wide-open tomb of the night.

But for the quiet groans of the wounded—and the ever-increasing sense of desolation as, moment by moment, hope for the lost stretcher-party ebbed away—we might have floundered into fuddled forgetfulness, wondering why we were groping about up here at all. So suddenly warless was the nocturnal catalepsy: so numb both body and ghost from shock and strain.

Who are these shufflers?

Make way for the slow march of skeletons moving to the rear.

Shuffle—halt—shuffle—bringing in the dead.

Deadbeat themselves, bringing in the dead.

Shuffle—halt—shuffle. . .

Not a drum to muffle—

Not a tear to shed . . .

"Seen any stretcher-bearers?"

"None but yourselves, surely, and it fadin' to the night. *Any wather?*"

No hope left. And no "wather". Killed—wounded—taken prisoner? Will any of them find their way back to us in the long drag of the dark? Too late to be looking for them now—we'd only break our necks down some splitfaced crag. Yet it's hard to turn our backs upon the high ridge and give up the search.

That's the sound of digging—clink—scrape—shovel.

They're digging down below.

There's a foot or two of soil below the broken ledges

Where the Gaunts and the Shaggies are digging in the dark...

Wearily and slow.
"Dig a little deeper boys, to circumflect the flies"—
To circumflect the flies from the soon-forgotten graves
That no one will be knowing:
Where no one will be keening when the dawnwind's blowing—
    No coffin lowered,
    And no Last Post. . . .
            "Any wather?"
There's cruel barren grandeur in an ordered retreat,
And solemn empty splendour in a moonstruck defeat. . . .
            " Any wather?"
Sergeant, call the roll!—it's the same old story:
"Fall in, the Dead!—they're dishing-out Glory!"
                "Any wather?"
We went down to the beach. No one said a word.

While we were searching for our lost stretcher-bearers on
the ridge, Hamilton had been ashore, seen de Lisle, and been
waylaid by Major-General Lindley, commanding the 53rd
(Welsh Territorial) Division. Under date August 18, the diary
tells us that—

> "Lindley asked if he might walk with me to the beach, and
> on the way down he told me frankly his Division had gone to
> pieces and that he did not feel it in himself to pull it together
> again."

So Lindley packed up and went. He was given a base job.

The Dublins and the Munsters were still burying their
dead—clink—scrape—shovel—as we fell asleep at Two-Tree
Hill.

On the morning of August 18 the 30th and 31st Brigades of
the Xth (Irish) Division were brought down from the Kiretch
Tepe to rest camps at A Beach.

Out of loyalty to "Old K." Hamilton would have fought to
the bitter end with ghost-divisions—the phantoms of the slain
floating in the morning mists and strange sea-frets. Was doing
just that, in fact. Was commanding a left-over army of sick
men—men who, day and night, had to run to the "lats" every
half hour or so.

Even now, on August 18, he was prepared to fight on with

nothing but sick men and the shadow-shapes of field artillery and howitzers that had never been landed—or had only just been landed (at Anzac!) and were "at the disposal of" General de Lisle "as soon as horses could be provided to mobilise them". At this moment there were three more field artillery brigades and two batteries of 4–5 inch howitzers waiting at Lemnos, "ready to be brought up as soon as they could be landed, but they would have to be landed without horses and taken into position by horses of other units". (See Dardanelles Report, Part II, Sec. 102, page 46.)

And this—*twelve days after the landing!*

Who was to blame for all this—no one? A week ago, on the evening of August 12, Hamilton had written in his diary:

"... I know equally well that he [K. of K.] is not capable of understanding how he has cut his own throat, the men's throats and mine, by not sending young and up-to-date Generals to run them."

It is clear that despite his almost idolatrous devotion to "Old K." he was aware of the "blind spot"—the blank—the fathomless emptiness behind the hypnotic stare of those diamond-hard, piercingly blue eyes. And it is clear that he had fixed the blame for this mountain of muddle upon the old and out-of-date generals who commanded us.

Hamilton's notion of the Suvla landing was summed up in his diary, under date—

"August 17th, Imbros. The surprise was complete, and the army was thrown ashore in record time practically without loss. . . ."

It sounds marvellous—everything went like clockwork! But he was not there, and did not see any of it. Six days later, on the 23rd, when explaining the Suvla landing in his "weekly budget", he writes:

"... Not that I have yet got any very clear conception of the details myself. It seems clear that this great mass of young inexperienced troops failed simply because their leaders failed to grasp the urgency of the time problem when they got upon the ground, although, as far as orders and pen and ink could go, it had been made perfectly clear."

The truth is that the "time problem" in his written battle orders had not been "made perfectly clear". Instead, as already stated, the fatal words *"if possible"* had taken all the "urgency" out of them, and reduced them to little more than polite requests.

The nearest Hamilton came to any self-criticism, or any inkling that his G.H.Q. staff might be too lightheartedly confident—counting their lighter-loads before they had landed —was a diary jotting dated August 26th:

> ". . . Anyway, whether by my own fault or those of others, one thing is certain, namely, that up to date there has been misunderstanding."

We may wonder whether, in fact, we are dealing with a pack of incompetent Old Army Generals who misunderstood their "perfectly clear" orders—or with various forms of dry-rot at the top of the Victorian/Edwardian social structure? Perhaps of our phase of civilisation?

And now, day by day, the Suvla command disappeared. Mahon had gone, Stopford had gone, Lindley had gone. One after another the Old Army Generals were packing up. In quick succession—

Sitwell was bundled off: August 18.

Hill, suffering from acute dysentery, had to go: August 22.

Hammersley was taken off in a state of collapse: August 23.

Others followed. Some were dismissed, some resigned, some were physical wrecks and could not carry on. All were haggard and distraught. Nearly all were angry. Never before in military history had there been such a drastic clear-out of brass-hats during a campaign. Six commanding officers in nine days, and none below the rank of brigadier-general!

They left, all unknowingly, one man without dismay: one solitary knight, one Chevalier de Bayard *"sans peur et sans reproche"*—Hamilton.

Without reproach, because he felt it his duty to obey Kitchener's impossible order of March 12, 1915. Yet the heart-rending truth is that, at this moment, no one had any firm faith in the Gallipoli venture except Hamilton himself. He stood alone—and did not know it.

From August 18th to the 21st the days ran into each other. It wasn't like the first lull. This one was full of frantic disquiet.

A kind of itch. Not from lice, although now, for the first time, we were "chatty" ("crumby", as the Cockneys put it), with "Scots Greys" drilling by whole battalions in the seams of our shirts—bodylice (*Pediculus vestimenti*).

But this was another itch going on all the time. A feverish determination to "grasp the urgency of the time problem"—to do something, somehow-or-other—quickly!—to regain the initiative. Surely it could not be too late to salvage something—if not victory—from that First Fine Careless Belly-Landing of August 6–7th, when a whole army was "thrown ashore" ("thrown" is the word) and then allowed to shamble around the beaches to a standstill?

No wonder this impulse was fretting Hamilton every moment of the day and night. His cable to K. of K., recorded in the diary on August 13, does not overstress the hardly-to-be-hoped-for triumph:

> "... Though we were to repeat our landing operation a hundred times, we would never dare hope to reproduce conditions so favourable as to put one division ashore under cover of dark and, as the day broke, have the next division sailing in to its support."

Who would abandon what had been so successfully begun without making a supreme effort? With de Lisle in command he hoped to retrieve the position. True, the new corps commander had reported that it would take "several weeks" to reorganise, whereas "we have to try to act within two or three days".

So the three-day lull was full of fidgety restlessness. Troops moving. Troops landing. A hither-and-thither of transports and lighters. "Something on," as Boler said.

Russia hardly came into our picture of the war on any front. Out here, we knew we were supposed to defeat the Turks and push on to Constantinople. Hamilton had written in his diary, you remember, of "our push for Constantinople". This was natural enough, because Kitchener's written instructions were to the effect that if the Fleet failed in its attempt to force The Narrows, he was to land his troops on the peninsula, hold it with a light garrison, and march on Constantinople.

The diary tells us that, when he returned to the War Office
on the morning of March 13, he found K. of K. "standing at
his desk splashing about with his pen at three different drafts of
instructions", and that—

> "He toiled over the wording of his instructions. They were
> headed 'Constantinople Expeditionary Force'. I begged him
> to alter this to avert Fate's evil eye. He consented and both
> this corrected draft and the copy as finally approved are now
> in Braithwaite's dispatch box more modestly headed 'Medi-
> terranean Expeditionary Force' ".

He adds that—

> "None of the drafts helps us with facts about the enemy; the
> politics; the country; and our allies, the Russians."

It was, however, hoped that if and when we marched
on Constantinople*—150 miles east of Suvla as the crow
flies—we should be joined by a Russian corps landed on the
Bosphorus.

So far, during the past fortnight, we had advanced about
two and a half miles. Changing the name of our expeditionary
force had not, alas! averted "Fate's evil eye". But soon the
regulars would show what could be done. De Lisle, having
"investigated the situation at Suvla, represented to G.H.Q. the
desirability of strengthening the force at his disposal by bringing
over the 29th Division from Helles". Which really was the
oddest thing to do, because, having been round "every corner
at Suvla", and being thereby convinced that there was nothing
for it but to pack up and go, our new corps commander

---

* Had we taken Constantinople, the Fleet would have been able to run
military supplies and munitions into Russia'a "backdoor" via the Black
Sea ports, and the collapse of the Czar's armies, due to lack of food, clothing,
and war materials, might have been averted. In the event, however, it was
amongst these thousands of demoralised peasant soldiers that the Bolsheviks
carried out their most effective propaganda during the summer of 1917,
when Kerensky issued his futile "blood and iron" orders in an attempt to
continue the Russian offensive against Germany.

Trotsky, writing at the time, said: "The material premises for an offensive
are extremely unfavourable. The organisation of supplies for the army
reflects the general economic collapse. No result is possible but the pro-
gressive breakdown of the army": and goes on to speak of the "mass
desertions" from the front then taking place. (See *The History of the Russian
Revolution*, by Leon Trotsky, English translation published by Gollancz,
1932, Vol. I, p. 392.)

"represented the desirability" of bringing in another division—his own—to make the next attack! So now another oddity had turned up in place of the oddly stubborn Stopford.

The 29th Division was "the famous 29th"—the crack division of the M.E.F.—which, however, had already been battered to pieces from April 25 in frontal attack after frontal attack on Achi Baba (709 feet) at Cape Helles: an utterly senseless slaughter, thanks to the "quite unconquerable optimism" of its then commander, the "gay and high-spirited" General Hunter-Weston, whose only idea of war was one massed frontal attack following another. When on July 25, he was invalided home, the command was taken over by Major-General Sir Beauvoir de Lisle, K.C.B., D.S.O.

It was now landing (Friday, August 20) and taking up its bivouacs on the westward slope of Lala Baba, in readiness for the new offensive—the last battle—fixed for tomorrow.

We saw them coming ashore. They looked pretty grim and woebegone. In fact they looked like the rest of us. And no wonder. They had come straight from the firing-line without a rest. By nightfall, more than one brigade had landed. But five battalions of their two remaining brigades were fighting in the front line trenches at Helles when they were ordered to embark that night for Suvla to take part in the next day's battle.

Neither Hamilton nor de Lisle had thought out any new stratagem for this new offensive. They decided to batter away at the same old objectives in a widespread head-on attack in broad daylight right across the Suvla plain—Hamilton with his never-failing birdlike hopefulness: de Lisle with plenty of driving energy, but knowing it was hopeless. A strange combination, this. Just about as odd as you could get it. And, of course, fatal.

De Lisle's plan, "which met with Sir Ian Hamilton's approval", was simple:

(i) On the left, the 53rd and 54th (Territorial) Divisions were to hold the enemy from Sulajik to the Kiretch Tepe.

(ii) In the centre, the 29th Division would make two attacks: the 87th Brigade on Scimitar Hill, the 86th Brigade on the Anafarta Spur and the W Hills (Ismail Oglu Tepe).

(iii) On the right, the 29th would be supported by the 11th

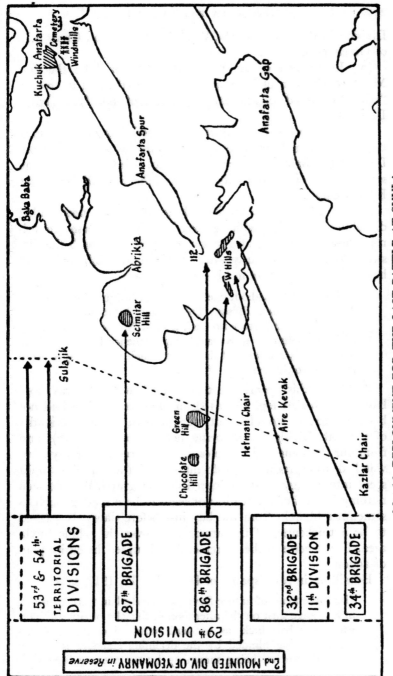

Map 16. DEPLOYMENT FOR THE LAST BATTLE AT SUVLA

Division in the attack on the W Hills, via Hetman Chair S.E. of Green Hill.

(iv) In support of the main advance would be the 2nd Mounted Division of Yeomanry (dismounted), and in reserve "what remained of the two Brigades of the Xth (Irish) Division".

(v) It had been arranged with Birdwood that a force of nine battalions from Anzac should co-operate by advancing from Damakjelik Bair in order to connect with the straggling southernmost tip of the outpost line of the 11th Division near Kazlar Chair.

August 21 broke cobweb-thick in the usual dew-chilled dishabille of floating white gauze. By mid-day these ground-mists had evaporated, and it was as hot as ever, with the flies swarming: but—curiously—the hills and the plain were still hazed. Hamilton wrote in his diary that evening:

> "Sailed for Suvla about one o'clock with Braithwaite, Aspinall, Dawnay, Deedes, Ellison, Pollen, and Maitland. The first time I have set forth with such a staff. Not wishing to worry de Lisle I climbed up Karakol Dagh, whence I got something like a bird's eye view of the arena which was wrapped from head to foot in a mantle of pearly mist."

By 2 p.m. this "pearly mist" had thickened, and was more like a translucent fog. It was strangely spectral. We had not been warned for stretcher-duty (as the 30th and 31st Brigades of the Xth Division were being held in corps reserve), and from our dug-outs and foxholes on Two-Tree Hill many of us watched this gradual transformation of the familiar sunlit scene into a foggy sun-illuminated shadow-graph. We had seen nothing like it before. It did not seem to be a sea-fog, such as sometimes blew in from the bay just before dawn. It seemed to be a thickening of the atmosphere over the whole Suvla area. It was eerie in the extreme. And it upset the entire plan of action.

Hamilton, in his dispatch of December 11, 1915, says:

> "By some freak of nature Suvla Bay and plain were wrapped in a strange mist on the afternoon of the 21st of August. This was sheer bad luck, as we had reckoned on the enemy's gunners being blinded by the declining sun and upon the Turkish trenches being shown up by the evening light with

singular clearness, as would have been the case on ninety-nine days out of a hundred. Actually we could hardly see the enemy lines this afternoon, whereas out to the westward targets stood out in strong relief against the luminous mist."

Then he adds—

"I wished to postpone the attack, but for various reasons this was not possible."

Almost as curious as the "luminous mist" was the fact that nothing our Commander-in-Chief wanted could ever be done. At a critical moment he always seemed to be balked in one way or another. Note also the attitude in which, attended by seven members of his G.H.Q. staff, he came ashore to watch this all-important attack—diffident, kindly, keeping well out of the way, plodding quietly up the Karakol Dagh, "not wishing to worry de Lisle".

As it was "not possible" to postpone the attack, it began at scheduled time, mist or no mist. At 2.30 p.m. the battleships in the bay, together with the scanty artillery ashore, opened up a thunder-cracking bombardment: and Hamilton adds rather forlornly, twenty-four machine-guns on Chocolate Hill "did what they could to lend a hand".

"It so happened," says the Dardanelles Report, "that a fog came on which seriously interfered with the preliminary bombardment," and Hamilton's dispatch admits that the gunnery was "none too accurate". The shells screamed over our heads, and burst shrouded in a veil of opalescent vapour that hung like sunlit muslin.

But when we turned about, and looked towards the bay, facing the sun, it was like staring at the white screen of a shadow-show lit from behind, upon which every object—the rocky headlands, warships, water-lighters, hospital ships, tents, store-dumps, mules, even a man walking along the rim of the shore—stood out in grey silhouette. We could be seen, the Turks were hidden! And the strange thing is that this "luminous mist" never again came up. Kemal was well served by the jinn of the place.

The haphazard bombardment continued until 3 p.m., when the advance began. The 34th Brigade of the 11th Division rushed the Turkish trenches south of Hetman Chair. Hamilton's dispatch says that this was done "practically without loss", but

Q*

Hammersley, who was still in command on August 21, stated before the Royal Commission that one battalion lost five of its seven officers before reaching the Turkish trenches, and that by the end of the day the losses in this sector were "extremely heavy".

The main objective in this battle was, once again, the W Hills and the Anafarta Spur, with the capture of Scimitar Hill as incidental to the main attack. But—once again—the actual lie of the land brought the dreaded Scimitar Hill into the foreground, and forced the battle to concentrate on its ravaged, burnt-out, and already blooksoaked flanks.

Captured on the night of the 8th by the pioneer battalion, and then voluntarily abandoned, it remained the key to the whole position, in spite of its paltry 229 feet above sea-level.

Although the 34th Brigade had rushed the Turkish trenches between Hetman Chair and Aire Kevak, it could not hold the position. On its left, the 32nd Brigade moved directly against Hetman Chair and the communication trench running eastward to the W Hills. This trench could not be seen from the brigade's front line. Moreover, the battalion on the left flank had been told to march by a compass bearing, owing to the fact that "a kind of Scotch mist enveloped the front, and only the silhouette of the hills was visible". Within the first few hundred yards this battalion "had no officers left", and, as no one else knew the compass bearing, it soon lost direction "by inclining too much to the north", and suddenly found itself under heavy enfilade fire from the communication trench, for which in fact it was then searching.

The two remaining battalions of the brigade were hurriedly pushed forward—and they also lost direction, coming under heavy fire from the same strongly held, many-loopholed communication trench. To avoid being wiped out, all four battalions had to fall back towards the southern slopes of Green Hill.

Shortly after 3 p.m. two battalions of the 33rd Brigade, held in divisional reserve at Lala Baba, moved towards Hetman Chair in support of the 32nd Brigade. But—it seems incredible —they also lost direction! Their advance being overtaken and cut across by the first wave of dismounted Yeomanry (now coming up), they became separated, one group bearing to the

north and the other to the south-east, where it joined up with
the 34th Brigade instead.

Thus, within half an hour of starting the attack, all was
confusion along this sector of the front: a confusion made worse
by a fierce bush fire that had broken out north of Hetman
Chair. By 5 p.m. hardly any advance had been made towards
the W Hills, and "so far as the 11th Division was concerned the
operation had failed".

Meanwhile, the leading battalions of the 29th (Regular)
Division from Helles, that had taken up positions overnight,
began their attack on Scimitar Hill, the Anafarta Spur, and
the W Hills at 3.30 p.m. The Irish troops of the 87th Brigade
stormed up to the crest of Scimitar Hill and carried the trenches
there, but were forced halfway down again by a tornado of
shrapnel and machine-gun fire from Anafarta Spur (Hill 112:
height 328 ft.)—where the advance of the 86th Brigade had
been checked by a raging bush fire, and by the fact that its
right was unsupported by the 32nd Brigade, still half a mile
to the rear on the southern slopes of Green Hill.

On the left, between Sulajik and the Kiretch ridge, the two
Territorial divisions had merely been requested to "take
advantage of any opportunity to gain ground", but as no
opportunity presented itself, they carried out their allotted
task of holding the line against an enemy who had no intention
of doing more than snipe and shell them.

Catastrophe now overtook the 29th Division. With the help
of another battalion, its 87th Brigade again stormed to the top
of the "fatal hill", but so decimating was the Turkish fire from
Hill 112 that they had to fall back, and could only make a little
headway on the south side. More scrub had been set alight by
bursting shrapnel. The fires spread rapidly, and once again
Scimitar Hill was a fiery furnace.

By 5 p.m. it was all ablaze on the south-west. From A Beach
we could see the hungry flames running in a red ripple over-
hung by choking columns of smoke that made the "luminous
mist" more strangely perilous. The far-off crackling roar
intensified the sense of ever-widening dread—the same hill-
contours all aflame again! We thanked God we were not on
duty over there. . .

Many men of the 29th Division were trapped on the hillside. The dead were left in a natural crematorium. The wounded out in the open "endeavoured to crawl back to cover, but many, if they did reach the scrub, perished in the flames". It was August 9 all over again: with de Lisle in command instead of Stopford. There was no difference—except that the holocaust was more frightful. On the 9th the dead and wounded totalled 1,500. Today another 5,000 were added to the casualty list. And not one inch of ground gained.

By 4 p.m., half an hour after the attack began, de Lisle and his staff at corps headquarters had pieced together reports brought in, and had come to the conclusion that—

(i) 11th Division troops had captured Hetman Chair.

(ii) The 86th Brigade was held up (which was true).

(iii) The 87th Brigade, having captured Scimitar Hill, had been forced down from the crest (which was true, but these troops were already making ready for their second assault).

On the above far from accurate information de Lisle based a corps order that reached the commander of the 29th Division at 5 p.m., when his troops were making their second assault, inching forward under heavy fire, with the scrub already ablaze behind them, but still pushing slowly up the southern slopes. The corps order informed him that the 2nd Mounted Division of Yeomanry would "push through" to the objectives originally set for his division.

He at once issued an order to the attacking troops to stand fast and await the arrival of the Yeomanry. So the advance was called off, and no further attempt was made for two and a half hours. It was almost dark before the battle was resumed.

From Two-Tree Hill we had a magnificent view of the dismounted, or rather unmounted, Yeomanry as they moved out from Lala Baba and began their march across the Salt Lake in open formation. This was some time between 3.30 and 4 p.m. On the Karakol Dagh, Hamilton and his staff were also watching. It was a sight to behold. There were five brigades, each nearly 1,000 strong, marching in extended order (column of squadrons)—wave after wave—with about seven paces between each man. They stretched from just below the Cut to the scrubby ground south of the Salt Lake, a distance of 2,000 yards. And they "presented such a target as artillery-men dream of".

They marched steadily, like an army of soldier ants that cannot be deflected, and almost as soon as they came into the open from their bivouacs behind Lala Baba, shrapnel began to thin them out. Nevertheless, these Yeoman of England, upholding the traditions of their forefathers at Poitiers, Crécy, Agincourt, kept their formation, "only moving at the double when ordered to do so".

In his dispatch of December 11, 1915, Hamilton wrote:

> "The advance of these English Yeomen was a sight calculated to send a thrill of pride through anyone with a drop of English blood running in their veins. Such superb martial spectacles are rare in modern war."

But whether this was the best way to get these troops across this salt-white plain is a very different matter. The dispatch says:

> "During this march they came under remarkably steady and accurate artillery fire. . . . Ordinarily it should always be possible to bring up reserves under some sort of cover from shrapnel fire. Here, for a mile and a half, there was nothing to conceal a mouse."

But, of course, a mouse would have had more sense. These bold Yeomen, Hamilton reported, "moved like men marching on parade". Without question the "wee sleekit" would have crept and scampered and sneaked his way around the southern edge of the Salt Lake, where at least there was "some sort of cover" in the shape of thick low scrub.

Ah, Mousie, hadst thou been i' charge! . . . but then our Commander-in-Chief could not have written in his dispatch:

> "Despite the critical events in other parts of the field, I could hardly take my glasses from the Yeomen. . . . Here and there a shell would take toll of a cluster; there they lay; there was no straggling; the others moved steadily on; not a man was there who hung back or hurried."

True, true—too deadfully true. (Already some of our stretcher-squads were moving across the Salt Lake—without waiting for orders—to help the regimental stretcher-bearers.) Hamilton ends his splendid eulogy by saying—

"But such an ordeal must consume some of the battle-winning fighting energy of those subjected to it."

No doubt about that, either. Nor about the ordeal to which our stretcher-bearers were subjected. Long after the last wave of advancing Yeomen had vanished into the "pearly mist" towards Chocolate Hill, they were bringing in the wounded under vicious bursts of shrapnel—and were still at it when darkness fell. The snipers were vicious too. One of our A Section bearers recalls (under date April 4, 1957)—"Getting a bullet through my rolled-up shirt-sleeve, while stretcher-bearing in the dismounted Yeomanry advance across the Salt Lake plain. I can't think now how I got mixed up in it, for I don't think I was supposed to be on duty . . ."

That night Hamilton wrote in his diary:

"By 6.30 it had become too dark to see anything. The dust mingling with the strange mist, and also with the smoke of shrapnel and the hugest and most awful blazing bush fire formed an impenetrable curtain."

In this ominous murk the Yeomanry reached Chocolate Hill, where a hurried and almost worthless briefing took place. One brigade was to advance on Scimitar Hill, now a sinister, smouldering-black hump. Three brigades were to advance on Hill 112, at the tip of the Anafarta Spur. One brigade was to be held in reserve. Without more ado, and without any idea of a co-ordinated attack, the Yeomen of England "stumbled blindly into battle".

Of the four brigadiers taking part in this advance, two had not the slightest notion of what they were supposed to do, and none of the officers had any inkling as to the lie of the land, the present British position in the battle area, nor where the Turkish lines might be. In fact it was a typical Suvla battle.

"The mist was growing thicker, scrub fires were raging, and pillars of smoke were blotting out the view," as the four Yeomanry brigades pushed forward, with no more than an hour of dimmed-out daylight in which to find their objectives.

Twilight had closed down when the Yeomanry came up on the left of the 87th Brigade on Scimitar Hill, and it was almost dark when they began their advance up the northern and western slopes. At the same time the 87th Brigade made their third assault, and again nearly reached the summit on the southern slopes.

The Yeomanry did in fact reach the crest of the hill—carried earlier in the day by the 87th Brigade in their first assault—but now, stumbling about in the darkness of oncoming night, the smoke-laden gloom lit only by shrapnel-bursts and the red glow of wind-fanned embers, they came under enfilade fire, and "blurred khaki figures disappeared in the darkness and smoke and were lost to view". It was impossible to hold the position, and they were forced to fall back to the original line halfway down the hill on the south side, where they found themselves again on the left of the 87th Brigade, who had also been forced back.

But this position would be untenable at dawn, swept by enfilade fire from the jutting spur east of Abrikja (328 feet) and from Hill 112 (328 feet). Knowing this, the Turks quietly withdrew—for the second time—from the crest of Scimitar Hill (229 feet) during the night, and left them to it.

De Lisle, recognising the danger of the British position, but giving no thought to the exhausted state of the troops engaged, already "tried beyond all endurance", issued an urgent corps order instructing the 29th Division to make a fresh attack on Hill 112 before daybreak, pending a new onslaught on the W Hills and the Anafarta Spur.

But the commander of the 29th Division had had enough of corps orders for one day. He ignored it altogether. During the night he withdrew his advanced battalions to the established British line east of Green Hill, and the Yeomanry marched back to their bivouacs at Lala Baba before daybreak.

So ended the last battle at Suvla. There were 5,300 casualties.

Result: one Turkish trench captured at Hetman Chair.

We never mentioned the lost squads now. That day's disaster was locked up somewhere at the back of our minds. I think we looked upon it as a kind of disgrace to us all. And, anyhow, we'd given up hope of ever seeing any of them again.

Having been warned for duty at Chocolate Hill the following

day, I was getting my clobber together when someone called out—"*Cor-blimey! look who's here!*"

Two little figures came shuffling into camp over the humpy ground. They might have been Scrag and Scrawny, if such outlandish nondescripts had names at all! and yet, after one long, astonished stare—as though they were men risen from the dead—we saw through their weazened masks, and knew them for two bearers from the lost squads.

But they eyed us with horrible suspicion, the glitter of sniper-madness darting from deep-sunken sockets. They edged away from us, keeping close together, their limbs trembling like dodder-grass. One had ginger hair, and a crop of ginger beard bristled his chin. He muttered to himself. Their lips were burnt black, swollen and cracked. They did not even ask for water. Their hair was matted with sand and wisps of pale dead grass. They had lost their pith helmets, and the sun had scorched and peeled the backs of their necks. Their puttees were stuck with prickles and spikes from thorn-bushes and thistles. Ginger had lost his belt. The other had no haversack. Both were begrimed with dirt and encrusted with sand.

We gave them Oxo from the special "medical comforts" store. The orderly officer came and looked at them. They were given blankets, but they were past sleep. Kept dozing off—waking with a start—muttering—". . . Don't move! . . . keep down! . . . wait till it's dark . . . might have a chance. . . ."

When they were questioned they could give very little information.

"Where is Lieutenant Smith?"

". . . Gone . . . all gone. . . ."

"We chewed grass . . . tried eating grass to fill up a bit . . . no food . . . no water. . . ."

"What happened to Lieutenant Smith?"

"He took us too far . . . we got cut off . . . we waved our stretchers when we found we'd gone too far. . . ."

"Once we 'ad to crawl back again," said the other, "where there was some bushes. . . ."

It was useless. Gradually the glint of sniper-madness left their eyes, but they were never the same again.

"After the failure at Suvla on August 6th and following days, the same question presented itself to the Dardanelles Com-

mittee and the Cabinet as in May, i.e., whether the Dardanelles operations were to be continued or abandoned, and, if
continued, in what way. . . . The matter was discussed at
many meetings of the Dardanelles Committee. . . .

"On August 27th, the Dardanelles Committee, after discussion, decided that no line of future policy could be framed
for the present . . .

"The final decision was not reached until December,
1915."

> —(Dardanelles Report, Part II, *The Operations at Suvla*,
> Secs. 115 and 118, pages 51–52).

The little tortoises were still asleep in the hot sand near A
Beach. . . .

On September 1 Hammersley was sent home with a clot
of blood in his leg, and that evening Hamilton wrote in his
diary:

> "Reports say that the least movement would kill him. And
> this was the man, remember, on whom, under Stopford,
> everything depended for making a push."

That night he had one of his premonitory dreams:

> "September 2nd, Imbros. An ugly dream came to me last
> night. . . . I was being drowned, held violently under the
> Hellespont. The grip of a hand was still on my throat, the
> waters were closing over my head as I broke away and found
> myself wide awake. I was trembling and carried back into the
> realms of consciousness an idea that some uncanny visitor
> had entered my tent . . . never have I suffered from so fearful
> a dream. For hours afterwards I was haunted by the thought
> that the Dardanelles were fatal: that something sinister was
> afoot: that we, all of us, were pre-doomed."

At 11.15 p.m. on September 22, in the seventh week of our
sojourn at Suvla, the 32nd Field Ambulance left Two-Tree
Hill for bivouacs at C Beach, a dreary two-mile trek along the
western rim of the Salt Lake to the miserable salt-flats south
of Lala Baba, where they left us to rot amidst the stink of
rotting seawrack rinsing in bubbled scum and matted tangles
at the water's edge.

We were now encamped upon a low-lying saltmarsh pockmarked with dried-mud potholes tufted with harsh beachgrass. A miasmic waste that would have drained the life out of a Samson. Even the flies became lethargic and more horrible, crawling slowly over the scruffy ground, over our faces, over our hands, over our food.

The weather had changed. The sky was overcast. Thin dry winds lifted the dust in blinding clouds that choked us, powdering our sunburnt skins until we looked like ghosts. We felt naked here, lost and forgotten. The daily shelling and sniping went on. Morning and evening the shells came whining over the Salt Lake. One of them—a "dud"—from a Turkish battery on the W Hills plunged into the dry sludge. As it hadn't exploded, we dug it out carefully. The shellcase was rusty, and on it was stamped in clearly incised letters—

WOOLWICH, 1911.

We just looked at each other, as much as to say: "Well, that shows you, doesn't it?"...

And while we were left moping at C Beach—because no one in Whitehall could make up his mind what to do about the Gallipoli Campaign—the situation was drifting and floundering on all fronts.

> "The Russian reverses were still continuing," says the Dardanelles Report (page 52). "On August 20th, Lord Kitchener pointed out that, owing to the situation in Russia, he could no longer maintain the attitude which was agreed upon ... the large divisional reinforcements asked for could not be sent to the Dardanelles, as they had been promised to France and could not be diverted. He said his inclination was to help Sir Ian Hamilton as far as was possible without interfering with the operations in France.... This was agreed to, and Sir Ian Hamilton was so informed. He replied that he would do the best he could with the forces at his disposal."

Three days later he had written in his diary:

> "August 23rd, Imbros. At 11.15 red hot from France there arrived Byng (to command the IXth Corps), Maude and Fanshawe (to command Divisions)...."

So now, at Suvla, we had three splendid new generals all ready to take over—the sand, the seabirds, and the tortoises? For the IXth Corps—including the 29th Division—as a fighting force, capable of making an advance against Kemal's

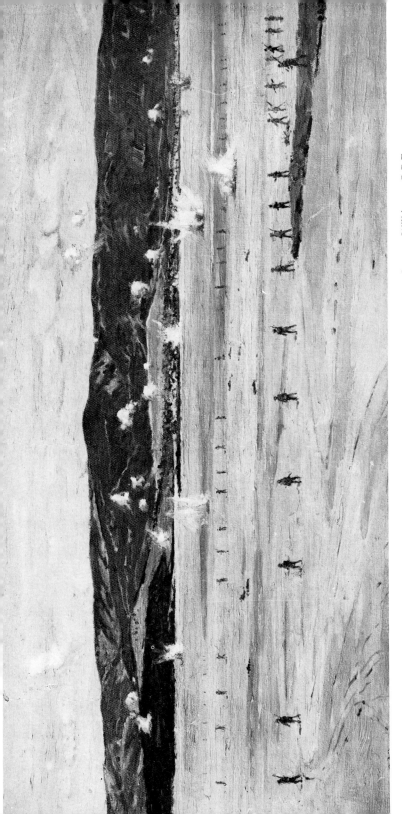

34. The Yeomanry crossing the Salt Lake, August 21, 1915, from a picture by Norman Wilkinson, O.B.E.

35. Sir Ian Hamilton saying Good-bye.

36. Stores burning after Evacuation at Suvla.

troops in the hills, simply did not exist. And every hour of the day and night it was dwindling away. Dysentery was doing Kemal's work for him *At this time* 800 *sick were being evacuated from the Peninsula every day.*

On September 3, Hamilton was writing that—

> "He [Maude] is convinced that . . . our hold-up here is not a reality but only a hold-up or petrefaction of the brains of the French and our Dardanelles Committee."

On September 7, he had cabled K. of K., and says in his diary:

> "Have told him I have had a nice letter from Mahon, thanking me for allowing him to rejoin his Division, and saying he hopes to stay with them to the end."

He is the same kindly creature. A week later he is just beginning to see what is happening:

> "September 13, Imbros. [Extract from a letter]. How is it that our letters from home are filled with lamentations and that . . . we see headlines in the papers such as 'The Gallipoli standstill', whereas it does not seem to occur to anyone to speak about 'The French standstill'?"

By September 14 he is writing, with perhaps a touch of bitterness?—

> "K. had an intuition at the back of his mind that victory would dawn in the East. But he is no longer K. of K., the old K. of Khartoum and Pretoria . . . he had a call (by heavenly telepathy I suppose) that his New Armies must go to the East."

On September 16, he records:

> "A cable from Dawnay saying Lord K. 'would not regard unfavourably a withdrawal from Suvla Bay.'"

At last he realised that the beginning of the end was at hand. But Old K. himself was still dithering—still torn between East and West. . . . Even as late as November 3 (when it had already been decided to send British troops to Salonika) he sent a cable to Birdwood:

> "Very secret.
> ". . . I shall come out to you; am leaving tomorrow night . . . I believe the Admiralty will agree to making naval attempt to force the Straits. We must do what we can to assist them . . .

R

"Examine very carefully the best position for landing near the marsh at the head of the Gulf of Xeros [the Bulair isthmus]* . . .

"I absolutely refuse to sign orders for evacuation, which I think would be the gravest disaster and would condemn a large percentage of our men to death or imprisonment."

Unknown to us, the Xth (Irish) Division, sick and shattered as it was, had been earmarked for the Salonika undertaking. Even now Hamilton was fighting tooth and nail against evacuation. His diary entry for September 26 says:

"Since the last abortive effort of the Turkish Command to get their men to attack, every soldier in the trenches knows well that the enemy are afraid of us."

And on the same date he cabled K. of K.:

"But even if this last step [total evacuation] were not necessary, the withdrawal of British soldiers from Suvla would be an overwhelming victory for the Turks."

Hamilton was not entirely alone in his fight against evacuation. Keyes was doing his damnedest to get the Fleet to have another go at The Narrows. But the tide of events was flowing strongly against them. When, on October 11, K. of K. cabled asking for an "estimate of the probable losses" to be expected "if the evacuation of the Gallipoli Peninsula was decided upon", Hamilton was aghast, and the next day wrote in his diary of—

". . . A disaster only equalled in history by that of the Athenians at Syracuse: a disaster from which the British Empire could hardly hope to recover."

He was thinking mainly, of course, of the hazards involved in getting his troops off the peninsula, especially at this time of year, with winter storms on their way. But in another sense his words were prophetic. The British Empire did not recover from the blow.

Three days after writing those words, on October 16, Hamilton was recalled.

Even the sea at C Beach had lost its colour: doleful, mudfish-grey, rocking the foul flotsam to and fro, to and fro, in a frothy cradle of bilgy slush. We rocked with it, to and fro, in the

* See footnote p. 136.

strangest melancholy that ever settled upon soldiers in the
field. And so for seven whole days, until rumour hatching
rumour caught us in a thin net of hope on September 29—
that we were going back to England! that the Italians were
landing troops to help the Australians at Anzac! that we were
to be sent to Egypt—to India—to Japan! Best of all—that the
Xth Division would be sent back to Dublin, where, after a
civic reception, it would reorganise for garrison duty in
Ireland! That civic reception was, as Sergeant Midwinter said
later, "a delightful touch".

Then, suddenly, came the order to pack up.*

At 11 p.m. on September 30 we moved off from C Beach
along the shingle-clattering shore—Hamilton's "silent army"
as silent as ever, stumbling into ankle-deep sandholes—to
Nibrunesi Point. The night was pitch black. We had the
sensation of sneaking away in the night-time: a long straggling
column heavy-laden with rolled overcoats, haversacks, water-
bottles, and folded stretchers—those hatefully bloodstained
stretchers. Once, when someone far away shouted, I found
myself instantly-on-the-alert, listening from sheer habit for
the long-drawn cry that did not come. . . .

Sneaking away in the darkness . . . leaving the dead—leaving
the dead.

We halted on the north side of Lala Baba. Here, in the
swarming darkness and troop-confusion, the bearers from our

---

* We were in fact leaving Suvla for the Salonika Front. The troops
remaining after our departure hung on for about two months, since it was
not until December 7, 1915, that the War Cabinet at home decided to
evacuate Suvla and Anzac. Later it was decided to evacuate all troops on
the peninsula. This involved the secret withdrawal and embarkation of
134,000 men, 14,000 animals, and nearly 400 guns. At some points the
Turkish trenches were less than ten yards from the British, and the open
beaches from which our troops had to be taken off were within effective
range of enemy artillery.

At Suvla, on the final night of December 20th, not a single casualty was
suffered, and "not a wagon, gun, horse, mule, or donkey was left ashore".
At Anzac the total casualties amounted to two men wounded.

The entire evacuation of the peninsula was completed on January 9,
1916, "without the loss of a single life, and with only three men wounded".

A military correspondent of the *Vossische Zeitung* wrote: "As long as wars
last the evacuation of Suvla and Anzac will stand before the eyes of all
strategists as a hitherto unattained masterpiece."

advanced dressing station on Chocolate Hill (Boler amongst them) met us. Interminable waiting now. Men pushing forward, little by little—officers nagging: "Keep together, there! keep together!"

Keep together!—the dead won't see us . . . sneaking away, sneaking away. . . .

Horses stamping—snorting—whinnying. Why do they stamp and snort and whinny? Horses know? Horses "see"? What can they "see" in the mole-dark gloom—what can they "see" that we can't see?—

Dead men watching us sneak away?. . .

(I don't see no dead, do you?—No, no, no, the dead are dead!)—

"Hey—you! put that fag out! No smokin'—didn't you 'ear?"

"Cor-blimey—no smokin'! 'Ow much longer before we go?"

Every unit of the Xth Division at Suvla assembled ready for embarkation.

Huddled together. Waiting, waiting. Fused into dark lumps of nodding apathy. Almost too weary to keep their eyes open. No singing, no whistling. Hardly any talking. A cough. A sneeze. A yawn . . . another yawn . . . another. . . .

"Pick up your kit, boys—and move along down to the lighter!"

So they picked up their kit. But they couldn't move for the troops in front of them, huddled together, waiting. One of our bearers said: "The Turks *must* have seen all these troops moving down. Can't understand why they aren't shelling us."

Another replied: "They're only too bloody glad to see us go!—more likely to come and wave us goodbye, if you ask me."

The first one whispered: "What's wrong with the Old Man?" He might well ask. Mad Jack was stamping up and down in one of his comical-crazy tantrums. Made worse, no doubt, by an enormous boil that had come up on the back of his neck during the last few days at C Beach. He had it tied up with a bandage that looked like a white choker. Couldn't turn his head. And now he couldn't find his new adjutant—poor Lieutenant Beverland, always so meek and mild and gentle—

who had replaced Captain Young, badly wounded near the Salt Lake, August 22, and taken off the peninsula. Beverland had been sent back for some papers, and had got lost. So here was Okie Mutt stamping about stiffnecked like a wooden doll, raving: "Where's my bloody fool of an adjutant?—where the devil's he got to?"

As there was no reply, it drove him almost demented. I took care to keep out of his way. He raved on in the crowded darkness, and everyone round about fell silent: "Has anyone seen that bloody fool of an adjutant of mine?—dammit! I can't wait all night for him! . . ."

Boler loomed out of the dim confusion, and a strong whiff of rum came with him. "See you later, Sarn't—lookin' after things—important—*prac*tically everythink—"

He was rum-happy, and in his hurry to look after things (mostly bottles) he lost some of his own kit. He worked hard getting our gear and equipment into the lighters, although he was "three parts canned". Every now and then he loomed up like a great shadow, only to fade away again to the secret hiding-place of, I suppose, a rum-jar. He had a wonderful nose for alcohol on occasions like this.

At last the new adjutant turned up—and got a verbal trouncing from the Colonel. And at last we went aboard the lighter.

Boler came lurching over the gunwale a moment or two before the lighter chugged away from the shore. Soon the dark hump of Lala Baba began to slide from us.

Boler was standing next to me. "Have you got my glasses safely?" I asked. "I got your glasses, Sar'nt", he said, "safe as—safe can be—roun' my neck." He took them off, but got the sling-strap twisted, and fumbled it. I saw them slip from his fingers—case, strap, and all—and heard the splash as they sank into the waters of the bay. Perhaps they are still there, somewhere in the rippled sand at sea-bottom north-west of Lala Baba? . . .

That was the last we saw of Suvla.

Besides a pair of good Zeiss glasses, I knew I had left something of myself behind. And every man who was at Suvla is somehow still there.

BIBLIOGRAPHY

Armstrong, H. C., *Grey Wolf* (Barker, 1932): a biography of Mustafa Kemal.

Ashmead-Bartlett, Ellis, *The Uncensored Dardanelles* (Hutchinson, 1928).

Aspinall-Oglander, Brig.-General C. F., *Military Operations: Gallipoli* (Heinemann, 1929–32).
   Roger Keyes (Hogarth Press, 1951).

Bean, C. E. W., *The Official History of Australia in the War*, Vols. I and II (Angus & Robertson, 1921).

Churchill, The Right Hon. Winston S., *The World Crisis* (Odhams Press, 1923–29).

Cooper, Major Bryan, *The Tenth (Irish) Division in Gallipoli* (Herbert Jenkins, 1918).

Dardanelles Commission, Final Report, Part II, [Cmd. 371] (H.M. Stationery Office, 1917).

Gunther, John, *Inside Europe* (Hamish Hamilton, revised edition, 1937).

Hamilton, General Sir Ian, *Gallipoli Diary* (Edward Arnold, 1920).
   Dispatch of December 11, 1915 (H.M. Stationery Office).

Hanna, Henry, *The "Pals" at Suvla Bay* (Ponsonby, Dublin, 1916).

Hargrave, John, *At Suvla Bay: Notes and Sketches* (Constable, 1916).

Herbert, A. P., *The Secret Battle* (Methuen, 1919).

"Juvenis", *Suvla Bay and After* (Hodder & Stoughton, 1916).

Keyes, Admiral Sir Roger, *Naval Memoirs* (Butterworth, 1934).
   The Fight for Gallipoli (Eyre & Spottiswoode, 1941).

Mackenzie, Compton, *Gallipoli Memories* (Cassell, 1929).

Masefield, John, *Gallipoli* (Heinemann, 1916).

Midwinter, Charles, *Memoirs of the 32nd Field Ambulance, Xth (Irish) Division* (privately printed, 1933).

Moorehead, Alan, *Gallipoli* (Hamish Hamilton, 1956).

Nevinson, Henry W., *The Dardanelles Campaign* (Nisbet, 1918).

North, John, *Gallipoli: The Fading Vision* (Faber & Faber, 1936).

Owen, Frank, *Tempestuous Journey: Lloyd George, His Life and Times* (Hutchinson, 1954).

Royal Army Medical Corps Training (War Office, 1911, reprinted 1914: H.M. Stationery Office, 1914).

Trotsky, Leon, *The History of the Russian Revolution*, Vol. I (Gollancz, 1932).

von Sanders, Field-Marshal Liman, *Five Years in Turkey* (U.S. Naval Institute, 1927).

INDEX

A Beach, 78, 80, 81, 84, 85, 86, 98, 99, 101, 102, 107, 113, 131, 145, 148, 194, 201 (footnote), 208, 223, 235, 245, 251

Abrikja, 160, 164, 203, 249

Achi Baba, 25, 188, 240

Agamemnon, H.M.S., 88 (footnote)

Aghyl Dere, 117, 182, 186, 187, 189, 194, 195

Aire Kevak, 244

Alexandria, 32, 40, 61, 62

Ali Bey Chesme, 169, 175

Allanson, Major, 185, 186, 187, 188, 188 (footnote), 189, 190, 196, 207

Anafarta Gap, 126, 130, 142, 151, 200

Anafarta, Kuchuk (village), 123, 125, 161, 163, 171, 179, 198

Anafarta Ova, Kuchuk (plain), 77, 104, 121, 123, 157, 203, 215

Anafarta Spur, 151, 159, 172, 175, 176, 179, 197, 198, 201, 203, 205, 240, 244, 245, 248, 249

Anzac (Cove), 41, 44, 70, 71, 81 (footnote), 95, 104, 112, 117, 127, 134, 137, 145, 150, 156, 173, 174, 181, 182, 185, 194, 196, 202, 207, 208, 228, 231 (footnote), 236, 242, 255 (footnote)

Apex, The, 190

Aquitania, 64

Ari Burnu, 81 (footnote)

Army Service Corps (A.S.C.), 55, 145

Arno, 143, 144

Asia Minor, 135

Askold, 88 (footnote)

Aspinall, Lt.-Colonel, 29, 138, 139, 142, 143, 145, 146, 147, 148, 149, 152, 153 (footnote), 154, 242

Military Operations: Gallipoli (quoted), 145, 146, 148

Asquith, Rt. Hon. H.H., 20, 43, 44

Australian and New Zealand Army Corps (Anzacs), 25, 70, 71, 81 (footnote), 190, 191, 192, 195 (footnote), 202

Azmak Dere, 124

Baka Baba, 203

Baldwin, Brig.-General, 186, 187, 189, 190, 191, 196

Balfour, Rt. Hon. A. J., 44

Baltic, The, 21

Basingstoke, 50, 55, 58

Battleship Hill, 112, 150, 191

B Beach, 78, 80, 81, 86, 103, 105, 106, 111

Beverland, Lieut., 256, 257

Birdwood, Lt.-General Sir William, 25, 26, 38, 70, 95, 104, 117, 151, 181, 182, 195, 197, 242, 253

Black Sea, The, 18, 239 (footnote)

Boer War, The, 76

Boler, Pte Fred, 90, 157, 191, 192, 195, 197, 214, 238, 256, 257

Bolshevik Party, 35, 239 (footnote)

Bosphorus, The, 28, 149, 239

Bouvet, 34, 35

Braithwaite, Major-General Walter, 27, 28, 144, 179, 197, 239, 242

Breslau, 18

British Naval Mission, 19, 30

Bulair, 104, 112, 119, 124, 126, 133, 135, 136, 136 (footnote), 138, 148, 149, 160, 161, 162, 169, 217, 254

Buller, General, 76

Byng, General Sir Julian, 202, 206, 227, 252

Canada, s.s., 59, 65

260